Lois Hole's
Favorite Bulbs

Lois Hole's *favorite* Bulbs

Better Choices, **Better Gardens**

EDITED BY

Jim Hole &
Valerie Hole

HOLE'S

PUBLISHED BY HOLE'S
101 BELLEROSE DRIVE
ST. ALBERT, ALBERTA, CANADA
T8N 8N8

Printed in Canada   5   4   3   2   1

National Library of Canada Cataloguing in Publication Data

Hole, Lois, (date)
  Lois Hole's favorite bulbs : better choices, better gardens / Valerie Hole and Jim Hole, editors.

  Includes bibliographical references and index.
  ISBN 1-894728-00-9

  1. Bulbs. I. Hole, Jim, (date) II. Hole, Valerie, (date) III. Title. IV. Title: Favorite bulbs.
  SB425.H64 2003   635.9'4   C2003-910235-1

Film and prepress by Elite Lithographers, Edmonton, Alberta
Printed and bound by Bolder Graphics, Edmonton, Alberta
∞ Printed on acid-free paper.

Additional Photography: Geoff Bryant (www.geoffbryant.com) p. 244; Jill Fallis pp. x, 10, 34 and 297; Internationaal Bloembollen Centrum, Hillegom, Holland pp. 9, 64, 71, 91, 92, 100, 110, 137, 169, 172, 173, 188, 192, 193, 212, 231, 232, 244, 246, 261, 268, 270, 274, 275 and 299.

Contents

Twenty Best Bulbs

Preface

Jim Hole

Valerie Hole

We've worked on plenty of publishing projects together over the last ten years, but it's fair to say that *Favorite Bulbs* is the most challenging book we've tackled yet—and one we were at first hesitant to take on. We knew the subject was complex. But like millions of other gardeners, we grow bulbs, and we wanted to get people excited about the unrealized potential of bulb gardening.

Once we decided to go ahead with the book, we divided up the work. Everyone involved had a goal to accomplish. There were myths to shatter, contradictions to explain and new information to share. In 1999, we started planting bulbs: to photograph, to experiment with garden designs and to test the newest varieties. Then there was the task of evaluating the existing bulb books, both to confirm our own research and to analyze the books' assumptions and gaps. It was the beginning of a long, exacting and very educational process.

The casual gardener may wonder what took so long to finish. It's not as if bulbs are very complex: you buy them, plant them and wait for the flowers to appear. From that perspective, bulbs should be among the easiest plants to discuss. And much of the time that's accurate; but after writing *Favorite Bulbs*, we can tell you that bulb gardening is often more complicated than it appears.

Providing reliable planting instructions for bulbs—a monolithic category of plants—proved challenging. For every rule we made, we found exceptions. But in the end, we answered all of our questions about bulbs, and made many new discoveries.

We found, for example, that the ornamental onion variety 'Purple Sensation' is not, in fact, a variety of *Allium aflatunense*, despite the common misconception. Rather, it's a hybrid and stands on its own as an original creation, not a subset of *A. aflatunense*. (We listed it with *A. aflatunense* anyway, since the other alliums are listed by species and splitting hairs on this issue would create more questions than it answered.)

We'd never suggest that the categories we've used are the only correct ones. They are choices, not absolutes, and they represent compromises between scientific organization, retail trends and gardening conventions. Our aim was to help gardeners grow bulbs successfully by making sound purchasing decisions and by providing appropriate care. For us, it comes down to understanding. The point of gardening is to enjoy the plants, not to get caught up in a maze of rules.

We began this project with a lot of enthusiasm, and now, four years later, we are proud to present a book that we feel is an excellent guide for anyone who enjoys bulbs. Now it's your turn. We encourage you to experiment, to discover the complex, fascinating world of bulbs, much as we did when writing this book. Anyone can plant tulips and enjoy a great show of colour in the spring, but the rewards of delving deeper into the mysteries of bulbs are much greater.

—Jim Hole and Valerie Hole

Foreword

I've loved bulbs ever since I was a little girl, when I admired the crocuses that grew by the thousands in a field not far from my home in Buchanan, Saskatchewan. Since then, I've grown hundreds of bulbs, from the paperwhites on my kitchen table to the alliums in my front yard. But gathering the knowledge to create this book was a much bigger venture that took many years. Most of the credit goes to my son Jim, my daughter-in-law Valerie (married not to Jim, but to my older son, Bill) and the many talented staffers at the greenhouse. My own contributions are rooted in the early years of our family greenhouse business.

I had a lot of experience growing vegetables, so the first time I planted tulip bulbs, I treated them much as if I were sowing a row of corn. I gave the bulbs ample space, planted them in nice, straight rows and walked away well satisfied with my work.

The results, as anyone with a little bulb gardening experience would expect, were disappointing. Spaced so far apart, the tulip flowers looked unimpressive, almost puny. But I learned from my mistake. The next fall, I planted the bulbs much closer together, in clumps that echoed the patterns of nature. And sure enough, when spring arrived those bulbs treated me to a lovely show.

Not long afterward, I was searching for begonias at Eaton's. I started shopping later in the season than I should have, so the selection was very limited. There were only three tubers in an unlabelled box. I took them home, planted them in a hanging basket and hoped for the best.

Well, the best is exactly what I got. Those mysterious tubers produced the most magnificent begonia I'd ever seen, a lush, full plant that produced dozens of gorgeous pinkish-orange flowers. I hung it up in the front greenhouse, and every customer who saw it instantly wanted to buy it. There must have been two hundred requests that first morning, so I had little choice but to put a big SOLD sign right on the basket. I didn't want any of our employees to sell that plant accidentally before I had a chance to save and propagate those precious, unknown tubers!

But then I made a fatal mistake. A dear friend of mine asked if she could have the plant for her garden. She had the perfect location for it, and I couldn't refuse her. "Just as long as I get the tubers back when the plant is finished," I told her.

Well, she went on vacation and forgot about the plant, and then the first heavy frost of the fall hit. And of course, the tubers were frozen solid. I was terribly disappointed.

Since then, plenty of beautiful begonia varieties have come along, many even more beautiful than the one I lost. Still, in my heart of hearts, I felt I lost an irreplaceable gem that day.

Those experiences, while instructive, weren't enough to put together a comprehensive book on bulbs. Today's gardeners are looking for ways to extend the season, enjoy bulbs indoors, keep their favourites over the winter—and they're looking for far more unusual plants than I ever grew. That's why I was happy to pass most of the responsibility for researching and writing *Favorite Bulbs* to Jim and Valerie.

It's not that I was uninvolved in the process. Despite my new role as Lieutenant Governor of Alberta, Bill, Jim, Valerie and I gather for lunch whenever our schedules allow, to catch up on greenhouse issues and family matters. And during the writing of this book, many of those noon-hour discussions revolved around our collective experiences with bulbs. My stories often served as a starting point for a more detailed examination by Jim or Valerie, and I'm happy to have given them somewhere to begin.

If there's one thing Jim and Valerie discovered while working on this book, it's that there's a lot of contradictory information out there. Once we established the direction of this book—to provide comprehensive information for home gardeners—it became much easier to resolve those contradictions. Valerie in particular had grown frustrated with the lack of a comprehensive, easy-to-use book on bulb gardening. She was determined to clear up common misconceptions and solve a number of perplexing mysteries. In doing so, she and Jim have opened up a whole new world of possibilities for bulb enthusiasts.

Jim, Valerie and the other experts at Hole's have created a wonderful book, filled with not only my favourite bulbs but also many exciting new varieties. Valerie has provided terrific history, variety recommendations and hands-on advice, while Jim has explained the wonders of the science behind bulbs. Together, they've produced a terrific book that novice gardeners and professionals alike will find indispensable.

And me? Well, I'm content to grow my tulips and alliums every year, and to enjoy paperwhites on my kitchen counter. But I'm also glad to know we've produced a resource for those who want to take their gardening and their knowledge much further. With the arrival of *Favorite Bulbs*, I hope that many more gardeners will enjoy, as I have, a lifetime of delight with these amazing plants.

Lois E. Hole
February 2003

Acknowledgements

We would never have completed *Favorite Bulbs* without the help of many talented people.

First and foremost, we are indebted to Carol Cowan, Director of the Netherlands Flower Bulb Information Centre in Toronto, and her associate Frans Roosen, Technical Director of the Internationaal Bloembollen Centrum (International Flower Bulb Centre) in the Netherlands. Carol and Frans generously provided their vast expertise and allowed us unfettered access to their research. They also provided several photographs of rare bulbs, filling in some of the gaps in our collection.

Paul Turmel and Alison Partridge of the Butchart Gardens in Victoria, BC shared their considerable knowledge and extended their hospitality, allowing us to take photographs of the hundreds of gorgeous flowering bulbs on display at the Gardens. Hans De Jongh from Paridon Horticultural was tremendously helpful. We would also like to thank Susanna Barlem and the other staff of the Calgary Zoo for their help in obtaining pictures.

We wish to acknowledge the following people for their assistance: John and Kay Melville, Janet Sparrow and her children, Dorothy and Jonathan Jedrasik, Danielle Entwistle, Kandace Kalin, Zachary Keith, Adrienne Farrell, Herv Benoit and Jill Fallis.

As always, the staff at Hole's made many invaluable contributions.

Finally, we must thank our readers for their loyalty and patience. We know that many of you have been eagerly awaiting this book, and we hope that the final result is as inspiring and informative as you anticipated.

Introduction

Some of the most popular, fragrant and gorgeous flowers in the garden are powered by enigmatic engines called bulbs. Packed with growing tissue and stored energy, bulbs come in a variety of forms and produce a dazzling array of beautiful flowers and foliage—and many of them do so year after year with little or no care.

But for novice gardeners, early experiments with bulbs can be intimidating, even overwhelming. Bulbs are among the easiest plants to grow, yet there are many choices to be made. Which of the thousands of varieties to choose? Where to plant—and when? Which bulbs stay in the ground and which must be lifted to survive the winter?

The contributors to this book have all been in the beginner's shoes. Some have learned through practical trial and error. For instance, the first time that staffer Marlene Willis planted tulips, she took great pains to follow the garden centre's instructions exactly. She handpicked her bulbs, amended her soil, planned a design, planted her bulbs early, watered the bulbs in gently and pampered them lovingly. What she didn't realize is that she had also planted each and every one of those bulbs upside down. Despite all the expert information she received, no one told her the basics.

Fortunately for Marlene, those tenacious tulips still bloomed. They had to struggle to emerge from the soil and were later flowering than expected, but they did come up—and as a bonus they taught her a lesson in perseverance.

Gardeners celebrate when they succeed and learn when they fail. Similarly, in creating this book we have compared our successes and failures, our triumphs and disasters, made notes on what worked—and what didn't—and brought it together in a practical, accessible format. *Lois Hole's Favorite Bulbs* is packed with sound advice for novice gardeners and insider tips for bulb enthusiasts.

A BIT OF BULB HISTORY

When people consider the history of bulbs, they usually think of Tulipmania, a period in which the economy of seventeenth-century Holland was nearly brought to its knees by out-of-control speculation on bulb prices. But the history of bulbs is much more interesting and complex than even that story implies.

Human beings have likely been eating the underground storage organs of plants since the dawn of our species, some discovering that potatoes and yams were quite palatable, others finding that narcissus bulbs were best left to produce flowers. Historical evidence reveals that the citizens of the ancient empires of India and the Far East, Egypt, Greece and Rome all used bulbs for decoration—bulbs such as scilla, gladiolus, muscari, allium, crocus and hyacinth. Three-thousand-year-old palaces on the island of Crete feature paintings of lilies—symbols of purity—on the walls. The Bible contains references to bulb-forming plants, as does a long tradition of English literature and folk songs—from Shakespeare's *azured harebell* to the schoolyard's *Bluebells, cockle shells, eevy, ivy, over.*

Bulbs also play a prominent role in our lives today. Many Canadians, for example, eagerly await the appearance of the tulips on Parliament Hill each year, and botanical gardens around the world create plantings for the enjoyment of millions of annual visitors. Bulbs continue to inspire our artists and visionaries—from Monet's majestic "Tulip Fields with Rijnsburg Windmill" to Tiny Tim's kitschy "Tip Toe Through the Tulips." The Canadian Cancer Society has adopted the daffodil as its symbol because the flower, which naturalizes readily all over Canada, is a powerful affirmation of renewal. And at a more basic level, many of the foods and flavours we enjoy—onion, garlic, fennel and saffron, for instance—derive from edible bulbs.

Simply by choosing which bulbs to cultivate, human beings have had a profound effect on them. Before humans came along, flower colour and size changed slowly. But once we brought bulbs into our gardens, breeders started crossing varieties in the hopes of producing more beautiful flowers, a wider range of colours, more robust growth and better disease resistance. As technology advances, humans will doubtless continue to shape the development of these versatile plants. Bulbs have grown alongside humans for millennia, providing both physical and spiritual sustenance, and that relationship is likely to go on for many years to come.

THE STRUCTURE OF THIS BOOK

This book is intended to provide all you need to know about bulbs to create beautiful gardens. Our goal was to present a complex subject in simple, but not simplistic, terms. No matter what your skill level, choosing from the myriad bulbs and growing them successfully can be challenging. For this reason we have structured this book to make finding the information you need easy.

The first section provides general information on getting started, caring for bulbs and planning your garden. We begin by exploring the nature of bulbs. Why do bulbs exist? What's the difference between a bulb and a corm? And, perhaps most importantly, what's the difference between spring-planted and fall-planted bulbs? It's much easier to grow and enjoy bulbs when you understand them. This section is filled with tips on shopping for bulbs, planting them properly and nurturing the plants through their growth cycle. We've also offered some of our favourite design principles, planting combinations and ways to use bulbs as cutflowers in bouquets and arrangements. Of course, these suggestions are just a beginning: the real fun of bulb gardening comes when you let your imagination run wild!

The second section, Twenty Best Bulbs, forms the body of the book. Here you'll find detailed accounts of our favourite bulbs, listed in alphabetical order by common name. The opening page of each account includes a quick fact box, designed to help you plan your gardening at a glance. There you will also find the Golden Rules: the three most critical things to know about a particular bulb, no matter which variety you plant or where you live.

Narcissus is among the best-known and best-loved bulbs

At the end of each account we've included a section called Try These! Here you'll find our top variety or species recommendations. Some bulbs, such as alliums, are listed by species or variety; others, such as daffodils and dahlias, are listed by division. The listings include common and Latin names, height, blooming season, hardiness, brief descriptions and notes on special requirements and features.

Some bulbs defied our basic categories and needed special handling. For example, we have divided the discussion of *Anemone* by species—*A. blanda*, *A. coronaria* and *A. nemorosa*—to reflect each species' particular care requirements. Similarly, we divided our discussion of tulips into cultivar and species varieties. While their care requirements are similar and the botanical differences are minor, there are so many cultivars that the species deserved their own treatment.

The third section of the book is intended for those who are ready to move beyond the basics. For the Adventurous is a listing of several dozen bulbs we encourage you to try. We have also included detailed explanations of how to force bulbs indoors and how to naturalize your yard or garden with bulbs.

Throughout the book, you'll find short discussions of the science behind the amazing transformation from humble bulb to radiant flower. Each sidebar is a short primer for gardeners who are curious to learn more about the biological, chemical and physical processes of bulb gardening. We encourage you to use these sidebars as a stepping stone to pursue your own research, if you are so inclined: the science of bulbs is fascinating!

After years of research, hundreds of photos and countless hours of writing and editing, our first book on bulbs is finally where we want it: in the hands of gardeners enthusiastic to experiment. We hope you enjoy our efforts.

What Are Bulbs?

Bulbs have a special appeal for gardeners, and no wonder. Their rapid development, as well as their ability to increase dramatically in size and number, is both fascinating and satisfying. They are one of the plant kingdom's most diverse groups—beautiful, varied and versatile. Close your eyes and think of a bulb. Perhaps you imagine a tulip, a daffodil or an amaryllis. But bulbs encompass a much broader array of plants than most of us realize—from elephant ears, muscari and water lilies to potatoes, asparagus and garlic.

In our common understanding, the word *bulb* refers to plants that share two important characteristics: when dormant, they can survive for weeks or months without soil or moisture; and when optimal conditions are available, they begin to grow. We refer collectively to plants with these qualities as geophytes. Geophytes are plants propagated by means of underground buds; they include true bulbs, corms, tubers, tuberous roots and rhizomes.

Bulbs come in a range of shapes and sizes

*A mass planting of
gorgeous 'Yokohama' tulips
at the Calgary Zoo makes
a stunning display*

Bulbs are amazing storage organs. The bulb contains all the plant parts, including the flower, and keeps them safely underground (usually), allowing the whole plant to survive adverse conditions. True bulbs, corms and tubers are similar because they are actually buds—that is, underground roots or stems bearing buds. They exist in a dormant state, waiting to resume growing when the proper conditions of moisture and temperature are available. They are like the buds on your flowering shrubs in appearance, but they differ because they are formed underground and are the nucleus of the entire plant, not just a plant part.

Bulbs also store the food and energy the new plants need in order to grow. The bulb supports growth until the root system develops. Once the plant is established, it manufactures new food energy, which it sends back to the bulb to prepare for the next dormant season. The foliage of flowering bulbs plays a vital role in manufacturing and storing reserve food supplies.

For true bulbs to reach their full size (that is, large enough to produce flowers and proper growth for the next season), the leaves must be allowed to complete their growing cycle after the flowers have finished blooming. (For most other geophytes, the foliage is irrelevant to replenishing the bulb.) Many gardeners cut down the foliage because it looks unsightly after the flower has faded. But without time to collect energy and store food, the bulb may not flower and may even die the following year. Instead of removing foliage, find creative ways to disguise it, perhaps among newly emerging perennials.

Bulbs are amazing storage organs

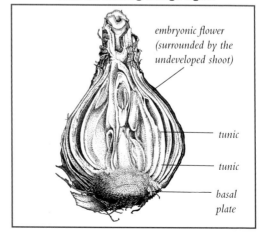

*embryonic flower
(surrounded by the
undeveloped shoot)*

tunic

tunic

*basal
plate*

Allium karataviense and Allium moly look stunning interplanted among small shrubs

TYPES OF BULBS

For the purposes of this book we will use *bulb* as the catch-all term to refer to bulbs and bulb-like plants. It doesn't matter what form of geophyte, or bulb, you grow, but it is useful to understand the differences between the types. Knowing the type of bulb will help you understand a plant's specific characteristics, including its growth habit and life cycle.

True bulbs ⤳ A true bulb is an underground stem with a growing point or bud surrounded by fleshy scales modified for food storage. The scales are held together at the base by hardened stem tissue called a *basal plate*. When the bulb begins to grow, the new roots develop around the edge of this disc.

Most true bulbs are covered by a thin, papery sheath called a *tunic* and are known as *tunicate* bulbs; the common cooking onion is a good example. The tunic offers protection and prevents moisture loss. A few true bulbs, such as lilies, do not possess a tunic and are called *nontunicate* bulbs. They have separate scales attached to the basal plate and are often more easily damaged in handling. They are also more susceptible to desiccation.

True bulbs are planted with the pointed end up. If a tunic is present, leave it intact, but don't worry if the tunic slips off. As long as the bulb is firm and shows no signs of bruising or fungal growth, it should grow well.

True bulbs in this book

- allium
- chionodoxa
- fritillary
- galanthus
- hyacinth
- iris
- muscari
- narcissus
- puschkinia
- scilla
- tulip

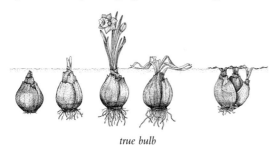

true bulb

Corms
in this book

- *Anemone coronaria*
- colchicum
- crocus
- gladiolus
- crocus

Corms ∽ A corm is a solid mass of fleshy tissue, a specialized underground stem with buds on the upper surface. Like true bulbs, corms have a basal disc of hardened stem tissue, from which the new roots emerge. The corm is a temporary storehouse for food. After the plant has used the food supply reserved in the corm, the corm withers and dies, and one or two new corms, called cormels, form on top of the old one.

Corms are usually rounded and slightly flattened. If a tunic is present, it is fibrous or netted. The tunic is composed of dried leaf bases held together by the basal disc. At the tip of the corm is a shoot that develops into leaves and the flowering shoot. Corms are planted basal disc down, with the terminal shoot pointing up.

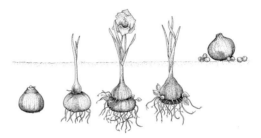

corm (gladiolus)

Tubers
in this book

- tuberous begonia
- elephant ear
- eranthis

Eranthis hyemalis, *commonly known as winter aconite*

Tubers ∽ Tubers are composed of solid swollen stem tissue; they vary widely in shape. Like corms, they have discernable buds—commonly called *eyes*—that eventually develop into growing shoots. But tubers lack a hard basal disc; they are really just modified stems. Roots emerge from many parts of the lower surface.

Just as the shapes of tubers vary, so do the planting instructions. In general, tubers that produce eyes over their entire surface, such as the potato, are simply dropped in the ground. Tubers that produce eyes on the upper surface are planted so the eyes face up.

tuber (begonia)

Tuberous roots ⌁ Like tubers, tuberous roots are made up of solid tissue and lack a basal disc. But tuberous roots are composed of root tissue; that is, they are modified roots, not stems. Tuberous roots do not themselves draw up water, but rather develop fibrous roots that absorb moisture and nutrients from the soil.

Some tuberous roots have *eyes* on their surface—sweet potatoes, for example. Others, such as dahlias, have eyes or buds only on the neck of the root (the point where it joined the old plant stem). New growth sprouts from the eyes, so tuberous roots are planted with the eyes pointing upwards.

Tuberous roots in this book

• dahlia

tuberous root (dahlia)

Rhizomes ⌁ A rhizome is composed of solid stem tissue like a tuber, but has an elongated, often branching shape like a tuberous root. Most roots develop along the lower surface of the rhizome, while the leaf and flower shoots emerge from the eyes on the upper surface.

Rhizomes vary in form and size. Some, such as *Agapanthus* and tuberose, have an upright, elongated, bulb-shaped rhizome; others, such as calla lily and canna lily, exhibit a more irregular, knobby shape. Regardless of their shape, rhizomes have surface buds that produce shoots and are always planted so the buds point upwards. If you can't see the buds, look inside the dry, scale-like leaf remains. These are the sites of potential buds.

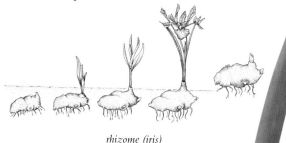

rhizome (iris)

Rhizomes in this book

• *Anemone blanda*
• *Anemone nemorosa*
• calla lily
• canna lily

Bulbs can be planted and enjoyed even in this narrow wall garden on Vancouver Island

the science behind it

Convergent Evolution

Why do geophytes take so many forms to accomplish the same purpose? The variety in forms—true bulbs, corms, tubers, rhizomes and so on—is the result of convergent evolution. Convergent evolution refers to the independent development of similar structures in organisms that are not directly related but are found in similar environments. Plants and animals from different backgrounds may arrive at the same evolutionary endpoint as a response to particular environmental factors.

Take the case of whales and fish, for example. They're not at all related, but both developed streamlined bodies with fins to solve the problem of propelling themselves through the water. In the same way, the various geophyte forms are different solutions to the common problems of changing seasons and adverse weather. The thick skin of begonia tubers conserves moisture to help the plant survive through the winter; the layered scales of tulip bulbs effect the same outcome. In the end, neither method is better than the other.

Had all flowering bulbs evolved in precisely the same habitats, they might have developed common solutions to common problems. But ours is a diverse world, with many different environments. Convergent evolution is evidence of nature's enormous problem-solving versatility.

Bulbs Are Beautiful

Most people plant bulbs to enjoy a show of gorgeous flowers. But gardeners can do the same with many annuals, perennials and ornamental vegetables. Bulbs deserve our attention because they form a category of plants for which there are no substitutes.

Fall-planted bulbs—crocuses and tulips, for instance— bring colour to the garden long before most annuals or perennials. Many naturalize and spread over the years, creating a garden landscape that other plants cannot duplicate. Here in St. Albert, for example, we garden in a northern climate, so squeezing a few extra weeks of colour into a dauntingly short growing season is crucial! Spring-planted bulbs, on the other hand, lend a tropical flair to the temperate garden. With their variations of foliage, texture, shape and colour, bulbs add dynamic interest to the garden throughout the year.

Spring-Planted Versus Fall-Planted Bulbs

Retailers divide bulbs into two major categories, based on their availability for planting. **Spring-planted bulbs** typically cannot endure extreme winter temperatures and require the moist warmth of spring to burst into flower. They are planted once the soil warms up; they provide excellent summer and early-fall colour. **Fall-planted bulbs**, on the other hand, are planted in the late summer and early fall, and most bloom the following spring, producing some of the earliest colour in the garden. Most fall-planted bulbs need a long period of cold temperatures during the fall and winter in order to flower in the spring. This process is called *vernalization*, which derives from the Latin root *vernus*, meaning spring. Hardy fall-planted bulbs must experience vernalization or else they will not bloom the following season.

In very warm climates, bulbs do not undergo vernalization. Tender bulbs go dormant during the cool or dry season, but they simply rest in the ground until sufficiently warm or moist conditions return and restart the growth cycle. Hardy (or cold-season) bulbs, on the other hand, require prolonged chilling by refrigeration—which mimics vernalization—in order to set flowers and bloom in the spring or summer.

The blooms of Allium *'Purple Sensation' illustrate the incredible diversity of bulb flowers*

Danielle Entwhistle and Kandace Kalin enjoy the beautiful tulips at the Calgary Zoo

the science behind it

Vernalization

Fall-planted, cool-season bulbs never truly go dormant. Bulbs are like biological computers, constantly monitoring their environment, waiting for the right time to resume active growth. This monitoring is one of the most important elements of vernalization. Before bulbs resume active growth, they must detect that they've been exposed to near-freezing temperatures for many weeks. The persistent cold signals that at least one winter has passed and it's safe to resume growth.

Scientists understand the mechanics of vernalization only vaguely. No one is sure, for example, which part of the bulb is the sensor that indicates how much time at cold temperatures has passed. Is it the nose of the bulb, the base or the bulb itself?

We do know a few things. Experiments suggest that vernalization is a chemical process, one that is effective only within a narrow range of cold temperatures. But it must be an unusual process indeed, since chemical reactions are generally retarded by cold. To explain this discrepancy, some scientists have theorized that dormancy in fall-planted bulbs could depend on a balance between gibberellic acid—a growth promoter—and abscissic acid—a growth inhibitor. Winter cold may slow down the growth-promoting process more than it slows down the growth-inhibiting process. When the cold ebbs, the gibberellic acid takes over and active growth resumes.

Other scientists have hypothesized the existence of a substance called *vernalin*. The existence of vernalin was originally inferred after an experiment that showed that when vernalized plant parts are grafted onto non-vernalized plants, the vernalization "spreads" to the grafted plant. Still, because vernalin has never been directly measured, its existence remains a contentious issue, even decades after the hypothesis was first raised.

We also know that vernalization is cumulative. As the number of cold days accumulates, the bulb becomes more effectively vernalized—that is, it gets closer and closer to the day when it will resume active growth. Experiments have also shown that vernalization can be reversed early in the process if the bulbs are subjected to heat.

There is still much work to be done before we completely understand the science of vernalization. Fortunately, experience has shown that gardeners can count on the process to work each year. As long as we continue to have winter (or, in southern climes, refrigerators), we can be assured that vernalization will work its magic on our bulbs.

This difference between spring and fall bulbs is crucial, yet it follows the basic logic of the garden. You plant gladiolus bulbs in the spring because they can't survive the winter months outdoors; for this reason, you cannot purchase gladiolus bulbs in the fall. Similarly, you won't find tulip bulbs for sale in the spring because tulips require exposure to 12 to 15 weeks of winter weather before they bloom; they simply cannot experience the conditions necessary to initiate flowering if they are planted in the spring. To enjoy flowers year-round, it pays to know which bulbs bloom when, and for how long.

Within the larger categories of spring- and fall-planted, bulbs may also be categorized by blooming season: spring-flowering, summer-flowering, fall-flowering and winter-flowering. By selecting a few species from each group, you can have flowering bulbs throughout the year for a modest investment.

Spring-flowering ❧ This group is probably the most familiar to gardeners. Spring-flowering bulbs include tulip, daffodil, hyacinth, crocus and many smaller species such as snowdrops, scilla and muscari. Purchased and planted in the fall, spring-flowering bulbs are hardy in most areas—depending, of course, on your climate. In very cold zones, spring-flowering bulbs may not survive unless planted in a sheltered location (near the foundation of a house, for example) and protected through the winter.

Summer-flowering ❧ Summer-flowering bulbs are purchased and planted in the spring, and bloom in the summer, typically June through September. There are two subgroups within summer-flowering bulbs: hardy (those that reliably overwinter in the ground) and tender (those that must be dug up and overwintered in storage except in very warm zones). The tender subgroup includes dahlia, gladiolus, tuberous begonia, canna lily, montbretia, *Tigridia*, *Caladium* and *Galtonia*.

Some very tender bulbs are best grown indoors (outside of tropical zones) and are most commonly sold as houseplants.

The 'Estella Rijnveld' parrot tulip is a lovely example of a fall-planted, spring-flowering bulb

Alliums are hardy spring-flowering bulbs

Fall-flowering ✺ Most of the fall-flowering bulbs are hardy. Interestingly, this group of bulbs receives minimal attention, which is a pity because these bulbs can provide a real blast of colour before winter sets in and after most of the annuals have died. Fall-flowering bulbs include fall-flowering crocus and colchicum. We've used them both extensively in our alpine show garden where they regularly draw comments and questions.

Winter-flowering ✺ The winter-flowering bulbs can be divided into two main groups: those that are very tender and bloom best in the house or a sunroom, and those spring-flowering bulbs that can be forced indoors to bloom during the winter months. The first group includes *Achimenes*, amaryllis, calla lily, hybrid cyclamen, gloxinia and gloriosa lily. In our garden centre, for example, we plant up colourful amaryllis for winter sale and they are always snapped up quickly. The second group includes the most common spring-flowering bulbs, such as tulip, narcissus, hyacinth, crocus, muscari and small irises. (Note that not all varieties of these species are suitable for forcing; see page 295 for a list of varieties you can force successfully.)

There is also a small group of very early spring-flowering bulbs that may appear in late winter in mild climates such as the southern tip of Vancouver Island. *Galanthus* and early crocus species are among the bulbs that may flower in February or early March.

The Growth Cycle of Bulbs

The growth cycle refers to the changes a bulb undergoes from the time it begins to grow actively, through its dormant period, to the point it begins to grow again the following year.

Typically, when gardeners speak of the dormant period of a bulb's growth cycle, they are referring to the period when no growth is visible above the ground. But bulbs undergo many changes, both physical and chemical, during dormancy, and their root systems may be growing actively even though no growth is visible above ground.

Regardless of when it is planted, as soon as a bulb is in soil it begins to produce roots and, eventually, stems. (In the case of fall-planted bulbs, the top growth remains underground until spring.) When conditions are right, foliage and flowers emerge. Without suitable growing conditions, the bulb remains dormant. For example, a canna rhizome planted outdoors in cold soil remains dormant until the soil warms up. If a dormant bulb remains in cold, moist soil too long, it may rot. To give tender bulbs such as canna lily, calla lily, tuberous begonia and elephant ear a sufficient growing season, start them indoors where optimum conditions can be provided, and then transplant them to the garden after the soil has warmed.

Each winter we plant up several large-growing tender bulbs specifically for transplanting. By the time the weather warms up, the bulbs have developed to more-than-respectable size and we use them throughout our show garden as focal points. These 'monster' pots draw a tremendous amount of attention from visitors who can't get over their size. Such terrific results would be simply impossible in our climate if we didn't invest the time to start the bulbs indoors.

When the conditions for growth are right, the tips of these species crocuses can be seen emerging from the warming soil

the science behind it

Reproduction of Bulbs

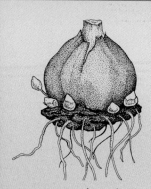

corms and cormels

Like all living organisms, geophytes exist to perpetuate their species. They accomplish this in a variety of ways, but the basic job is the same. A particular adaptation of bulbs is that they reproduce both sexually and asexually. Seed production is the sexual means; bulb formation is the asexual means.

Reproduction by seed is most common among bulbs grown for commercial purposes; in fact, it is essential to the development of new varieties. Plant breeders cross-pollinate varieties of bulbs and collect the resulting seed. By crossing varieties, breeders hope to produce new offspring with superior characteristics. Asexual reproduction takes a variety of forms, depending on the bulb species. True bulbs produce daughter bulbs called offsets during the growing season. The mother bulbs often die after flowering, to be replaced by the daughter bulbs; this process is called annual replacement.

So producing a new variety of tulip, for example, requires years of laborious cross-pollination (sexual reproduction) followed by several more years of bulb multiplication (asexual reproduction) to produce enough bulbs to sell. Once a superior bulb is bred, asexual reproduction through bulb growth followed by division is essential; only this process will yield the numbers of genetically identical bulbs required by the retail bulb market.

Some bulbs—such as daffodils, tulips and tiger lilies—reproduce by splitting (that is, by forming new, small bulbs called bulbils that eventually separate from the parent bulb). Similarly, corms produce cormels, miniature corms that form in addition to the new, full-size corm. Gladiolus, for example, frequently produces cormels.

Some tubers decompose at the end of their lifespan, leaving a cluster of new, smaller tubers in their wake. Dahlias, for instance, reproduce this way. Other tubers, such as begonias and gloxinia, reproduce simply by increasing in size. They produce additional eyes but do not split to form separate new plants. Rhizomes, on the other hand, branch during the active part of their growth cycle. Each branch produces a new eye or growing point, and new growth begins at these eyes.

Most bulbs can reproduce asexually indefinitely if conditions are favourable. Bulbs spend most of the growing season collecting and storing the energy photosynthesized by the foliage. But at some point, active reproduction begins. Depending on the species, reproduction may be triggered by environmental factors such as day length, temperatures, light intensity or low mineral content; or by internal factors such as plant hormone levels. In essence, bulbs attempt to reproduce when their local environment approximates that in which the species originally evolved.

Begonias, for example, evolved in temperate zones, where days shorten as the summer progresses. The diminishing day length signals that the growing season is reaching its end and the time has come for the plant to channel its energies to reserves that can be drawn upon in the reproductive phase. Top growth and flowers fade, and the tubers increase in size, storing up the energy necessary to produce next year's flowers and foliage. That foliage will, in turn, soak up the sun's energy to produce the next generation of tubers.

Bulb Hardiness

Hardiness is usually determined by the plant's physical characteristics, whether they were developed through evolution or introduced by plant breeders. *Winter hardiness* refers specifically to a plant's ability to survive the cold season.

Plant hardiness varies according to where you live. If your climate and growing conditions differ significantly from the environment that the bulbs you're planting are used to, you may face some hardiness issues. The most common problem occurs when gardeners try to grow a bulb in a region considered too cold for the plant—although the opposite can also occur, as any Californian who has tried to grow tulips will tell you.

Hardiness is not an exact term, however, because a bulb may not survive even in a zone milder than the bulb's rated hardiness. That's because even a hardy bulb may be affected by a wide range of factors. Too much or too little moisture may kill a hardy bulb, as may a lack of consistent snow cover during the winter. Conditions that are either

Our perennials manager Bob Stadnyk once received some Tecolote hybrid ranunculus in February. The bulbs were soaked overnight, potted and grown indoors. In the spring, once the danger of frost had passed, the ranunculus were planted outdoors. They bloomed in May and looked great. In July, the foliage died down and their location was marked. In the fall, the tuberous roots were dug up and stored indoors. But some of the roots were inadvertently left in the ground over the winter and, to our surprise, bloomed again the following spring. Amazingly, a Zone 9 plant survived the winter in a Zone 3a location.

There were several reasons that the ranunculus survived. First, it was a particularly mild winter. The bulbs were planted against the north side of a house, a thick layer of early snow provided a blanket of insulation before the ground froze and the temperature remained consistently mild—there were no harmful cycles of freezing and thawing. We were lucky that year—they didn't survive the following winter.

too warm or too dry during dormancy may harm or even destroy a bulb. Exposure to strong winds may dry a bulb out. Even the amount of time the bulb has to establish itself in the fall after planting—that is, the degree to which new growth develops before winter arrives—may determine whether or not a bulb survives the winter.

Hardy bulbs can survive outdoors in a given area through the winter without protection. For our purposes, when we call a bulb hardy, we mean that it's hardy in the Prairie provinces and other areas with similar climates, such as the Plains of the United States. Bulbs that are hardy on the Prairies may not be hardy in Alaska or the Yukon; bulbs hardy on Vancouver Island may not be hardy in North Dakota. Once established under typical conditions for that area, hardy bulbs should survive year after year.

Typically hardy bulbs include tulip, hyacinth, crocus, scilla, *Galanthus*, *Leucojum*, some varieties of lily, most varieties of narcissus and most varieties of muscari, to name a few. But even some of these bulbs will not survive without protection (such as thick mulch) in areas with really harsh winters. Microclimates—locations in your yard that are warmer than the surrounding area—can moderate a harsher climate. Trees, shrubs and fences slow chilling winds and capture insulating snow at ground level. House walls offer shelter and raise the nearby temperature by a few degrees. With a little ingenuity, you can manipulate the effects of climate on borderline-hardy bulbs in your area.

Semi-hardy bulbs are hardy in climates with mild or moderate winters; they will not survive in areas with harsh winters. As a rule, these bulbs will withstand soil temperatures at or near zero degrees Celsius if they have protection. Bulbs in this group include ranunculus, bulbous irises, some anemones and some varieties of narcissus.

Tender bulbs will not tolerate frost and overwinter only in warm climates. In cooler climates, these bulbs must be dug up after light frosts have killed the foliage. They may then be stored over the winter or treated as potted plants and overwintered indoors. Bulbs in this group include dahlia, calla lily, canna lily, elephant ear, gladiolus, tuberous begonia, amaryllis, montbretia, *Galtonia*, *Caladium*, eucharist lily and gloriosa lily.

Although 'Scarlet Gem' is a tazetta narcissus, it is hardy outdoors, unlike the better-known paperwhites, which are also in this division

Here's a method for preparing cold-season bulbs like tulip, crocus, colchicum, muscari and hyacinth if you live a mild climate. Place the bulbs in the refrigerator in a ventilated bag (a mesh bulb bag or paper bag with holes poked in it works well). Remove any fruit from the fridge, since the ethylene gases it gives off may injure the flowers inside your bulbs. Keep the bulbs for 8 to 15 weeks (depending on the variety or species) at 4 to 7°C. When spring arrives in your area, take the bulbs out of the fridge and plant them in the garden.

HARDINESS AND ZONES

The accepted standard for determining a particular plant's hardiness is its zone rating. Zone maps, which divide the continent into areas of similar climates, are based primarily on the minimum winter temperatures but also take into account other factors such as length of the growing season, soil conditions and fluctuating winter temperatures.

North American plant hardiness zones run from 0, the coldest, to 11, the warmest. In Canada the warmest zone is 8a, which occurs only on the West Coast; Zone 11 occurs in Hawaii and in Mexico.

In St. Albert, Alberta, where our greenhouse is located, the average frost-free growing season is 140 days. This zone is classified as 3a: in theory, a plant that is capable of surviving temperatures as low as -37°C will grow in this zone but will die at lower temperatures. In reality, however, we can successfully grow many so-called out-of-zone plants. With protection, plants rated for Zone 4 regularly survive the winter, while plants rated for Zones 5 and 6 survive some years and not others. Microclimates within a zone—and even within a yard—make an enormous difference to overwintering success. Experience has taught us that zone ratings should be used as a general guide rather than an absolute rule.

Zone ratings are also significant to the individual gardener's preferences and attitudes. Some gardeners want a very low degree of risk and a high rate of success. These gardeners should follow the zone recommendations. Others are more experimental and philosophical in their approach; they're more likely to enjoy their win-some-lose-some experiences with out-of-zone plants.

Of course, some gardeners—those who live in regions with very mild winters—face a special challenge with fall-planted bulbs. Many of these bulbs require a period of extended cold to initiate flowering; without it, the bulbs remain dormant. In these climates, gardeners must fool the bulbs into responding as if they've lived through winter (see sidebar above).

It's true that only so many species of plants can be grown in any zone. And there is no sure way of determining precisely which plants will survive in your garden and which will not. Zone ratings may not accurately reflect the specific conditions in your backyard. Don't be afraid to push the limits!

Shopping for Bulbs

Your bulb-shopping experience may be different every time, thanks to the arrival of new varieties (and the disappearance of old ones) each year. Crop failures may play a role: your favourite Darwin tulip may be in short supply if the weather in Holland has been unfavourable. Gardening trends also have an effect—if orange is in and pink is out, for example, you may find your choices governed by prevailing tastes.

Even so, some things remain constant. Bulbs for planting—whether they be true bulbs, rhizomes, corms or otherwise—are sold primarily in three ways: in packages at garden centres, as open stock at garden centres, and through mail-order and Internet catalogues. Each outlet may offer some exclusive varieties, but most carry a wide range of products. Regardless of how you buy your bulbs, you need some basic information to make an appropriate purchasing decision. Keep in mind both your level of gardening experience and your long-term goals for your yard, and make your choices accordingly. Many bulbs are easily replaced as your plans and tastes change, while others naturalize readily, giving you an attractive, low-maintenance option.

Sometimes it's best to start with something reliable and easy to grow, such as tulip or gladiolus bulbs. As you gain experience and confidence, you'll become more

Bulb season comes twice a year and is an exciting time in the garden centre, offering numerous choices

A true bulb must reach a minimum size before it flowers. We might refer to this size as the bulb's 'critical mass.' Bulbs that lack critical mass simply do not have enough stored energy to flower.

adventurous. Spend some time flipping through bulb catalogues and books. Note the species and varieties that catch your eye. Then it's time to do some research. Consult your local garden centre to determine the suitability of your choices to your zone and local conditions. Check the species descriptions (pages 61 to 276) in this book to find out cultural details, such as height, spread and growth habit. With this basic information, determine the categories of bulbs best suited to your gardening situation. Crosscheck the species and varieties that originally caught your attention against your list of the most suitable categories for your location, and make your choices accordingly; you'll have much greater success.

Once you've narrowed down your choices, check their blooming period. If you plant bulbs that bloom in succession, you can enjoy a long-lasting, dynamic display of colour. To extend the blooming period, plant early-blooming, mid-season and late-blooming varieties in the same area of the garden. For even more dazzle, choose contrasting or complimentary flower colours, working with the colours and tones in your existing garden plan.

An advantage to buying from a garden centre is the opportunity to see the stock for yourself and choose the best product available. Many retailers carry only stock suited to the local conditions, so you may be assured of buying bulbs that will thrive in your zone. Knowledgeable garden centre staff can help you select species and varieties best suited to your garden situation. Most importantly, you can buy fall-planted stock early and get it into the ground promptly, to give your bulbs the best start possible.

The first time you walk into the garden centre to buy bulbs, it may be difficult to distinguish between a high-quality product and a bad bargain. If you keep the following factors in mind, you should have no problem finding the pick of the offerings:

- **Firmness:** Bulbs should feel plump and fairly hard, not squishy or loose.
- **Weight:** Bulbs should feel relatively heavy for their size.
- **Outer condition:** The bulb skin should be smooth, bright and free of blemishes and mechanical injury (cuts and bruises).

Beware of bargains that seem too good to be true: they probably are! Bulbs offered at prices well below normal should be checked carefully. Can you see and handle them to determine their health and firmness? Bulbs tend to dry out after a few weeks on display and may not be viable if they've been sitting too long—small bulbs are particularly prone to desiccation. What size are the bulbs? If they are undersize for their species, they may not flower well in the first season—if at all. Be wary of buying spring-flowering bulbs in the late winter: if the bulbs require a cool period to initiate flower production, you won't get any blooms in the first growing season.

the science behind it

Latin Names

Scientists, horticulturists, plant breeders and many gardeners use Latin to name plants. *Muscari azureum*, for example, is the Latin name for one of the earliest-flowering species of grape hyacinth. *Muscari* is the genus, which describes a group of plants that have certain characteristics in common; *azureum* is the species, a narrower category that includes only plants that interbreed naturally. This two-part system of naming (called binomial nomenclature) was created to eliminate the confusion produced by multiple common names for plants and animals.

Carolus Linnaeus introduced binomial nomenclature in his book *Species Plantarum* (1753). Linnaeus catalogued more than 6,000 plant species and more than 4,000 animal species using the system of classical taxonomy, which groups organisms by their structural characteristics. All living things are classified into broad groups, called taxa, identified by Latin (or Latin-derived) names. For example, plants belong to the plant kingdom, Plantae; animals (including humans) belong to kingdom Animalia. Each kingdom then splits into increasingly narrow categories—phylum, class, order, family—also using Latin names, until identification reaches the level of interbreeding organisms, identified by genus and species. Binomial nomenclature is an efficient way to identify plants because no two species have the same Latin name.

The International Association for Plant Taxonomy governs the selection of plant names. New names are added as new species are discovered, and old names are changed as species are reclassified. Subspecies of plants exist, too, and when a plant name includes a genus, species and subspecies, we call this trinomial nomenclature.

So, although many plants go by the common name "grape hyacinth," Latin names allow us to distinguish between *Muscari armeniacum*, *Muscari azureum*, *Muscari botryoides* and *Muscari neglectum*. Thus, the key to getting the plant you want is knowing how to ask for it by name—the Latin way!

Marlene Willis, one of our resident experts on bulbs, recalls an experience she had years ago. After moving into a new home, she planted dahlia tubers in the one corner of the yard that wasn't covered by sod. Marlene amended the soil with mushroom manure and—without consciously deciding to do so— provided the tubers with the perfect growing conditions. Nature cooperated that year. The results were amazing, with varieties that normally grow 1-1.5 m reaching heights of 2–2.5 m and boasting stunning displays of blooms. "Even though I'm almost six feet [180 cm] tall, I felt dwarfed by those towering giants!" Marlene calls her accidental success a delightful surprise. The union of perfect site, soil and weather inspired her to try many other kinds of bulbs. Staff member Christine Cassavant, on the other hand, deliberately plants her tulips under the large spruce trees in the front yard, knowing they won't last long in such adverse conditions. As she says, "They'll last two years, tops—but what a stunning combination!"

SIZING BULBS

With true bulbs, the size of the bulb you plant makes a difference to both the size and the number of blooms. If properly planted and cared for, large bulbs should produce large, healthy blooms. Small bulbs, on the other hand, may not be mature enough to produce flowers at all in the first year. Similarly, a rhizome or tuber with many eyes, or growing points, will thrive considerably better than one with few eyes.

The largest true bulbs are often referred to as *top size*. With true bulbs, the larger the bulb, the larger the flower it will produce. Tulip bulbs, for example, are graded by circumference, and top-size tulips have a circumference of 12 cm or greater. Daffodil bulbs are sized based on their noses. Species and cultivars of species bulbs are not graded by circumference because their sizes vary so greatly that grading would not be relevant. The only criterion is that the bulb be of sufficient size for its species or variety to produce flowers during the growing season.

Planting Bulbs

Now that you've purchased your bulbs, it's time to give them the right conditions to resume growth. Whether they're fall-planted or spring-planted, bulbs have specific soil and light needs. The wrong environment will hinder a bulb's growth and may even prevent it from flowering or coming back in subsequent seasons.

The information provided below refers to bulbs in general. See the section In the Garden in the species descriptions (pages 61 to 276) for specific cultural information.

John Gabriel, one of Hole's experienced staff, plants large quantities of bulbs in our show garden each fall

SOIL

Soil is important to growing bulbs successfully. Soil provides a physical home and protects the bulb from frost, extreme heat and drought, predators and disease. Soil supports the roots and aerial shoots, and it retains the moisture, nutrients and air that all plants need. Soil type can be crucial to the survival of many bulb species.

Most bulbs grow fairly well in a range of soil conditions, including clay, loam and sandy loam. However, some require specific soil conditions to thrive. To flower well year after year, Darwin tulips, for example, require rich, heavily fertilized soil, whereas species tulip bulbs prefer a leaner soil. Most bulbs prefer a compost-rich sandy loam, which drains well but doesn't dry out too quickly. A good mix is two parts loam, one part peat moss or compost, and one part coarse sand.

Although most bulbs tolerate a wide range of soil conditions, they are very intolerant of poor drainage. They will not grow well in soils where the water level is consistently close to the surface. Any area of your garden that remains wet for long periods after it rains or in the spring when the snow is melting is not suitable for growing bulbs. Most bulbs will rot in these boggy conditions (with a few exceptions, such as *Colocasia esculenta,* which lives happily in standing water, and water cannas).

the science behind it

Amending Soil

Some gardens have "perfect" soil, usually defined as a loam that holds moisture and nutrients without getting waterlogged, but also dense enough to anchor plant roots firmly. If you can pick up a fistful of soil and squeeze it into a soft, springy ball that holds its shape yet crumbles easily between your fingers, you probably have good soil.

Unfortunately, the soil in many gardens is composed mostly of heavy clay, coarse sand or spongy peat. Heavy clay soils are very dense, with little air space for roots to grow or water to drain. Heavy clay soils often become waterlogged, causing bulbs to rot in the ground. Sandy soil, on the other hand, is so coarse that water doesn't stay in the root zone long enough to irrigate the plants properly. Peaty soil, like sandy soil, contains so much air space that water drains too rapidly to support flowering bulbs.

To provide a healthy environment for bulbs, it's necessary to amend heavy clay and sandy soil. To do so, you must add organic matter such as peat moss, well-rotted manure or compost. Organic matter will loosen heavy clay soil, creating air spaces for roots and water to move through. And it will add needed bulk to sandy soil, preventing water from draining too quickly. Aeration and drainage are vastly improved by organic matter, but you must be prepared to add sufficient quantities. Depending on the size of your bed and the quality of your soil, it could take several seasons and many loads of organic matter to create the soil you want. Changing the composition of your soil is a big job, but your plants will thank you for it.

Sun or Shade?

The majority of bulbs prefer sun—the more sun, the better. Remember, though, that most spring-flowering bulbs bloom before the trees have leafed out, so as long as their area of the garden is sunny at the time they bloom, it doesn't matter if the garden becomes shadier later in the season. Locations near or under evergreens are unsuitable for bulbs, however, because the soil is dry, shady and often acidic. Most bulbs need some sun after they finish blooming because the foliage continues to develop, replenishing the energy in the bulb for growth the following season.

Specific location recommendations are designed to elicit the bulb's best performance. For example, a plant recommended for full sun may survive with only morning sun, but it will not likely reach its full potential. For best results, choose your bulbs according to the light levels in their intended location.

Full sun ‒ Bulbs in this category require a minimum of five hours of direct sunlight for best performance. Gladiolus, dahlia, tulip and crocus fall into this category.

Shade to morning sun ‒ These bulbs require cooler, less intense light. They can tolerate full sun from morning until noon, but will wilt if exposed to hot afternoon sunlight. They also do well in areas that receive dappled shade all day. Tuberous begonia, hyacinth, muscari and *Galanthus* fall into this category.

Bulbs that thrive in full shade are uncommon, but they do exist. Such bulbs require a cool, moist soil and are usually native to forests, where they receive low-intensity, early-spring sunlight through the leafless canopies of the trees. Their blooming period usually finishes early in the season before the deciduous trees and shrubs have leaves.

Crocus chrysanthus *'Snow Bunting' thrives in a location that receives a minimum of five hours of direct sunlight*

the science behind it

Stretching

When light levels are low, plants may stretch—that is, grow tall and lanky—in an effort to reach more sunlight. Plants that grow beneath other plants stretch because they are searching for a different quality of sunlight. All plants need the right spectrum, or quality, of light to grow properly, and they seek it actively, guided by their photoreceptors, which can sense differences in light waves. Red light, in particular, is most sought.

Plants growing in unobstructed sunlight are bathed in light from across the spectrum. But the light received by shaded plants is filtered by their taller neighbours; instead of the feast of red light they crave, shaded plants absorb relatively greater quantities of "far-red" light. Because far-red light doesn't suit their needs as well as ordinary red light, the plants stretch in an attempt to correct the ratio of red to far red.

The problem is that stretching stems stretches resources. Tall, lanky stems are weaker and more prone to insects and diseases than shorter, sturdier growth. Stretched plants may topple over and die. And if they do survive, they likely won't capture enough energy to regrow or rebloom the following year. Clearly, it's important not only to plant your bulbs in an appropriate location but also to space them so that tall plants don't overshadow short ones.

INTO THE EARTH

You've chosen the perfect location. Now what? It's time to put the bulbs into the soil. Depth and spacing are important considerations in planting bulbs, not just to provide the best growing conditions possible, but also to create the aesthetic effect you desire.

At its most basic, the process of planting bulbs is very simple:

1. Dig a hole to a depth of three times the bulb height (to the base of the bulb).
2. Place the bulb in the hole.
3. Fill the hole with appropriate soil.

These general guidelines will work most of the time with most bulbs. The specific directions we provide in the accounts that follow are intended to help you make better choices based on light, location and climate, to help you get the best results from your bulbs.

Remember that bulbs are fairly forgiving. Even if you plant them upside-down, they will likely grow. Most bulbs also signal their distress at being planted in the wrong location or receiving improper care. If your bulbs are slow to produce shoots and flowers, or if the foliage is stunted, the bulbs may be trying to tell you that they need help. Don't be afraid to dig the bulbs up to solve a problem—or to try again next year if something goes wrong.

DEPTH

There are two basic approaches to depth, depending on your overall garden plan. You can dig a wide area of soil to the desired depth, set bulbs onto the exposed surface and then replace the soil, or you can dig individual holes for individual bulbs. The first method is typically used when planting the bulbs in a formal design pattern, while the latter is used more often for smaller clusters of bulbs and for large feature plantings.

Depth is variable with spring-planted bulbs. Consult the species descriptions that follow (pages 61 to 276), the product packaging or your local garden centre for details. The general rule for fall-planted bulbs is to plant large bulbs (those 5 cm or greater in diameter) to a depth of 2

Large fall-planted bulbs, like these tulips, are usually planted to a depth two to three times their height to the base of the bulb

to 3 times their height and to plant small bulbs to a depth 3 to 4 times their height. Depth should be measured from the base of the bulb to soil level.

In light, sandy soils that dry out quickly, bulbs should be planted at the deeper end of the range; in heavier soils, they should be planted at the shallower end. In very cold climates where the ground freezes hard to a consider-able depth, borderline-hardy bulbs must be both planted deeply and mulched for the winter months.

Planting your bulbs deeply may delay flowering slightly but not significantly. Other factors that determine when bulbs flower include the amount of sun they receive, how early the soil warms up and the climate in which they are growing. Bulbs planted in shadier locations flower later than the same bulbs planted in a sunnier location. Bulbs planted in northern climates flower later than the same bulbs planted in a milder climate simply because spring arrives later. The ability of bulbs to delay growth until conditions are right reduces the chance of frost damage in early spring.

Bulb dust contains a fungicide and an insecticide, which helps keep bulbs from rotting in the ground and protects them from many soil-borne diseases

Spacing

Spacing is also variable for most bulbs—it's more of an art than a science. Your choice depends on your sense of aesthetics, the surrounding garden and the amount of effort required for continuing care.

With spring-planted bulbs, you must take into account the mature height and width of the plant. Consult the species descriptions that follow (pages 61 to 276), the product packaging or your local garden centre for details.

As a rule, fall-planted bulbs are spaced according to their height. Leave a space 1 to 2 times the bulb height between large bulbs (5 cm or greater in diameter); for small bulbs, leave a space 2 to 3 times the bulb height. But note that many gardeners leave less space between their bulbs with no negative effects—other than, perhaps, having to thin the bulb bed a little more frequently than they might otherwise.

Spacing depends on the effect you want to achieve. Plant closely for a dense, solid mass; allow greater distance for feature plantings and borders. Dense clusters typically look more natural than sparse plantings. Regularly spaced plantings look formal, even stately, if applied to a large bed or along an extended path. Be careful not to space too widely. A solitary bulb or a single row of very widely spaced bulbs has little visual impact in the garden.

WHEN TO PLANT

It's best to plant your bulbs as soon as possible after purchasing them. If you cannot plant them right away, store them in a cool, dark, well-ventilated location. If the storage location is very dry, cover the bulbs with moist peat moss.

Gardeners worry about planting their fall bulbs too early. They fear the bulbs will emerge through the soil surface and freeze with fall frosts. Relax! Fall-planted bulbs begin to develop roots as soon as they are in the soil, but without the cold treatment provided by a long winter, they will not begin to produce top growth or flowers. In fact, the earlier the bulbs are planted, the more extensive the root development before freeze-up and the greater the chances of winter survival.

Both hardy and borderline-hardy fall-planted bulbs should be watered in well after planting. These bulbs grow and develop roots and shoots underground in the fall, and water promotes the development of a strong, healthy root system. Bulbs won't initiate root development in dry soil, and if the bulb is not rooted by the time the ground freezes, it may not survive the winter. Good root development anchors the bulbs in the soil and lessens the possibility of damage or injury. The root system is also in place in the spring for immediate access to water and nutrients once top growth begins.

When to Plant Bulbs

When to plant fall bulbs	Zone	When to plant spring bulbs
August to early September	1	Late May to early June
August to early September	2	Mid to late May
September	3	Mid May
Late September to early October	4	Early to mid May
Late September to early October	5	Mid April to early May
Mid October	6	Early to mid April
Early November	7	Late March to early April
Mid November to early December	8	Early to mid March

In general, the warmer the zone, the later you can plant in the fall and the earlier you can plant in the spring.

How to plant bulbs

Wondering how to plant an unfamiliar bulb species? It's easy! Compare your bulb to the images in the chart below and follow the directions.

Bulb	Bulb type	Planting directions
	true bulb	Plant pointed end up
	corm	Plant basal disc down, shoot pointing up
	tuber, eyes scattered across surface	Simply set in the ground with the majority of eyes facing up
	tuber, eyes on upper surface	Plant with eyes facing up
	tuberous root, eyes scattered across surface	Simply set in the ground with the majority of eyes facing up
	tuberous root, eyes on root neck only	Plant with eyes facing up
	rhizome	Plant with buds pointing up; buds may be inside scaly covering

If you have planted your bulbs upside-down, don't despair. Although upside-down planting sets their progress back, some emerging stems will eventually find their way to the surface. It's also possible to dig bulbs up and reposition them, particularly those bulbs with a definite growing point, like tulip and gladiolus.

Spring-planted bulbs can go directly into the garden once the soil warms up. The date of the average last frost in your community is a valuable guideline for when to plant spring bulbs. Assuming the weather is warm, you can safely plant on or after this date. (Tender tropical bulbs should be planted about two weeks after the date of average last frost.) Bulbs planted too early into cool, wet soil will stall and may even rot. If your spring bulbs begin to sprout while waiting for warm weather—or if you want to get a jump on the season—start the bulbs indoors in pots and transplant them after the danger of frost has passed. In particular, if you live in a cool climate with short summers, start long-season tender bulbs indoors and transfer them to the garden once the weather is consistently warm. Starting bulbs indoors helps to produce big, robust plants—so you don't run out of summer before the flowers arrive!

the science behind it

Gravitropism

Gravitropism describes the phenomenon that causes plant roots to grow downward in response to gravity. Plants normally exist in a state called *anisotropic* growth; in simple terms, the stems grow upward (negative gravitropism), and the roots grow downward (positive gravitropism). Thanks to gravitropism, this tendency continues even if a plant is turned sideways or upside down.

Stem and root tissues contain substances that affect plant tropism (movement). Stems grow away from the ground because of the hormone auxin. When a plant is oriented away from the vertical axis, auxin moves to the part of the plant that is closest to the centre of gravity. If a bulb is lying on its side, for example, auxin causes the lowermost side of a developing shoot to grow faster than the uppermost side. This uneven growth naturally results in a curved shoot, bending upwards, away from the centre of gravity. Once the shoot is vertical, the auxin moves back to the growing point at the shoot's tip.

Root tissues, on the other hand, contain starch granules called statoliths that act as gravity receptors. The statoliths pile up at the bottom of plant cells, shifting the weight load and triggering downward growth. To imagine this process, think of two large boxes, each containing a dozen baseballs. One box has foam chips between the balls, distributing the weight load evenly from top to bottom. The other box has no packing chips, and the balls pile up at the bottom. Both boxes weigh the same (if we discount the weight of the foam chips, of course), but the distribution of the mass is different.

Although gravitropism helps the shoots and roots of improperly planted bulbs to grow in the proper direction, the process may set back the plant's development and may delay flowering. Gravitropism is a powerful force, but gardeners should not rely on it to reorient improperly planted bulbs.

Bulbs in the Garden

We have learned through experience that most bulbs need regular care through the season. Your care schedule needn't be formal or involve a lot of work, but it should be consistent. Just a few basic duties will keep your flowering bulbs looking their best.

Water

Water is most crucial from the time the bulbs begin to produce flower buds until they come into bloom. For those bulb species that do not develop their foliage fully until after they have flowered, such as tulips and daffodils, ensure that the bulbs receive adequate water (either from rainfall or supplemental watering) until the foliage has a chance to mature. Once the foliage turns yellow and begins to die, stop watering.

The first time Christina McDonald, one of our staff members, planted gladiolus bulbs, she didn't bother to stake the plants, believing that her small enclosed garden would offer sufficient protection. She still regrets that decision: "They were so beautiful and being a new gardener I was so proud of that bed, but all it took was one bad storm and all my lovely glads were face down in the mud! I've since learned to be a little more diligent."

A large planting of narcissus bulbs makes a strong statement in the garden as well as providing lots of blooms for cutting

compost the infected plants; destroy them. There is no chemical treatment for *Fusarium*.

Blue mould (*Penicillium*) ↝ *Penicillium* is the most common garden fungus, but it rarely causes problems for bulbs in soil. Blue mould grows on the bases of bulbs. The spores enter the plant tissue through bruises, scratches, insect holes and other wounds.

A little blue mould on the skin of a bulb isn't normally a problem; a few spots on the scales won't impair the development of the bulb. Avoid heavily infested bulbs that appear soft and blue around the base. A badly infected bulb may decay completely after planting. There is no chemical control for this fungus.

ぷ ぷ ぷ

Most disease problems can be avoided by growing robust, healthy plants and choosing disease-resistant varieties. Diseases are far more likely to attack plants that are stressed by underwatering, underfeeding or lack of light, or that have been handled roughly during harvest and storage.

Sanitation is the other cornerstone of control. Keep your garden clean and limit the risk of introducing and encouraging disease. Don't rely on chemicals in lieu of proper sanitation and regular care. Such controls have their place, but they're no substitute for a neat, well-maintained garden.

Black aphids

TINY PESTS

Bulbs are largely resistant to insect pests. The majority of damage is caused by four insects: aphids, mites, thrips and whiteflies.

Aphids ↝ There are about 4,000 species of aphids in the world, and about 250 species are plant pests. Aphids are small, soft-bodied insects with piercing, sucking mouthparts specialized for feeding on plant sap. As aphids feed, they secrete a sticky liquid waste called honeydew, which is visible on foliage.

Aphid populations can explode during the summer months, so vigilance is the key to control. At least once per week, check the growing tips and undersides of the leaves where aphids like to feed. A thorough spraying of a mild insecticide, such as insecticidal soap, can prevent an aphid population explosion. Weekly sprayings may be required to keep aphid numbers down. Don't let aphid populations rise to large numbers; if you do, control may become virtually impossible.

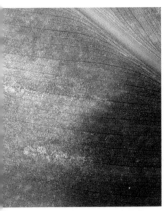

*Two-spotted spider mites
on a canna leaf*

Thrips on a gladiolus leaf

Two-spotted spider mites ✌ Although there are many species of spider mites, the two-spotted spider mite is the most destructive to bulbs. They feed by sucking sap from plant cells, robbing the plant of nutrients and providing an entry point for disease. Early control is critical.

Insecticidal soap is an effective treatment, provided the mites are sprayed directly. Be sure to spray the mites hiding on the undersides of the plant leaves, and treat the bulbs when mite numbers are low. Only live mites, and not the eggs, are affected by the soap, so multiple applications may be necessary.

Thrips ✌ Anyone who has grown gladiolus is familiar with the damage caused by thrips. These tiny, slender insects feed on the stems, leaves and flowers of gladiolus plants, causing brown streaks or stippling of the plants.

You can eliminate overwintering thrips on your corms by dipping them in a solution of Lysol before planting. However, this treatment does not deter thrips that migrate to the plants during the growing season. Thrips like to be enveloped in plant tissue for security, which makes it difficult to control them with insecticidal soaps. Malathion is the preferred control.

Whiteflies ✌ Whiteflies are usually thought of as greenhouse pests, because they cannot tolerate cold. Whitefly infestations on garden plants often originate from infested plants moved from the greenhouse to the garden. If you discover whitefly populations on your garden plants, treat them with insecticidal soap three times at five-day intervals.

BIGGER PESTS

Although we often think of insects as the main garden pests, larger creatures—such as mice, chipmunks, squirrels, porcupines, rabbits and deer—can also be a nuisance. There are several ways to deal with these intruders. You can try to frighten the animals away, use a commercial repellant, modify your garden habitat to make it less enticing or erect physical barriers to exclude animals.

Burrowing rodents, such as squirrels and moles, are the most common pests in the garden. They feed on bulbs underground. For example, the grey squirrel, a common city dweller, seems to target tulip bulbs and can dig up entire beds of newly planted bulbs in short order.

Repellants are one way to discourage feeding. Treat the bulbs with repellant before you plant. Thiram, for example, adds a bitter taste to bulbs, rendering them unpalatable. Thiram is also a fungicide, used for controlling rot on a number of crops, including bulbs. For best results, follow the application instructions on the label.

Where squirrels are particular pests, some gardeners provide them with a feeding station stocked with peanuts. As long as the feeding station is filled, there's little incentive for squirrels to seek out other food sources—such as bulbs. This may seem like a protection racket, but bulk peanuts are a lot cheaper than bulbs!

Browsing animals, such as rabbits and deer, eat the growing bulb foliage and flowers. You must spray the emerging growth with foul-tasting repellant to protect the plants from nibbling. Scent repellants are sprayed or scattered around the base of the growing bulbs; the odour discourages feeding. We do not recommend mothballs as repellants because they contain naphthalene, a chemical that may cause respiratory problems in humans.

A dog in the yard discourages deer and rabbits, but may provoke squirrels. Some gardeners have had success with ribbons or fabrics that flutter in the breeze; the motion discourages nervous browsing animals. Lights and water sprinklers activated by movement may also be effective, but only if the animals are large enough to trigger the sensors.

Exclusion is the most effective control. Place fine-meshed chicken wire or old screening over the bulb bed to stop squirrels and other burrowing creatures. A high, solid fence discourages deer, who are reluctant to jump a visual barrier, and shuts out rabbits, who cannot leap over.

Interestingly, animal pests do not feed on narcissus. Interplanting narcissus among your bulbs may discourage their activity. (See page 300 for a list of other bulbs that most animals won't touch.)

The results of a squirrel feasting on hyacinth foliage

One of the ways the staff at the Butchart Gardens prevent squirrel damage is by covering the bulb beds with large nets

Deadhead blooms as they fade to maintain an attractive and productive garden

Drying gladiolus leaves may look unsightly, but they have an important function to perform, so allow the foliage to die back naturally

DEADHEADING

Once the flowers fade, deadhead them—that is, pinch off the dying bloom with your fingers (use scissors for larger blooms). This step accomplishes a number of purposes. Deadheading dahlias allows the plant to devote more energy to producing additional blooms; deadheading single-blooming species, such as tulips, allows the foliage to start feeding the bulb for next year's growth, rather than expending energy producing seeds. It also helps control species that self-seed readily, by preventing seed heads from forming. Finally, deadheading improves the look of your plants and encourages more flowers.

Deadheading is one of the simplest tasks in the garden, and one of the most enjoyable. Just pick a sunny afternoon and wander through the garden, using your fingers gently to pinch off any faded or wilting blooms. This task is relaxing and productive!

AFTER-BLOOM CARE

Once the blooms have faded, the question of what to do with the foliage becomes paramount. The foliage may look unsightly, but it has an important function to perform. Allow the foliage to die back naturally so that the plant can continue to store energy for the next growing season. Bulbs continue to require water and fertilizer to build food reserves in the bulb for the next year's foliage and flowers.

There are various ways to camouflage dull or fading bulb foliage, some more labour intensive than others. Try planting bulbs among larger perennial plants, whose later growth hides or minimizes the view of the dying foliage. For example, daylilies and daffodils work well together, because their foliage is similar. You can also plant annuals in front of spring-flowering bulbs to hide the withering leaves and stems. You can cut the foliage back by half, to reduce its straggly, unkempt appearance, and fertilize every two to three weeks to encourage bulb development. Some gardeners gather or braid the foliage, but this treatment reduces the bulb's energy-collecting ability and may compromise its growth in the next season—we don't recommend that you try this.

Some really energetic gardeners dig up the fading bulbs, foliage and all, and replant them in a less visible spot specifically for the purpose of letting the bulbs finish the season.

Of course, if you don't want the bother of tidying up after the flowers have faded, treat your bulbs like annuals and remove them from the garden once blooming has finished. You can start fresh with new bulbs next season. This strategy is particularly useful for gardeners who grow bulbs in containers and have limited gardening space.

the science behind it

When Something Goes Really Wrong!

Bulbs are beautiful and largely trouble-free additions to the garden. However, a few unusual—and vividly named—problems may afflict flowering bulbs: horse's teeth, nose rot and stem topple.

A bulb is said to be suffering from horse's teeth when its main shoot is lost to injury or disease and the growing plant instead produces side shoots, resulting in a bushy plant without flowers. There is no cure for horse's teeth, but if the bulb is hardy, don't uproot the foliage. It may feed the bulb enough to produce new bulbs and new flowers next year.

Nose rot usually begins because of a physical injury to the nose, or tip, of the bulb. The nose is vulnerable to rot because its growth is still tender, unlike sturdier, more disease-resistant old growth. The nose also isn't as well sealed against infection as the rest of the bulb.

Before shipping their crops to retail, most bulb growers cure the bulbs, drying them so that the vulnerable noses will be nearly as tough, woody and resistant to infection as the rest of the bulb. That's why nose rot is rarely a problem with store-bought bulbs. Of course, if you harvest your own bulbs for further propagation, you'll have to cure them yourself.

Stem topple of tulips occurs because of a lack of the element calcium. Calcium builds strong cell walls in plants, and without enough of it, the walls—and the stem—may collapse. Most soils have sufficient calcium to support the needs of tulips. If many of your plants are suffering from stem topple, you may need to add calcium to the soil. Commercial calcium supplements will do the trick.

Horse's teeth, nose rot and stem topple are relatively rare ailments. But it never hurts to be prepared.

John and Kay Melville of St. Albert prepare their canna bulbs for winter storage

Overwintering Bulbs

Hardy bulbs, such as tulip, narcissus and crocus, do not require protection over the winter to survive in most zones. However, after they are planted in the fall, these bulbs require a minimum of 3 weeks of daytime temperatures of at least 10°C to root properly before winter sets in. Gardeners in areas with harsh climates should plant their fall bulbs as early as possible to ensure the development of a good root system and thus their survival through the winter.

To overwinter borderline-hardy bulbs successfully, you can plant them deeper, mulch them or locate them close (but not too close) to buildings or sheltered areas where other perennials or shrubs catch the winter snow. These plants also act as additional insulation and protection from the wind. This extra insulation minimizes the freezing and thawing of soil that plagues regions with widely fluctuating winter temperatures. Remember, the purpose of winter protection is not to keep the soil warm but rather to keep it evenly cool, so that warm spells don't trigger premature growth and severe cold spells don't damage the bulbs.

Some hybrid tulips come back well for years, provided the foliage is left to replenish the bulbs, but eventually they produce smaller flowers that begin to fade. For this reason, in major show plantings, such as Parliament Hill in Ottawa and the Calgary Zoo, tulips are treated as annuals and replaced each year.

Tender bulbs must be dug up, stored indoors and replanted in the spring if you want them to bloom in subsequent seasons. Dig up summer-flowering bulbs in the fall after the first fall frost has touched the foliage. (If you wait too long, the soil will chill, frost will touch the bulb itself and the bulb will be lost—tender bulbs do not recover from frost injury.) *Do not* wash the bulbs to remove the excess soil; clinging dirt can be brushed off once it has dried. Allow the bulbs to dry on all sides and dust them with bulb dust. Store the bulbs in peat moss or vermiculite in mesh bags, nylon stockings, boxes or buckets in a dark, cool (but not cold) location. The bulbs will remain dormant until they are planted in the garden again when warm weather returns.

Many of our staff members have great success planting tender bulbs in containers and moving them to a cool, dark indoor location (a vegetable cellar is ideal) when the season turns. Christine Cassavant, for example, plants *Colocasia* in pots. Each fall she cuts the plants back and puts the pots in her cold storage room. If she has space, she brings the pots into her cool sunroom in late winter or early spring to give them a headstart before they move outside. Once the risk of frost has passed, the pots go back into the yard, and she waters and fertilizes as usual.

Not all tender bulbs can be treated this way—dahlias and begonias, for instance, tend to rot if they're kept in soil over winter. You must also be careful not to allow the storage temperature to drop below freezing. If you find it's too much trouble to dig up and store tender bulbs, treat them like annuals and plant new bulbs next year.

Two of our call centre staffers have enjoyed success with container planting. Betty Sampson filled a large pot with canna lily 'Pretoria' and sweet potato vine 'Marguerite', along with a few other annuals. "The colour combination was stunning and the size—well, it was just enormous!" she reports. Pat Lewis prefers to grow her dinnerplate dahlias in pots (with tomato cages for support). She finds this method allows an earlier spring start and makes removing the tubers for fall storage easy. According to Pat, "I use the pots in groups around my deck; they make a really attractive screen."

GROWING BULBS IN CONTAINERS

There are several good reasons to grow bulbs in containers. For one thing, it's easy. There are few disease problems, there's little weeding and, best of all, a container full of flowering bulbs looks wonderful. And if you don't like the look of the foliage after the flowers have faded, you can move the container to a less conspicuous part of the garden.

If you've grown bedding plants or vegetables in containers, you can follow many of the same rules for bulbs. First, choose large pots—at least 45 cm in diameter—to give the bulbs enough room to develop a healthy root system and to provide a large reservoir of water. Make

sure the pot has three or four drainage holes in the bottom. Next, fill the pot with high-quality potting soil. Unlike garden soil, potting soil is largely free of disease and insect pests, and won't clump or harden. Plant bulbs to the same depth and spacing as you would in the garden. Water them in well, and feed with water-soluble 10-52-10 or a slow-release granular fertilizer. Place the containers in a location that provides the necessary amount of light, and then sit back and enjoy. (Remember, however, that container growing reduces a bulb's hardiness because the bulb loses the insulating effect of the ground.)

Containerized plants require diligent watering. Because the soil volume is limited, pots dry out quite quickly, especially on hot summer days, so you may need to provide extra water. Check the containers regularly during the blooming season; when the soil surface begins to dry out, water thoroughly.

To extend the blooming season, consider planting bulbs in layers, like a lasagna (see illustration, left). We've produced some stunning window boxes and planters this way. Using a large, deep pot, plant different species at different depths. The varying blooming periods will ensure continuous colour, and the new growth will help to camouflage the dying foliage of the finished bulbs.

We've enjoyed great success planting bulbs in layers in windowboxes and containers

Fall-Planted Bulbs
in Containers

Growing spring-planted bulbs in containers is simple; you plant them at the same time as you're preparing the rest of your garden. But fall-planted bulbs in containers require a little more preparation, since the bulbs must spend the winter in a limited volume of soil, which compromises their hardiness.

Plant up fall-planted, spring-blooming containers as soon as you purchase the bulbs. Move the container into a cold room, cellar or garage where the temperature is no warmer than about 8°C but never below freezing. Once spring arrives, move the container back outside.

Alternatively, you can bury the entire pot. Dig a hole in your garden deep enough to accommodate the entire pot, and turn the pot slightly on its side. Bury it deep enough so that when you fill in the hole, there's at least 10 cm of soil covering the pot. (To keep the pot clean, wrap it in burlap before you bury it.) Once the ground has thawed in the spring, dig up the pot, brush off the soil, put the pot in a suitable location and wait for the blooms. Remember that, even in containers, the hardiness of bulbs overwintered outdoors will be limited by your zone.

Canna *'Richard Wallace'*
in a large planter

We have found that tulips and other bulbs fall-planted in containers are best treated as annuals or replanted into the garden after flowering finishes. We plant up numerous pots each year, and the sheer number of containers makes overwintering labour intensive. Tight spacing in the container also makes bulbs less likely to rebloom consistently year after year.

Judith Fraser, our indoor plants manager, overwinters narcissus, hyacinth and other spring-flowering bulbs in containers in her garage. She keeps the temperature at about 0°C and the soil just damp. Judith offers this advice: "The trick is to bring them into strong sunlight as soon as they are a few centimetres high, in late February or early March. This helps to prevent the emerging shoots from stretching. It's important to keep them cool at this time. Sometimes I put them outside during the day if the temperatures aren't too cold, and bring them back indoors at night."

Enjoying Bulbs

The versatility of bulbs, combined with their relatively modest care requirements, makes them an excellent choice for all kinds of gardeners, from novice to expert. Bulbs can be used in rock gardens and woodland settings, among shrubs and in perennial beds, in either sunny or shady locations. They can even be used in an environmentally conscious way. Scott Messenger, one of our watering crew leaders, is a big advocate of xeriscape gardening. He suggests replacing a traditional lawn with tufting grasses like fescue and planting drifts of bulbs among the tufts. As Scott says, "You get a really nice effect in the spring with all the blooms, and you'll use a lot less water than on a traditional lawn."

The best way to begin building a bulb garden is to start small and expand your collection each year in both variety and number. This way, you'll find your personal favourites, discover the species and varieties that grow best in your garden and come to understand the vast array of choices within each bulb category. Most bulbs require minimal to moderate care, and within a few years many readily naturalize and spread.

Lucas Sparrow and his sister enjoy the beautiful tulips at the Calgary Zoo

Bulbs do not usually require frequent dividing and re-planting. And unlike annuals, many bulbs are hardy and come up year after year. For this reason, choose your planting location carefully.

To get the most from bulbs, spend some time thinking about what you want to accomplish with your garden. For maximum impact, try to imagine the look of your garden as it evolves over the course of the growing season, or even several growing seasons.

BASIC DESIGN PRINCIPLES

Our most successful garden designs have incorporated a wide variety of plants. An interesting selection of shapes, sizes, textures and colours provides glorious bursts of colour and dynamic focal points throughout the season. Regardless of their varying garden styles, most gardeners share three common goals: to create a continuous show of flowers, to keep the different types of bulbs from over-growing one another and to get maximum results with minimum work. Achieving these goals requires planning. Start your planning by answering some basic questions.

- Where will the bulbs be planted? Along a walkway, in front of the house, beside a patio? Backed by a fence or in the middle of the lawn, like an island? Knowing their intended location will help you decide which bulbs are most suitable.

- How much sun or shade does the location receive? Of course it's either sunny or shady, but to what degree? Sunny all day, or only in the morning? Is the entire bed sunny, or is it shaded by a tree at one end? What direction does it face? Southern exposures are generally the hottest, while north-facing beds receive less warmth.

- How much area do you have? Measure the location's length and width. In a narrow bed you may have to put plants in a single row; in a wide bed you may prefer to plant lush-growing bulbs close together to create a solid mass of colour and texture.

If you're creating a bed of nothing but bulbs, you can save some effort by digging one large hole and planting all the bulbs at the same time. First, outline the area of the planting. Then completely excavate the soil to the desired depth—you can leave raised areas or dig deeper depressions for bulbs that require different planting depths than the majority. Rough out a grid and place the bulbs accordingly. Then gently replace the soil, completely covering the bulbs without dislodging them from their positions. This method of mass planting is much easier than digging dozens of individual holes.

Dorothy Jedrasik and her son Jonathan enjoy their garden, which features this gorgeous containerized dahlia

- Do you prefer tall or short plants? What colours do you like? Do you want a monochromatic display or a mix of colours? Keep your personal preferences in mind; there arc no best answers to these questions.
- Which bulbs do you like? Make a list. Talk to other gardeners and ask for recommendations. Look at neighbouring gardens and flip through this book. If you see a picture of a flowering bulb you like, take it to the garden centre.

Remember to consider foliage when planning your garden. Bulbs have specific flowering times and their foliage usually lingers, collecting energy for the next season's growth. Think of a garden in terms of various heights, levels and shapes that continually change, complementing, contrasting and playing off each other. A mixture of plants with contrasting leaf shapes, textures and colours is more interesting than a garden made up of many plants with similar qualities.

Don't worry about matching flower colours. Think of a bouquet of fresh flowers: no matter how different the flower colours, the blooms look great together. And although each of us has colour preferences, in a garden setting most schemes won't clash. If you like bright colours, choose varieties that flower in scarlet, crimson and golden-yellow. If you prefer pastels, choose plants that bloom rose-pink, pale blue, lavender or white.

You can even choose colour as a design theme. Tanja Pickrell, one of our garden centre supervisors, decided to try a red-and-white theme. She planted white crocuses, red and white tulips, and red and white lilies that would come up just in time to replace the fading tulips and crocuses. Along her fence she planted red and white gladiolus. She calls the result her 'Canada Bed.' Tanja recalls a neighbour who planted a mass of single tulips in his vegetable patch, all in one colour. Each spring the bulbs produced a brilliant, solid display of yellow blooms. "Simply stunning!" remembers Tanja.

If your garden is situated so that it is seen only from one side (against a fence, for example), the general rule is to put short plants in front, medium plants in the middle and tall plants at the back. But don't be reluctant to mix them up a little to avoid monotony. Put a few taller-growing plants in the middle row, and some medium-height plants close to the front. In island beds, which can be viewed from all sides, put taller varieties in the centre, with medium-height varieties surrounding the tall plants and shorter flowers around the edges. A particularly effective show can be created by sloping the bed gently from a central high point to the outer edges.

Make a survey of your garden and decide which locations are best suited to bulbs and which types of bulbs grow best in those locations. Get to know your yard; check out where the sun shines at different times of the day and season, evaluate the wet and dry spots, and identify sheltered areas where borderline-hardy plants could be located.

Bob Stadnyk, our perennials manager, plants a variety of spring-flowering bulbs in his alpine garden

Now it's time to sketch out a plan. This plan can be altered over time, as your tastes and needs change, but as with any project, it helps to know where you are headed. Your plan does not have to be complicated, nor do you need to be a landscape designer. If your plan is simple, a rough sketch will do; for more elaborate plantings, create a scale drawing on graph paper. Your first bulb experience may involve planting only a single variety of bulb, incorporated into your existing landscape. The key is to use four-dimensional thinking: considering how the garden will evolve during the growing season, and in seasons to come.

A garden plan can be particularly useful when determining how many bulbs to buy. How are you planning to use the bulbs—are you dedicating a whole bed to bulb plantings or filling in established spaces? Note the dimensions of the bed, and then use our recommended spacing or the average spread of each bulb to calculate the number of bulbs it will take to fill the area. The number of bulbs you'll need depends on the growth habit of the bulbs you're using, the area you wish to cover and the visual impact you want to create.

Sparse plantings tend to have less visual impact than tightly spaced ones. If you need to stick to a budget, it's better to focus the bulbs you have into a smaller location. A small, densely planted bed offers much more bang for your buck than a large bed with huge gaps between the flowers.

Triumph tulips 'Princess Irene' interplanted with 'Jack Snipe' narcissus have great visual impact

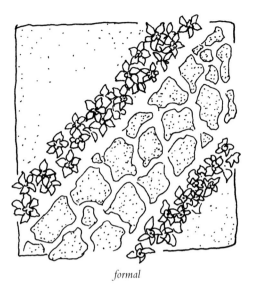

formal

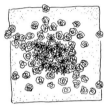

geometric

naturalistic

PLANTING PATTERNS

We're lucky enough to have a large garden where we can experiment and lots of interesting bulbs to play with. Over the years we've tried dozens of designs and have discovered that the outcomes can change dramatically depending on the plants and varieties we grow. Although there are almost limitless ways to arrange bulbs in the garden, the following basic patterns will work well in most yards.

Formal ✋ Formal gardens are composed of regular patterns not normally found in nature: straight lines, circles, triangles and other even shapes. In general, formal beds should be used sparingly, as a single focal point. A triangle filled with Darwin hybrid tulips with a border of muscari, for example, looks quite striking, as long as it's the only planting so formalized.

Geometric ✋ Within a formal garden, nest patterns within patterns—a square within a circle within a triangle, for example. This effect works especially well with bulbs that have rigid forms, like narcissus and tulip.

Naturalistic ✋ Scatter bulbs randomly in woodland gardens or open beds. For an authentically natural look, space bulbs closely in a central clump, and more sparsely as you move outward, thinning irregularly toward the edges of the planting.

Mixed ↝ Mixing bulbs with perennials is a great way to add interest to the garden, and maturing perennials can hide dying bulb foliage. For example, plant muscari and hostas together, so that the hostas are emerging just as the muscari fade.

River ↝ Plant bulbs in long, flowing, slightly weaving patterns that resemble rivers or streams. This pattern creates informal masses that look great in perennial beds or grassy areas.

Layering ↝ Put bulbs in the garden in layers. Plant large bulbs deeply and put a layer of soil over them; then plant the medium-sized bulbs and cover them with soil; then plant small bulbs close to the surface and top with more soil. For example, plant daffodils at about 25 cm deep; single early, double early or species tulips at 15 cm; and crocuses or muscari at 8 cm. In this way, you can enjoy a succession of blooms in one bed: the crocus or muscari will bloom first, followed by the tulips and then the daffodils.

↝ ↝ ↝

When setting out bulbs in small groups or clumps, always plant in odd numbers (e.g., 5, 9, 13). A cluster of five or seven tulips is much more visually appealing than a block of four or eight. Set the bulbs out in the desired pattern before you start digging. With formal patterns, use sticks or stakes to create a regular grid; in informal plantings, you can estimate the spacing by eye. This step is important for checking that you have enough bulbs to create your desired effect. Many people plant bulbs too far apart, and the result is less effective than it would be with more bulbs planted closer together.

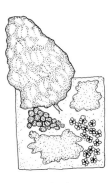

mixed

layering

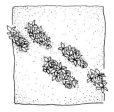

river

Natural Habits

Many bulbs will naturalize, or spread; others will not. If you plant naturalizing varieties, you must take their spread into account. Some are quite aggressive under the right conditions, so be sure you do your research. Use bedding plants or single-season bulbs to fill in the blank spaces while you wait for naturalizing bulbs to spread across the garden.

When you plant naturalizing bulbs, space them closely near the centre of the area and further apart as you move outward. Place just a few bulbs at the outside of the planting, and keep the planting rough and uneven. This effect mimics natural growth, as though the bulbs had spread from a small original clump. (For detailed information about naturalizing bulbs, see pages 297 to 299.)

Planting Along Walls and Fences

Bulbs can be used effectively along the wall of a house or to fill in the area between a pathway and a fence. When you plant in these locations, be sure to leave adequate space. Leave at least 30 cm between bulbs and the walls of the house. The overhang from the roof creates a dry zone close to the house. By planting bulbs further from the protection of the wall, you ensure that the plants enjoy the benefits of rainfall. The sun's heat can also reflect off the house and bake mature plants. Leave as little as 15 cm between bulbs and a fence, since overhang and reflection aren't problems.

Getting to know your garden will help you make the right location and bulb choices

CREATING WITH CUTFLOWERS

Creating arrangements with cutflowers from your bulb garden is another wonderful way to enjoy bulbs. A bouquet of tulips, for example, can be just as stunning as a bouquet of roses. Bulbs also offer a wide variety of colour choices, giving a larger palette from which to work. Of course, when creating cutflower bouquets from your bulb garden, there are a few facts you should keep in mind.

Bulb flowers for bouquets and arrangements should be cut just after the tight-bud stage—that is, just as the blooms are starting to open. If flowers are cut at this stage, they should last for a week or longer, depending on the species harvested. Many people make the mistake of cutting flowers in full bloom and are frustrated when the flowers begin to fade within hours.

When cutting flowers, leave as much foliage with the plant as possible to replenish the bulb. Tulips are the important exception to this advice. With tulips, the foliage normally comes with the long stem, which means sacrificing the renewable bulbs for the sake of the cutflower. If you want to enjoy tulips both indoors and out, consider setting aside part of your garden specifically to be harvested as cutflowers. Once the blooming period is finished, remove any stem remnants and fill the area with other plants until late summer, when you can plant new bulbs and begin the process again.

The best time to cut flowers for long-lasting bouquets is early in the morning when the day is still cool. Immediately after cutting, plunge the stems into cool water. It is a little-known fact that many bulb flowers grow a few centimetres in the vase after being cut, so wrap the flowers in a tube of newspaper for the first 24 hours to ensure that the stems remain upright in the vase.

Keep cutflowers out of direct sunlight and away from warm drafts. Put the vase in a cool room at night. Change the water every two days and add floral preservative to extend flower life.

To look their best, most vases need at least 12 stems. For a lush, full look, use 24. Solid colours have a very different impact from a mix of colours. A large mass of a single colour is more elegant and stately than a mix, instantly drawing the eye. As our florists like to say, solid colours create a huge "Wow!" factor—they leave a lasting impression. Colour mixes, on the other hand, tend to distract the eye and play off surrounding colours, creating a fresh, informal appeal.

When creating a fragrant bouquet, tend toward simplicity. Use one scent at a time or group flowers that share similar scents. Choose one type of flower as the focus of your aromatic arrangement and complement it visually with unscented partners. For example, you could create a bouquet with hyacinth in the centre, surrounded by clusters of single tulips around the base, and supported by any deciduous or perennial foliage with appealing texture and colour. Strongly scented bulbs include hyacinths, paperwhites and Oriental lilies. Double-flowering tulips and freesias have a sweet, spicy aroma. Lightly scented bulbs include muscari and scilla.

Buckets of fresh-cut tulips in our floral department are a sure sign of spring

the science behind it

Harvesting Hazards

Some plants aren't just touchy—they're down-right irritating! After handling certain flowers, such as tulips, some people suffer from dermatitis, a skin ailment. This particular form of dermatitis is often called "tulip fingers." People get tulip fingers because tulips—and other plants—contain an allergen found in chemical compounds called glyco-sides. To avoid this condition, simply wear gloves when handling the flowers.

"Daffodil itch," whose symptoms include dryness, scaling and redness, and fissures in the skin, is a similar skin ailment. The rash is caused when a gardener comes into contact with the sap of narcissus.

Narcissus sap contains calcium oxalate, a chemical that forms crystals that take the shape of raphides, just like those that cause tulip fingers. Daffodils contain up to six percent calcium oxalate, more than enough to damage the skin. Calcium oxalate exists in at least 215 plant families and can be found in any part of the plant. Although this chemical may irritate our hands, it has a purpose: it deters most animals from feeding on the bulbs, foliage and flowers.

Bulb flowers should be harvested just before they open

The harm caused by the chemicals in daffodils isn't restricted to humans and animals. Although scientists haven't yet been able to pin down the exact cause, the sap of freshly cut daffodils has been shown to have a harmful effect on other cutflowers in the same vase. Other cutflowers draw in the narcissus sap as they take in water, and something in that sap causes them to wilt.

This problem can be overcome, however. Other flowers can be placed in the same vase as daffodils if you leave the daffodils in water over-night, then rinse the stems before placing them in a vase with the other flowers. This treatment will wash away most of the sap. You may also create a sort of sterilization chamber for daffodils by adding 20 to 25 drops of bleach for every 4 litres of water in a vase. Place the daffodils in the solution for one to six hours. Rinse the stems, and you can freely mix daffodils with other cutflowers.

Tips for Enduring Arrangements

Our florists offer these tips for lasting enjoyment of bulb arrangements. Clean your vase with bleach, soap, and very hot water before adding any water or flowers. Cleaning kills lingering bacteria that could shorten the life of your cutflowers. (Washing your vase in the dishwasher works well.)

Fill your vase with water (lukewarm water encourages buds to open, while cold water preserves already-opened flowers). Add a floral preservative to extend the life of your bouquets. Floral preservatives contain simple sugar solutions that are food for the flowers, plus chemicals to inhibit the growth of fungi and bacteria, and pH adjusters that lower the pH of your vase water to the ideal, disease-inhibiting range of 3-4. (Lower-pH water is also more readily absorbed by cutflowers.) Add floral preservative each time you add water to your arrangement. Using distilled water may also extend their life.

Using a clean, sharp knife, harvest flowers at the late-bud stage, just before the flowers open. Just before putting the flowers in the vase, re-cut the stems with a sharp, sterile knife, since the cut ends rapidly close after cutting, forming a seal that prevents the flowers from drawing up water. Immersing the fresh cut immediately prevents the seal from forming.

A simple bouquet of tulips makes a stunning arrangement

*These cannas make an
awesome display at the
entrance to this yard*

BETTER CHOICES,
BETTER GARDENS

Years of experience have taught us that no matter how diligently you prepare your garden or nurture your plants, the most important contributor to your success remains choosing the right varieties. An inferior variety can only perform to the best of its limited potential, while a superior variety has been bred to perform well despite less than ideal conditions.

In the following section, you'll find comprehensive descriptions and care instructions for twenty of the most popular bulbs, with our recommendations for the best varieties for each. If you try these varieties, bred for colour, size, disease resistance, versatility and overall excellence, you'll find bulbs an absolutely dazzling addition to your garden. By making better choices, you'll enjoy a better garden.

Twenty Best Bulbs

ornamental onion

Type
True bulb

Planting season
Fall

Blooming season
Late spring to
mid summer

Hardiness
Zones 3–10

How many
Large varieties: start
with 3 bulbs; small
varieties: start with
9 to 25 bulbs

Golden Rules

- Never plant a single
  bulb by itself
- Provide consistent
  moisture through
  the growing season
- Allow seedheads
  to mature for
  naturalizing and
  self-sowing

Alliums

Allium spp.

If you've never planted ornamental onions, we urge you to try at least a few. We believe you'll be hooked after the first bloom. Alliums are long-lived perennials that require very little maintenance. They are inexpensive, extremely hardy, reliable and easy to grow. They bloom in a beautiful range of colours, from pink to rose, mauve to purple, true blue to clean white. The seedheads are attractive even after the flowers have finished blooming, and many species look gorgeous in flower arrangements. In short, they're perfect for almost any gardener or gardening situation.

Plant alliums in irregular groupings among small shrubs and perennials. The surrounding plants will make the allium flowers look spectacular and offer support to taller varieties. Remember always to plant bulbs in odd-numbered, informal clusters: formal, even-numbered plantings look unnatural.

Allium moly

Planting

- Plant as early as possible in the fall. Some alliums (especially smaller species) multiply quickly, so expect many more blooms in subsequent seasons. Larger species are slower to multiply.
- Plant larger varieties 6 to 10 cm deep, smaller varieties 3 to 5 cm deep. Space 2 to 3 times the bulb height apart.
- Full sun. A sunny location is best for alliums, although they tolerate light shade. The short species suffer less in shade than the large alliums do.
- Plant in well-drained, sandy soil.
- Add granular bulb food to the planting area.
- Water well after transplanting.

Alliums were among the first plants cultivated by humans, although they were originally cherished as edible, not ornamental, species. Not until the mid-nineteenth century did gardeners finally pay attention to ornamental onions.

The Allium *cultivar 'Globemaster' was discovered in 1964, when a bee inadvertently cross-pollinated* A. Macleanni Baker *and* A. christophii. *It forms large lavender umbels and grows to 100 cm. The flowers do not produce seed so they last longer.*

GROWING

- Alliums like moist but not wet soil. The bulbs prefer regular moisture during the growing season so supplement seasonal rain with additional water as necessary. They will usually flower under drought conditions, but the flowers will be smaller and won't last as long.

- Apply a good dose of water-soluble 20-20-20 fertilizer as the leaves begin to emerge and again when the flower buds are forming. Do not fertilize or water after the plants have finished flowering.

- Unlike most true bulbs, alliums flower at the end of their growing cycle. The foliage has already provided both the flowers and the bulb with enough energy to meet their needs by the time flowering occurs, so once the blooms have finished, the foliage turns brown and dies. (On some of the larger species, this process begins before the flowers have finished.) Allow the foliage to die back naturally.

- Deadhead finished blooms or allow them to dry on the stems so seeds can be blown to other parts of the garden. After the flowerheads turn brown, the florets open to reveal shiny black seeds. The seeds will eventually fall and produce new alliums.

- Every eight to ten years, dig out the old bulbs and discard them. Thin out the patch, and replant or give away the extra bulbs.

- Early autumn is the best time to divide alliums, when the foliage has died down, the bulbs are dormant and there's still time for replanted bulbs to develop strong root systems before winter sets in.

Allium *var. 'Purple Sensation',* A. aflatunense *and* A. *'Mount Everest'*

Allium caeruleum

Emerging flower bud on Allium karataviense

TIPS

- If your garden has clay soil, follow the shallower depth recommendation for alliums; if your soil is very sandy, follow the deeper recommendation.

- Add a handful of bulb food to the hole before you set the bulbs. This slow-release fertilizer is specially formulated to encourage good root development in the fall. It will also provide additional nutrients in the spring when top growth commences.

- Right after the bulbs have finished flowering, they are ready to be harvested or, if you desire, moved to another spot in the garden.

- Larger allium species may need staking.

IN THE GARDEN

- Alliums make a versatile addition to the garden. Try shorter varieties in rock gardens, mixed borders and naturalized gardens.

- Mix alliums with purple-flowering perennials such as heather, iris, pyrethrum, lavender, salvia and flowering sage.

- For a stunning contrast, plant allium with yellow-flowering perennials such as perennial daisies, lilies, foxglove, sedum and solidago.

- Interplant alliums with small shrubs and tall perennials. They will not only set off the allium flowers but support taller varieties and hide the dying foliage.

Many alliums make great cutflowers, but stick to those that lack the familiar onion scent, such as **Allium aflatunense,** **A. giganteum** *and* **A. karataviense.** *Cut umbels when about half the flowers are fully open. They will last up to three weeks.*

Allium *cultivar 'Lucy Ball' was created by crossing* **A. aflatunense** *and* **A. Macleanni Baker.** *It produces large dark lilac-purple umbels and grows to 100 cm.*

TRY THESE!

Most allium flowers are shades of purple. However, today it is possible to grow alliums with white, pink, yellow, blue and even black flowers! Of the more than 900 allium species, the following are our favourites.

Allium aflatunense

Allium aflatunense
(A. hollandicum)

Common names ❧ ornamental garlic, ornamental onion, Persian onion
Height ❧ 60–90 cm
Blooming season ❧ Late spring
Hardiness ❧ Zone 3

This is one of the easiest *Allium* species to grow. It's reliable and hardy, and the flowers last a long time. It is similar to *A. giganteum*, but it is smaller and tends to flower two to three weeks earlier. **Flowers** ❧ The flowers are produced in spherical, lilac-coloured umbels, 10 cm in diameter. **Requirements** ❧ This species prefers a sunny location but will tolerate light shade.

❧ **'Purple Sensation'** • Very darkpurple flowers make this variety especially gorgeous—well worth seeking out

Allium atropurpureum
(A. nigrum var. atropurpureum)

Common name ❧ black onion
Height ❧ 60–90 cm
Blooming season ❧ Late spring to early summer
Hardiness ❧ Zone 3

This is another drumstick allium. **Flowers** ❧ It produces intense darkpurple, globular umbels, 3–7 cm in diameter, with star-shaped flowers. The purple is so deep it often looks black, hence the common name. Excellent for cutflowers. **Requirements** ❧ This species prefers a sunny location with well-drained soil.

Allium caerulum
(A. azureum)

Common name ❧ blue globe onion
Height ❧ 30–60 cm
Blooming season ❧ Early summer
Hardiness ❧ Zone 3

This species is widely available and very popular because of its true blue flowers—*caerulum* means "blue of the heavens." This bulb naturalizes easily and self-sows readily. Closely plant a clump of at least 25 for best effect. **Flowers** ❧ *A. caerulum* produces masses of vibrant sky-blue, cup-shaped flowers in globular umbels 3–4 cm in diameter. **Requirements** ❧ The plants have thin leaves and stems, and may flop over in strong winds. Plant this bulb among medium-size perennials to provide support. This species prefers full sun and will tolerate a drier location. If planted in partial shade, the bulb forms weak stems and the flowers fall.

Allium christophii

Allium cernuum

Common names ✂ nodding onion, wild onion
Height ✂ 20–30 cm
Blooming season ✂ Early summer
Hardiness ✂ Zone 2

One of the few ornamental onions that does not have spherical flowerheads, *A. cernuum* is easy to grow, undemanding and reliable. The flowers lack an onion scent, stand up well to rain and wind, and make excellent and unusual cutflowers. It's also extremely hardy and is an excellent choice for areas with harsh winters. The leaves tend not to turn brown and dry, and the flowers are long-lasting and very pretty. **Flowers** ✂ It produces clusters of 25 to 40 small, cup-shaped, medium-pink flowers on crooked stems held in loose, drooping umbels like little chandeliers. Planted in groups of 13 to 15, these bulbs grow into attractive, vigorous clumps with tufts of narrow leaves and gorgeous, unusual bright-pink flowers. This species naturalizes readily. When the seeds have formed in the individual flowers, the flowerheads tilt upwards, almost as if to offer one last opportunity to remove them before they release the seeds.

Allium christophii
(A. albopilosum)

Common name ✂ star of Persia
Height ✂ 30–45 cm
Blooming season ✂ Early summer
Hardiness ✂ Zone 3

This is one of the best-known and most spectacular alliums. **Flowers** ✂ This species produces huge (15–25 cm), globular umbels of star-shaped silvery-purple flowers on short, stocky stems. The leaves are long and straplike, and appear early. In milder zones, this species will naturalize, but not as readily as many of the smaller species. **Requirements** ✂ This bulb prefers a sunny location with well-drained soil.

Allium cernuum

Allium giganteum

Allium giganteum
(A. procerum)

Common names ᔋ giant garlic, giant onion
Height ᔋ 100–150 cm
Blooming season ᔋ Early summer
Hardiness ᔋ Zone 4 (Zone 3 with protection)

This is one of the largest species of *Allium*. It has large floppy leaves that grow to half the height of the plant; they may be unsightly when they die back. **Flowers** ᔋ The flowers are usually violet-purple and huge, in umbels 10–15 cm in diameter. **Requirements** ᔋ This bulb must have well-drained soil and a warm, sheltered location that provides protection from the wind. Plant among small shrubs or medium-sized perennials, which will help support the plant and hide the dying foliage. Mix in a handful of sand when you plant *A. giganteum* in heavier soils, as it is more sensitive to rotting than other species.

Allium karataviense

Common names ᔋ Turkestan onion, ornamental garlic
Height ᔋ 15–20 cm
Blooming season ᔋ Late spring
Hardiness ᔋ Zone 3

A. karataviense is a durable species that naturalizes slowly. A patch planted in our show garden grew beautifully for seven years, through widely varied winters, without any problems. The leaves do not turn brown and appear fresh at bloom time. The flowerheads dry well and are lovely when used in dried-flower arrangements. **Flowers** ᔋ *A. karataviense* produces 15- to 30-cm beige-pink umbels—an unusual flower colour. The wide blue-grey, violet-speckled leaves contrast beautifully with the flowers, which have a faint fragrance. **Requirements** ᔋ This species requires full sun and good drainage, and prefers a sheltered location. If you want to try forcing an allium in a pot, this species is the best choice.

ᔋ *A. karataviense* var. 'Ivory Queen' • A really pretty variety with silvery-white flowers, grey-green foliage and wide-spreading leaves. Generally listed as *A.* 'Ivory Queen'.

Allium karataviense

Allium moly

Allium moly
(A. luteum)

Common names ᛣ golden garlic,
lily leek
Height ᛣ 25–30 cm
Blooming season ᛣ Late spring
Hardiness ᛣ Zone 3

This species naturalizes aggressively. It
is a sturdy plant that grows in clumps.
Flowers ᛣ The flowers are bright
golden-yellow and grow in umbels 6–
8 cm in diameter. They look spectacular against the bluish-green leaves. Not
recommended as a cutflower because
of its onion odour. **Requirements** ᛣ
Tolerant of light shade, it grows well
in woodland areas. Plant among small
shrubs and in rock gardens.

ᛣ **'Jeannine'** • A taller variety (30–40
cm) with larger flowers (8–10 cm) than
its species cousin. Usually produces two
flower stalks per bulb.

Allium neapolitanum
(A. cowanii, A. album, A. lacteum,
A. sulcatum, A. sieberianum)

Common names ᛣ daffodil garlic,
Naples garlic, bridesflower
Height ᛣ 25–45 cm
Blooming season ᛣ Late spring
to early summer
Hardiness ᛣ Zone 5 (Zone 4
with protection)

Easy to grow in warmer climates.
Flowers ᛣ The blooms make nice
cutflowers, with a pleasant fragrance.
Each bulb produces three slender
flower stems bearing loose, erect, shuttlecock-shaped umbels of star-shaped,
white flowers. **Requirements** ᛣ This
species prefers sandier, well-drained
soils, so mix some coarse sand into the
planting area.

Allium oreophilum

Allium nigrum (A. multibulbosum, A. monspessulanum, A. magicum)

Common name ➸ black onion
Height ➸ 60–90 cm
Blooming season ➸ Late spring to early summer
Hardiness ➸ Zone 3

This species looks great interplanted with medium-sized perennials in a mixed-flower border. It is not always readily available and is often confused with *A. atropurpureum*. If you want very dark-purple flowers, don't buy *A. nigrum*. **Flowers** ➸ Despite its common name, this species produces white or pink blooms; they form in globular umbels, 5–7 cm in diameter, with starry flowers. The common and Latin names both refer to the greenish, black-lobed ovaries. **Requirements** ➸ *A. nigrum* prefers a sunny location with well-drained soil.

➸ *A. nigrum roseum* • Pink-flowered variety; uncommon, hard to find

Allium oreophilum (A. ostrowskianum, A. platystemon)

Common name ➸ ornamental garlic
Height ➸ 15–20 cm
Blooming season ➸ Late spring
Hardiness ➸ Zone 3

One of the best 'old-fashioned' alliums, this species forms attractive clumps of flowers. It's hardy and reliable, readily self-sowing. Try planting in patches of 13 to 15 bulbs. Within a few years your patch will expand to three times its original size. **Flowers** ➸ This species produces rose-pink umbels, 4–6 cm in diameter, with star-shaped flowers. **Requirements** ➸ *A. oreophilum* tolerates poor soils but needs a full-sun location. Because this bulb naturalizes so readily, you may have to thin it out, but normally not for years.

➸ **'Zwanenburg'** • Has particularly pretty dark wine-rose, saucer-shaped flowers set off by silvery foliage

Allium roseum

Common names ✒ rosy garlic, rose garlic
Height ✒ 30–40 cm
Blooming season ✒ Mid to late spring
Hardiness ✒ Zone 3

A pretty little species, similar to *A. oreophilum* but shorter and with smaller flowers; it's also not as widely available. *A. roseum* propagates easily from bulbils; it also self-sows readily and naturalizes well. **Flowers** ✒ The pale-pink or white bell-shaped flowers grow to 1–2 cm and have a nice fragrance.

✒ ***A. roseum* var. *roseum*** • Produces numerous light-pink flowers and no bulbils; forms fertile seeds

✒ ***A. roseum* var. *bulbiferum*** • Sterile variety that produces numerous bulbils. Light-pink flowers

✒ **'Album'** • Produces white flowers

Allium roseum

Allium schubertii
(A. bucharicum)

Common name ✒ tumbleweed onion
Height ✒ 30–45 cm
Blooming season ✒ Late spring to early summer
Hardiness ✒ Zone 4

A beautiful species with huge flowers atop stiff, strong stems. Tumbleweed onions are stunning planted in front of pink rosebushes or in mixed flowerbeds. **Flowers** ✒ The spidery umbels, 30–40 cm in diameter, are made up of purple flowers radiating out like shooting stars. Before the seeds form in the flowerhead, the base of the stem withers and becomes brittle. Eventually the umbel snaps off. When the wind blows, the umbel rolls across the ground, scattering seed as it goes, just like a tumbleweed. **Requirements** ✒ *A. schubertii* needs full sun and well-drained soil. This species may be difficult to find.

Allium schubertii

Allium sphaerocephalon
(A. descendens)

Common names ᦸ drumstick allium, round-headed leek
Height ᦸ 50–60 cm
Blooming season ᦸ Early to mid summer
Hardiness ᦸ Zone 3

This extremely hardy species is inexpensive and widely available.
Flowers ᦸ The flowers form in reddish-purple, egg-shaped umbels 2–6 cm in diameter on long, wiry stems. The flowerheads bob attractively without damage in the wind, making it an excellent choice for windy gardens. Bees love this species! The flowers remain attractive even when they have finished blooming, and dry well for floral arrangements; they also make excellent cutflowers. **Requirements** ᦸ Try planting a patch of at least 25 of these bulbs among medium-sized perennials, in a sunny location with good drainage. This species will multiply to a degree, but it will naturalize only in warmer climates.

Allium unifolium
(A. grandisceptrum,
A. unifolium lacteum)

Common name ᦸ one-leaved onion
Height ᦸ 30–45 cm
Blooming season ᦸ Late spring
Hardiness ᦸ Zone 4

Despite its common name, this species actually produces two or three short, flat leaves on strong stems. The parent bulb reproduces by forming bulbils on short stems. **Flowers** ᦸ Gorgeous, glistening, sugar-pink, bell-shaped flowers form in open umbels. **Requirements** ᦸ A. unifolium likes a moist, sunny location.

Allium 'Mount Everest'

Height ᦸ 100 cm
Blooming season ᦸ Early summer
Hardiness ᦸ Zone 4

This hybrid variety was created by crossing A. stipitatum Regel and A. stipitatum album. **Flowers** ᦸ It produces baseball-sized frosty-white flowers on strong 60-cm stems. **Requirements** ᦸ This cultivar prefers full sun and well-drained soil. With its height and huge flowers, it is best planted in a sheltered spot.

Allium 'Mount Everest'

Nectaroscordum siculum

Nectaroscordum siculum
(Allium siculum, A. nectaroscordum, A. bulgaricum, N. siculum, N. discordis, N. bulgaricum)

Common name ∿ honey lily
Height ∿ 60–90 cm
Blooming season ∿ Late spring to early summer
Hardiness ∿ Zone 4

It was recently determined that these bulbs do not belong to genus *Allium*, although they are related. They now belong to a new genus, *Nectaroscordum*. The flowers are quite striking, even when they are finished. They remain erect and dry to a deep cream, so they are particularly prized for dried floral arrangements. The flowers are long-lasting and bees love them, but the plants exude a strong onion smell if bruised.

Flowers ∿ Each bulb produces up to 30 pendent, bell-shaped flowers held in loose umbels. Flowers are cream flushed with light pink, and have maroon and green tones toward the bases. **Requirements** ∿ This species tolerates some shade but prefers a sunny location. It requires very well-drained soil and a drier location. If your soil is heavy, mix some coarse sand into the planting spot. Since these flowers grow quite tall, plant them toward the back of the flowerbed in a round clump for a beautiful effect. They are particularly attractive planted among evergreens; the dark background of the trees is very striking.

Anemones

There is no such thing as a typical anemone. *A member of family Ranunculaceae (the buttercup family), genus* Anemone *contains about 65 species that thrive in temperate climates throughout the world. Some grow from corms, others from rhizomes; most are ordinary perennials. And because the anemone species and their growing requirements vary so widely, chances are good that no matter what conditions exist in your garden, a suitable anemone is available. In this section we deal with the three most significant bulbous species:* Anemone blanda, A. coronaria *and* A. nemorosa.

These anemones have a few qualities in common. All are susceptible to drying out, so buy them as soon as they become available at the garden centre, and plant them promptly. A. blanda *and* A. coronaria *will also benefit from soaking in tepid water for 24 hours before they are planted. They should all be planted in fertile, well-drained soil in informal drifts or clusters. Finally, all three prefer some protection from strong winds and exposed locations, although* A. blanda *has a higher tolerance for exposure than the other two.*

Anemones are commonly called windflowers. The genus name derives from the Greek word anemos, *which means wind. It's a fitting name because these light, lovely flowers tremble in even a gentle breeze. Whether you prefer the tough* A. blanda *or the heat-loving* A. coronaria, *in the next few pages you're sure to find an anemone that's perfect for you!*

The flowers of *Anemone blanda* and *Anemone coronaria* close at night and during cloudy weather.

Grecian windflower, winter anemone, daisy-flowered anemone

Type
Rhizome

Planting season
Fall

Blooming season
Mid spring

Hardiness
Zones 4–7

How many
Start with 13
to 15 rhizomes

Golden Rules

- Plant in a dry, sunny location

- Choose location carefully—this species naturalizes readily

- Best grown in informal drifts or clumps

Greek Anemones
Anemone blanda

Anemone blanda *is the first of the windflowers to bloom each year. It's a tough, robust little plant whose starry flowers are quite delightful when they blow in the wind, hence the common name. This anemone has a vigorous, spreading growth habit and will readily naturalize in Zones 4 to 7.*

Blanda *means beautiful and it's an appropriate name for this plant. The flowers are usually blue, but there are pink, white and mauve cultivars. The bright-yellow flower centres make a striking contrast to the pretty daisy-like petals that form each bloom. It may be common, but it's lovely—and highly underrated. Give this windflower a try: you're sure to love it!*

Anemone blanda *'Blue Shades'*

Planting

- Plant as early as possible in the fall so the plants have a chance to root well before winter sets in.
- Before planting, soak the rhizomes in tepid water for 24 hours. Plant immediately after soaking.
- Full sun. This species grows best in a dry, sunny location. It will tolerate light shade or dappled shade, but bulbs planted in shady locations naturalize less readily, flower later and have smaller blooms.
- Well-drained neutral to alkaline soil. A soil rich in humus or organic matter is ideal, but this species also tolerates poor soil.
- Plant 5 cm deep; space 3–5 cm apart.

Growing

- Divide mature clumps of *Anemone blanda* in the late summer, after the leaves have died back. Allow the new clump sufficient time to become well established before winter sets in.
- This species may self-seed quite freely, but some cultivars will not grow true from seed.

The Big Issue

Anemones are particularly susceptible to desiccation, so avoid buying dried-out rhizomes: they are unlikely to grow. If you find a bargain on anemones late in the season, check the rhizomes carefully before buying and be prepared for them not to grow. Desiccation is a particular problem for *Anemone blanda* and *A. nemorosa*, but may also affect *A. coronaria*— your best defence is to shop early.

Anemone blanda *flowers bloom for four to six weeks in the spring*

TIPS

- Mulch the planting area with bark mulch to insulate the bulbs and prevent the plants from emerging prematurely in the spring and being damaged by a late spring frost. Or put the bulbs in a spot that receives dappled shade, to ensure the soil warms slowly.

- Try planting a few *Anemone blanda* bulbs in the hollow of an old tree or among larger rocks in your rock garden. In a few years, they will grow to a dense, beautiful clump that produces masses of starry flowers in the spring.

- Anemones produce narrow leaves that take up little space, so they may be planted fairly close together (as close as 2–3 cm). In fact, they look better when they are closely planted. If you plant closely, be prepared to divide the bulbs in a few years if the clump becomes too crowded.

- If you want to have a large number of anemones quickly, you can propagate them by cutting the rhizomes in pieces. Be sure each piece has an eye, or growing point. The roots develop along the lower surface of the rhizome, while the stems and leaves grow from the eyes on the upper surface of the rhizomes. Allow the newly cut surface to air-dry for a few hours, to prevent disease organisms from infecting the rhizome, then plant as usual, eyes facing up. Propagation is best done in the late summer, after the leaves fade.

Anemone blanda *is native to the dry mountains of the Balkans and Turkey. This bulb is on the endangered species list in the wild; be sure the bulbs you purchase were grown from cultivated stock.*

In the Garden

- Under favourable conditions, this species quickly forms sizeable patches and is best planted beneath shrubs or in rock gardens, alpine gardens, informal mixed borders and perennial gardens. It can also be planted in outdoor containers.

- Windflowers look best planted in small informal groups among shrubs, small deciduous trees or mixed perennials. They also look great beneath almost any of the larger fall-planted bulbs, such as daffodils, tulips, fritillaries and scillas. They are just gorgeous mixed with winter heathers and hellebores!

- Windflowers are stunning planted in masses of a single colour. Although the cultivars are often sold as mixes, it's worth the effort to buy individual varieties. Different cultivars tend to bloom at slightly different times and also vary in vigour; white-flowered varieties tend to take over the patch.

- This species naturalizes readily, eventually forming a lovely carpet of colour. This growth habit is particularly effective in woodland gardens because the flowers typically bloom before the deciduous trees and shrubs leaf out.

- These anemones look absolutely beautiful planted in meadow or wildflower gardens, or in any area where grass is allowed to grow a little longer than on a typical lawn.

Try these!

The average height of *Anemone blanda* is 15–20 cm. White-flowered varieties tend to be a little taller; other cultivars may be slightly shorter.

✥ **'Blue Shades'** • Light- to dark-blue, daisy-like flowers

✥ **'Charmer'** • Deep-pink, daisy-like flowers

✥ **'Pink Star'** • Large, pale-pink, daisy-like flowers

✥ **'Radar'** • Deep-pink, daisy-like flowers with white centres

✥ **'White Splendour'** • Large, pure-white, daisy-like flowers. The tallest and most vigorous cultivar of this species; easily outgrows both the blue and pink cultivars.

Anemone blanda *'White Splendour' looks beautiful in front of the burgundy-streaked foliage of greigii tulip 'Pinochio'*

windflower, florist's
anemone, poppy-
flowered anemone,
cutleaf anemone

Type
Corm

Planting season
Spring (Fall in Zones
8–10)

Blooming season
Late spring through
mid summer

Hardiness
Zones 8–10 (Zone
7 with protection)

How many
Start with
7 to 13 corms

Golden Rules
- Plant in a warm,
  sunny location
- Provide a sheltered
  spot in the garden
- In cooler climates,
  plant outdoors only
  after the risk of frost
  has passed

Poppy Anemones
Anemone coronaria

*This species produces some of the most vibrantly
coloured flowers in the garden: rich raging reds,
fabulous royal purples and beautiful rosy pinks,
most with gorgeous contrasting black centres. These
anemones are also perfectly suited to growing in
containers. Container growing allows you to move
the plants to shelter during blustery weather and
makes their maintenance easy.*

*Poppy anemones require a warm, sunny location to
thrive and in most zones (Zone 7 or lower) must either
be treated as annuals or be lifted and saved at the end
of the season. Give these bulbs a sheltered spot in the
garden and they'll produce a gorgeous blast of summer
colour with their large, showy, poppy-like flowers.*

Anemone coronaria *is grown commercially for cutflowers.*
The blooms last about a week in a vase.

PLANTING

- Soak the corms in tepid water overnight before planting to ensure they are fully rehydrated. Plant them immediately after soaking or flowering will be diminished.

- Full sun. These anemones require at least a half day of afternoon sun or they will not produce flowers.

- Sheltered location. Shelter is necessary both for winter protection and because wind and heavy rains will damage the blossoms.

- Light, sandy, well-drained soil. These anemones prefer neutral to alkaline soils.

- Plant 5–8 cm deep; space 10–15 cm apart.

GROWING

- Cut rather than pull the flowers from the plants to ensure you don't damage them.

- Divide mature clumps of *Anemone coronaria* in the late summer. When the plants are crowded, the flowers are smaller.

- If you live in a zone where *Anemone coronaria* is hardy or borderline hardy, leave the corms in the ground over the winter (in borderline areas, mulch the corms for insulation). In cooler zones, treat this species as an annual. The corms are difficult to store successfully.

*Anemone coronaria is
native around the
Mediterranean Sea
in southern Europe.
In the wild, the red
form is most common.
Red is also popular in the
garden, as seen in this St.
Brigid cultivar 'The Goveror'*

Anemone coronaria *'The Admiral'*

Tips

- The corms should feel rock hard when you buy them. If they are soft or pliable, they have dried out and are probably not viable.

- The size of *Anemone coronaria* bulbs varies widely, especially in mixed bags (which is how these bulbs are usually sold). But don't worry: even the small, 2- to 3-cm corms readily produce flowers. Bulb size also varies somewhat between cultivars.

In the Garden

- *Anemone coronaria* is best planted in mixed perennial beds or among smaller deciduous shrubs. It also looks great planted in formal borders. This species is an excellent choice for container planting.

TRY THESE!

Anemone coronaria bulbs are classified as single-flowered and double-flowered cultivars. Single-flowered cultivars are referred to collectively as De Caen cultivars; double cultivars are called St. Brigid cultivars. Both are available in a wide range of brights and pastels as well as bicoloured varieties. They are usually sold as mixes—'De Caen Mix' or 'St. Brigid Mix'—and the contents vary depending on the availability of corms.

De Caen Cultivars

'Hollandia' • Single red flowers with a halo of white around the darker centre

'Mr. Fokker' • Single violet-blue flowers

'His Excellency' • Large, single scarlet flowers with a white eye

'Sulphide' (also known as 'Sylphide') • Single mauve-purple flowers

'The Bride' • Single white flowers with contrasting apple-green centre; also known as 'Die Braut'

De Caen cultivar 'Sulphide'

St. Brigid Cultivars

'The Governor' • Vibrant-red semi-double flowers

'The Admiral' • Deep pinkish-purple semi-double flowers

'Lord Lieutenant' • Blue semi-double flowers

'Mount Everest' • White semi-double flowers; the semi-double form of 'The Bride'

De Caen cultivar 'His Excellency'

true windflower,
European wood
anemone

Type
Rhizome

Planting season
Fall

Blooming season
Spring

Hardiness
Zones 4–8

How many
Start with 3 to 5
rhizomes

Golden Rules
- Plant promptly after buying or dividing
- Provide a shady or partly shaded location
- Best used in informal garden settings—naturalizes readily

Wood Anemone

Anemone nemorosa

This tiny anemone—growing just 10 to 15 cm high—is often called the true windflower. It has delicate white flowers whose softly pink-toned petals quiver in the slightest breeze. In its native habitat, wood anemone is found in shady spots in forests and on hillsides. This species requires cool, woodland conditions and consistent moisture. But once planted in the right location, these bulbs naturalize readily, producing dainty, charming, carefree blooms in mid spring.

PLANTING

- Plant as early as possible in the fall. These bulbs are small and dry out quickly.
- Shade or partial shade. Some protection from the wind is also beneficial.
- Plant 3 cm deep; space 8–10 cm apart.
- Light, humus-rich, well-drained soil. These bulbs do not tolerate dry soil and prefer acid to neutral soils, soils typically associated with woodland areas.
- Ensure good, consistent moisture.

GROWING

- Once the foliage appears, water regularly to keep the soil moist.
- Wood anemone does not like to be disturbed, so be patient. It may not really take off until the second season. Once the plants are content, they will spread rapidly.
- Divide this species in late summer. Replant thinned bulbs promptly—don't allow them to dry out.

Anemone nemorosa is native to northern Europe as far east as Turkey and northwest Asia

Tips

• Wood anemone is an excellent choice for shady gardens as long as the soil doesn't become too dry. Avoid planting the bulbs too close to spruce or pine trees, which may outcompete the anemones for soil moisture.

• This species spreads quickly by rhizomes, especially when the soil is rich in organic matter.

In the Garden

• Wood anemone is best planted in woodland gardens or in mixed, informal perennial gardens. The bulbs naturalize readily and are excellent planted among smaller trees and shrubs.

• This species looks great planted alongside hellebores and primroses.

Try these!

๛ *Anemone nemorosa* • This species produces masses of beautiful white flowers and has long-lasting deep-green foliage.

๛ **'Robinsoniana'** • Light-blue flowers; one of the earliest cultivars to flower; long-lasting dark-green foliage tinged with purple

Anemone ranunculoides is closely related to A. nemorosa and has similar growing requirements. It produces dark-yellow flowers with bronzy-green foliage and grows to 8–10 cm. It grows best with fine bark mulch mixed into the planting soil—the mulch simulates woodland conditions and helps keep the roots moist.

Type
Tuber

Planting season
Late spring

Blooming season
Late spring until frost

Hardiness
Zone 10 (Zone 9 with
protection)

How many
Start with 5 to 7
tubers

Golden Rules
- Plant no deeper
  than 5 cm
- Provide a shady,
  well-drained location
- Water moderately
  but frequently

Tuberous Begonias
Begonia x *tuberhybrida*

For years, tuberous begonias have been extremely popular in Europe but considerably less so in North America. Many gardeners here believe begonias are unreliable or too challenging to grow successfully. But this attitude is unfair: given the proper growing conditions, these begonias can produce a beautiful, exotic show. They feature a wider variety of forms and colours, and flower over a longer period, than any other bulbous plant, and they thrive in shade—even in northern latitudes.

It's true that begonias struggle in some areas, particularly in very hot, dry climates or very cold, wet climates. And begonias are a bit temperamental. They don't like strong sun but can't tolerate frost. They don't like windy locations and their soil must be neither too dry nor too wet. But give them a shady, well-drained spot and water them regularly, and they will yield a bounty of large, vibrantly coloured blooms in red, white, pink, orange, yellow, purple, apricot and many shades between.

Begonia *x* crispa marginata *'Apricot Lace'*

Most begonia tubers are produced in Europe, primarily in Belgium, which is the largest producer of begonia tubers in the world. Several companies in North America—primarily in California—also produce varieties of tuberous begonias.

Begonia *x* rosiflora *'Apricot'*

PLANTING

- Start tubers indoors in early spring, 4 to 6 weeks before transplanting outdoors. Plant outside after all danger of frost has passed—at the same time as your tomatoes.

- Shade. Tuberous begonias do not like hot sun. Choose an area of the garden that receives only morning sun or 50 percent shade. Too much direct sun can scorch the leaves and flowers or dramatically reduce their size.

- Rich, porous, well-drained soil with lots of organic matter. Begonias are surface rooters and produce shallow roots.

- Plant no deeper than 5 cm. Begonia tubers will rot if planted too deeply.

How to force begonia tubers

Begonia tubers can easily be forced indoors. Fill a seeding flat with 6–8 cm of good-quality potting soil. Moisten the soil without waterlogging it. Push the tubers, concave side up, into the soil until the top is slightly below the surface. The soil should just cover the tuber. Space tubers 5–8 cm apart in the flat. Erect a tent of plastic sheeting over the flat or use a clear plastic tray cover. Water as required, but only to ensure the soil stays moist. If the soil is too wet, the tubers will rot. Soil temperatures should be no lower than 12°C at night and 21°C–26°C during the day. Place the tubers in a warm location with good air movement; remove plastic covering after the shoots emerge. Once the tubers have produced four to six large leaves, they may be transplanted to larger containers or outdoors. To remove the tubers, simply lift them. Any excess soil will fall away, leaving a fairly large plant and a clump of fine, shallow roots around the outside of the tuber. Tuberous begonias typically flower 12 to 15 weeks after forcing.

Begonia *x* camellia *'Ruffle Picotee Rose & White'*

Begonia *x* camellia *'Ruffle White'*

Multiflora group cultivar

The Big Issue

Begonia tubers dislike being forced in deep soil or large containers. The root system is very small and shallow when top growth begins. If the soil is too deep or the container too large, the tuber struggles to maintain moisture levels, and the soil may easily become waterlogged. Transplant forced tubers to fairly small pots (11–13 cm) initially. As the plants mature and the roots reach the edge of the pot, transplant the tubers to larger pots or outdoors.

GROWING

• Pinching promotes bushier plants, strong stems and numerous flowers; begonias respond well to pinching. Pinch soft (taking off one or two leaves) or hard (taking off three, four or more leaves); pinch often if necessary. The best time to pinch begonias is when the plants are still developing.

• Provide abundant, consistent moisture. This requirement becomes especially important during hot weather. Tuberous begonias require moderate but frequent watering to keep the shallow root system moist without waterlogging the plant.

• Water the soil surface, never the leaves or flowers. Water early in the day to prevent the development of powdery mildew—avoid watering in the evening.

• Because of their large, heavy blooms, most upright tuberous begonias require support or staking. Gently tie the stems to a small bamboo stake to hold them upright. They may be injured if the ties are too tight or too sharp. Be sure the stake does not pierce the tuber when you position it.

• Once they begin flowering, fertilize begonias every 2 or 3 weeks with water-soluble all-purpose fertilizer (20-20-20) until the end of August. Do not overfeed: excess fertilizer causes soft growth that rots easily.

How to lift begonia tubers

Shortly before the average date of first fall frost in your area, stop watering. If the plants are in pots, they may be brought indoors to finish flowering, but this is not necessary. Leave the begonias in the garden until there is a light frost, frost that blackens the upper leaves of the plant but does not harm the main lower stems or tubers. (Begonia tubers cannot withstand a hard frost. If the first frost is likely to be hard, dig the tubers out of the garden or protect the plants by covering them with a blanket or towel.) Gently lift the plants out of the ground, trying to retain as much adhering soil as possible. Do not remove the tops. Set the plants between light layers of newspaper to dry for a couple of weeks; keep them in a cool but not cold location (such as a corner of the basement). •
After two weeks, cut back the tops, leaving 8–10 cm of the main stem attached to the tuber. Do not remove the soil from the tuber (it's OK if some soil falls off). Allow the remainder of the plant to dry gradually—this may take several weeks. When the stubby stems fall off with a light touch, remove them and shake the tubers free of soil. Pack the tubers in vermiculite, dry peat moss or dry, sterilized sand. You can also hang them in old nylon stockings packed with peat moss. Store at 7–15°C; do not store at temperatures below 5°C. Force stored bulbs in early spring, four to six weeks before the date of average last spring frost in your area.

Begonia x camellia 'Rose'

Begonia tuber freshly lifted for storage at the end of the growing season

The Big Issue

Tuberous begonias are just one form of a diverse group of plants. As the name implies, tuberous begonias grow from tubers that may be lifted and stored through the winter. Other begonia types include fibrous, fibrous-rooted, Iron Cross, Rex and Angelwing. These forms are known as bedding-plant begonias; they are distinct from the tuberous begonias and are not dealt with in this book.

Begonia x pendula cultivar 'American Hybrid Yellow'

Begonia *x* gigantea *cultivar 'Pin-up'*

Tips

- If you are growing begonias to produce large, showy flowers, pinch off any flower buds until the plant reaches 25 cm tall. This helps promote sturdier growth, which supports large flowers better, and means that fewer, larger flowers will be produced high on the plant. If you are interested in growing tuberous begonias only as bedding plants, don't worry about removing flower buds.

- Avoid windy locations: foliage and flowers may break off. Strong wind may cause scorching and damage to leaves and flowers. Wind also tends to dry out the soil quickly, especially for container-planted begonias and begonias in hanging baskets. Begonias do not like to dry out.

In the Garden

- Begonias are extremely versatile. They look great used as edging in flowerbeds or borders. They make a pretty feature planted together in groups of three or five, and are beautiful tucked into small shady spots around the garden. The shorter varieties look wonderful planted in shady rock gardens.

- Begonias are one of the best bulbs for planting in containers. Their growth habit is especially suited to small pots and hanging baskets. Set the container or basket in a warm, sheltered location on a deck or patio, or near the house.

TRY THESE!

All begonias available today have been bred by horticulturists. *Begonia* x *tuberhybrida* refers to a group of cultivars that have been derived through selection and hybridization from species native to the Andes. There are no principal varieties. Some named cultivars exist, but they are rarely offered except through specialty mail-order companies and very specialized growers.

There is no official internationally recognized system of classification for tuberous begonias. The classification system has evolved based on commercial trends and industry categorization, and tubers are typically sold in North America by colour and flower type. We have chosen to organize this section by dividing the various begonia types into the most widely recognized categories based on plant habit, flower colour and flower type; there is certainly a degree of overlap between categories.

Begonia *x* camellia *'Ruffle Mix'*

single group

Begonia x *gigantea*

This group produces large single flowers with four petals, usually flat.

crispa (frilled) group

Begonia x *crispa*

This group produces large single flowers with frilled or ruffled petal margins.

cristata (crested) group

Begonia x *cristata*

This group produces large single flowers with a frilled tuft or crest near the centre of each petal.

narcissiflora (daffodil-flowered) group

Begonia x *narcissiflora*

This group produces large flowers whose central petals spread erect, forming a trumpet that resembles the corona on narcissus flowers.

camellia (camelliiflora) group

Begonia x *camellia*

This group produces large double single-coloured flowers that resemble camellias. The petals are never ruffled. This group is one of the better-known groups, commonly referred to as camellia-flowered begonias (also known as the roseform group); it is also one of the most widely available types.

ruffled camellia group

Begonia x *camellia* (Ruffle)

This group has the same characteristics as the camellia group except that the petals are ruffled.

rosiflora (rosebud) group

Begonia x rosiflora

This group produces large double flowers with raised centres that resemble rosebuds.

fimbriata plena (carnation) group

Begonia x fimbriata

This group produces large double flowers with fringed petal margins that resemble carnations. This group is commonly referred to as carnation-flowered begonias.

picotee group

Begonia x camellia (Picotee)

This group produces large, usually double, camellia-form flowers. The petals have a thin outer band of colour that blends with the main or dominant flower colour.

ruffled picotee group

Begonia x camellia (Ruffle)

This group has the same characteristics as the picotee group except that the petals are ruffled.

marginata group

Begonia x crispa marginata

This group produces large, usually double flowers, but the petals are edged with a precise line of colour that is distinctly different from the main or dominant flower colour.

Begonia *x* fimbriata *'Mix'*

marmorata group

Begonia x marmorata

This group produces large double flowers like the camellia group, but the petals are rose-coloured, blotched or spotted with white.

pendula (hanging basket) group

Begonia x pendula, Begonia x Lloydii, Begonia x Lloydii pendula

This group produces many trailing or pendulous flowers ranging in size from small to large; they may be single, semi-double or double. The stems are also pendulous.

Begonia *x* camellia
'Rose and White Picotee'

The hardy begonia

One tuberous begonia is hardier than the others: *Begonia grandis* ssp. *evansiana*. Unfortunately, this variety is rare today and survives mainly through trading between avid gardeners.

B. grandis reaches 60–75 cm high with a 30-cm spread, and is hardy from Zones 6 to 10 (will grow in Zone 5 with protection). It grows from a small tuber and produces clusters of pink flowers. The plants begin to grow in the late spring and thrive in light shade or filtered sunlight. They bloom in late summer and continue to flower until frost. The leaves are wing-shaped, 10 cm long and olive-green with red tones on the underside. A white variety, known as *B. grandis* ssp. *evansiana alba*, is also available.

multiflora group

This group is an umbrella group for many different begonia cultivars and includes *Begonia* x *floribunda*, *B.* x *maxima*, *B.* x *multiflora*, *B.* x *multiflora gigantea*, *B.* x *multiflora grandiflora*, *B.* x *multiflora maxima*, *B.* x *tuberosa floribunda* and *B.* x *tuberosa multiflora*. These are low, bushy, compact plants that branch more freely than the other categories. They produce numerous smaller single, semi-double or double flowers and bear relatively small leaves. These begonias tolerate sunnier conditions than the other categories and are most likely to overwinter successfully.

This category includes the well-known series 'Nonstop'. Nonstop begonias are compact plants with a mounding growth habit. They reach a final height of 15–20 cm and flower earlier than any other tuberous begonias. They also flower consistently for the entire season. Nonstop begonias are more tolerant of windy conditions than many of the taller types. They are also more mildew resistant than most. This series currently dominates the tuberous begonia market.

bertinii group

Begonia bertinii

This group produces single, pendulous flowers with long, pointed petals. The stems of the plants are long and thin, but not pendulous.

compact bertinii group

Begonia bertinii compacta

This group produces both single and double flowers with no special characteristics. They differ from multiflora group because the leaves are a little larger and pointed, and both the flower stalks and stems are upright.

duplex group

Begonia x 'Duplex'

This group produces flowers that resemble poppies. The flowers are semi-double rather than fully double, and the petal edges are often ruffled.

arum lily

Type
Rhizome

Planting season
Spring

Blooming season
Early spring
to early summer

Hardiness
Zones 9–11

How many
Start with
2 or 3 rhizomes

Golden Rules
- Plant outdoors only after all risk of frost has passed and the soil has warmed
- Manage water carefully through the growing season
- Provide a warm, sunny, sheltered location

Calla Lilies

Zantedeschia spp.

After years of popularity as a prized cutflower with beautiful waxy flowers and a large golden spadix, the calla lily is gaining popularity as a garden plant. This interest is partly due to the availability of gorgeous new cultivars, featuring unusual flower colours and eye-catching leaves. Many of these new cultivars are 'miniature' forms, better suited to growing outdoors.

Calla lilies are the tenderest of the tender bulbs commonly available for temperate gardens. They cannot bear even a hint of frost—temperatures a few degrees above zero are enough to cause chilling injuries. Enjoy this tropical beauty indoors until the spring days are consistently warm and welcoming.

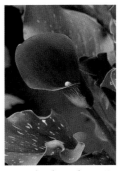

Zantedeschia rehmanii
x Z. elliottiana *cultivar*
'Majestic Red'

Calla lilies are not
related to true lilies,
which belong to the lily
family (Liliaceae). They
are, however, closely
related to jack-in-the-
pulpits (Arisaema spp.)
and caladiums (Cala-
dium spp.).

Zantedeschia elliottiana *(yellow flowers)*, Z. 'Mango' *(or-*
ange-red flowers) and Z. 'Majestic Red'

PLANTING

- Force calla lilies indoors 2 to 3 months before transplanting them outdoors in areas with short growing seasons or cooler summers (Zones 2–8).
- Moist, well-drained, humus-rich soil.
- Plant 10 cm deep; space 35–40 cm apart.
- Full sun in a sheltered location. In very hot areas, provide light shade; do not allow the plants to dry out.
- Water thoroughly after transplanting.

How to force calla lilies indoors

Plan for a single rhizome per 15-cm pot. Plant the rhizome 10 cm deep in good-quality potting soil. Water thoroughly; you may wish to apply fungicide at this time. Place pot in a warm, sunny location and do not water again until the first shoots emerge unless the soil dries out. Water sparingly until the foliage is fully unfurled; then water regularly until the callas are planted outdoors. The soil should not remain constantly wet or completely dry out. Callas prefer soil temperatures of 18–21°C until the new shoots have emerged fully; after the leaves begin to unfurl, soil temperature may be reduced to 15–17°C. Warmer temperatures will reduce the time to flower, but the plants will be softer.

Genus Zantedeschia *is a member of the arum family (Araceae). The genus name honours Italian botanist Giovanni Zantedeschi (1773–1846).*

Radical poet and artist Mina Loy was the original designer of the calla lily lamp, an Art Deco classic.

Zantedeschia elliottiana

GROWING

- Provide regular, plentiful water. Callas must not dry out during their active growing period, but the soil must be well-drained.

- Callas are not heavy feeders. Mix in a granular bulb fertilizer at time of planting or water with water-soluble 20-20-20 fertilizer every couple of weeks until the first flower is produced.

- After the flowers have faded, remove the flower stems. The foliage will continue to look attractive. Reduce water but keep the plants moist. Towards the end of the summer, begin to cut back on the water to encourage the foliage to die back and allow the bulb to go dormant before there is any risk of frost.

- Divide large clumps in late summer, near the end of the active growing season.

How to lift calla bulbs

After flowering has finished, reduce watering to encourage the bulbs to go dormant; cooling temperatures will also bring on dormancy. After frost has touched the foliage but before temperatures are cold enough to injure the rhizome, dig up the rhizome, taking care not to damage or bruise the roots. It is important not to lift callas until dormancy begins, signalled by yellow, decaying foliage. (As dormancy sets in, the tuber surface becomes tougher, which helps the tuber last in storage.) Unlike most bulbs, calla rhizomes should be washed gently with tepid water to remove as much of the soil as will easily come away. Be careful not to injure the rhizomes. Dip the rhizomes in a fungal solution or dust with soil and bulb dust to prevent the development of disease during storage. • Cure the rhizomes for 3 to 7 days at 21–26°C, ensuring good air movement. (Curing helps to form a tough outer skin that prevents both dehydration and disease.) Store rhizomes in a single layer on mesh trays or in paper bags in a cool (5–10°C), dark location. Ensure the rhizomes do not touch—this way, if one bulb becomes diseased in storage, it doesn't infect the others. • Remove the rhizomes from storage when you are ready to force them. Check for any diseased rhizomes and remove them. Rhizomes can also be split in the spring; be sure each piece has at least one eye or growing point on it (follow method for cannas, page 104). Allow any cut surfaces to air-dry for a few days before transplanting.

Zantedeschia *cultivar 'Mango'*

The Big Issue

Water management is critical to growing calla lilies successfully. Most disease problems with callas are associated with water management, provided the bulbs were healthy when they were planted. Water the bulbs thoroughly when you first plant them, and then leave them alone. Once the first shoots emerge, water the plant sparingly until the foliage opens. Gradually give the plants more water until they are transplanted outside. Once the callas are in the garden, water them liberally until flowering is finished. At this point, reduce watering to encourage the bulbs to go dormant before fall.

Callas are native to temperate and subtropical southern and eastern Africa.

Calla lilies make excellent cutflowers.

The Big Issue

Calla lilies are vulnerable to a disease called soft rot, caused by *Erwinia* bacteria. The infection is brought on by a combination of poor cultural practices, less-than-optimal growing conditions and unhealthy bulbs. Callas in these conditions are vulnerable to comon diseases such as pythium; once infected they are susceptible to secondary infection by *Erwinia*. If *Erwinia* becomes established, improved cultural practices won't help: improvements to correct the primary disease, such as heat and moisture, create an optimal environment for *Erwinia*, which may overcome the plant.

Resistance to soft rot is linked to genetics, but the issue is not clear-cut. Most calla lily bulbs are commercially produced by tissue culture. The first generation of tissue culture-produced bulbs (that is, the first group produced from the mother bulb) is called T1. Subsequent tissue culture-produced bulbs (that is, those produced from the first generation of offspring) are called T2. Commercial producers may take tissue from the second generation of tissue-cultured bulbs to produce offspring called T3. Some commercial growers who produce top-quality callas will grow only from T1 bulbs. They believe these bulbs are healthier and more vigorous than those produced from second- and third-generation tissue cultures. They also believe that first-generation bulbs are more resistant to *Erwinia*. Whether this belief is true is still open to debate.

It is almost impossible to tell whether bulb stock is T1, T2 or T3. T1 bulbs tend to look more like corms than do T2 and T3 bulbs; the latter bulbs are often larger and have significantly more growing points.

Whether a calla develops soft rot seems to depend as much on overall plant vigour as on resistance to *Erwinia*. For instance, cultivars with spotted leaves tend be more prone to soft rot, but spotted-leaf cultivars are also not as vigorous as green-leaved ones. Breeders are aware of these traits and are working hard to improve them.

In the meantime, the best control method for *Erwinia* is prevention. Choose firm, blemish-free bulbs, provide optimum growing conditions and keep your plants as healthy and vigorous as possible.

Zantedeschia '*Lavender Gem*' (top), Z. '*Cameo*' (bottom)

Zantedeschia *cultivar 'Flame'*

TIPS

• Callas are very soft tender plants and cannot tolerate any degree of frost. They also dislike cold, wet weather.

• In spring, you can purchase calla lilies that have been forced by the grower. Plant them directly into the garden once the risk of frost has passed.

• Rather than transplant the growing calla into the garden, plunge the pot directly into the flowerbed. When the bulb has finished flowering, dig up the pot and put it in a less-visible location while the bulb finishes its growing cycle. Watch the moisture level carefully.

• If you prefer to avoid the trouble of lifting and dividing calla lilies each year, treat the bulbs as annuals and allow the plants to remain in the garden until fall clean-up. Start with new bulbs each spring. This allows you to experiment with more colours and varieties.

• Depending upon the size of the rhizome, each bulb will produce 1 to 5 blooms. Each flower normally lasts 3 to 4 weeks. When the weather is especially hot and dry, or if the plant is stressed, the blooming period will be shortened.

IN THE GARDEN

Callas can be planted in mixed flowerbeds, borders or formal flowerbeds, provided they have a fairly sheltered location. Their elegant, upright growth habit is particularly suited to formal gardens and makes an excellent choice for outdoor containers.

TRY THESE!

As calla lilies have increased in popularity, breeders have been working hard to develop new varieties. Today many species and hybrids are available in a wide range of heights and flower colours. We mention some of the principal varieties here.

Zantedeschia aethiopica

Common names ⋗ white arum lily, white calla, florist's arum lily
Height ⋗ 1 m

This is the largest of the callas and many of its cultivars are grown for commercial cutflowers. **Flowers** ⋗ It produces white flowers up to 20 cm long. **Requirements** ⋗ It prefers moist, fairly boggy conditions and grows well beside ponds and water features. It can also be grown as a marginal plant in up to 30 cm of water.

⋗ **'Green Goddess'** • The best-known cultivar of this species; produces a succession of beautiful white flowers mottled with green. Leaves are arrow-shaped, deep green. A smaller cultivar (45-80 cm), well-suited to growing in pots.

Zantedeschia albomaculata

Common names ⋗ spotted calla, spotted arum lily
Height ⋗ 60 cm

The descriptor *albomaculata* refers to the translucent, silvery-white blotches on the leaves. **Flowers** ⋗ This species produces widely funnel-shaped ivory flowers with dark-green, white-spotted, heart-shaped leaves.

Zantedeschia albomaculata

Zantedeschia elliottiana

Common names ↝ golden arum, yellow calla, golden calla
Height ↝ 60 cm

Flowers ↝ This species produces golden-yellow flowers with silver-splotched, deep-green, heart-shaped foliage with translucent spots. The flowers are less open and more cowl-shaped than those of other *Calla* species.

Zantedeschia rehmannii

Common names ↝ pink arum, pink calla
Height ↝ 30 cm

This species is especially suited to growing indoors as a potted plant, but it also does well outdoors. **Flowers** ↝ It has small, reddish-pink flowers with yellow spadixes and dark-green leaves.

Zantedeschia rehmannii x Z. elliottiana cultivars

Height ↝ 30–60 cm

These are dwarf-growing types with smaller flowers. They are grown commercially as potted plants but also perform well in the garden.

↝ **Z. 'Cameo'** • Apricot flowers with dark throats; grows to 35 cm

↝ **Z. 'Mango'** • Orange-red flowers; grows to 35 cm

↝ **Z. 'Black-Eyed Beauty'** • Dark-yellow flowers with a touch of chautreuse and a black heart; grows to 35 cm

↝ **Z. 'Lavender Gem'** • Beautiful, clear-lavender flowers

Zantedeschia rehmanni x
Z. elliottiana *cultivar 'Cameo'*

Indian shot plant,
Indian reed flower

Type
Rhizome

Planting season
Spring

Blooming season
Summer

Hardiness
Zones 9–11 (Zones 7–8 with protection)

How many
Start with 2 or 3 rhizomes

Golden Rules

- Plant outdoors only after all risk of frost has passed and soil has warmed

- Provide regular moisture

- Plant in a hot, full-sun location

Canna Lilies

Canna indica

Canna lilies produce large, exotic blooms, and the plants grow fairly tall, from 75 centimetres to more than 2 metres. Their strong vertical growth habit brings a real presence to any garden, and their large, colourful, banana-like leaves are just gorgeous. Cannas were first introduced in Europe in the 1600s but quickly lost favour—they simply didn't suit the stiff, formal gardens of the day. But cannas are perfect in today's garden, where foliage and texture feature importantly, and they're a popular choice in many landscape designs.

Canna lilies are treated as annuals in most zones, but they can be left in the ground in areas with mild winters (Zone 8 and warmer). Anyone who loves a lush, tropical look should save space in the garden for a few cannas. They're low maintenance but have high visual impact.

Canna *cultivar 'Apricot Dream'*

Canna *is the only genus in the canna family,* Cannaceae. *The name derives from the Greek word* kanna, *which means reed-like plant.*

Canna *cultivar 'Phasion'*

Planting

- Plant outdoors after all danger of frost has passed and the ground warms up. In colder zones, cannas should be started indoors at the end of winter (about six to eight weeks before planting outdoors) and grown until they can be planted in beds or containers. Canna bulbs can be transplanted as late as June, but they will produce only foliage, not flowers.

- Full sun with good air circulation. Anything less than full sun will reduce overall growth and flower production.

- Rich, moist soil with lots of organic matter. Cannas will tolerate a range of soils, as long as there is adequate moisture and the soil is fertile and well drained.

- Plant about 10 cm deep to the base of the bulb. Cannas prefer to be shallowly planted, just deep enough that the top of the rhizome is covered with soil.

- Lay the rhizomes flat when you plant them. Cover with no more than 5 cm of soil.

- Space 45–60 cm apart. Small cultivars can be planted closer together, but medium and tall cultivars should be widely spaced. As a rule, cannas are greedy for space.

GROWING

- Cannas require a regular supply of moisture. They will not tolerate dry conditions.

- During active growth, fertilize every two weeks with water-soluble all-purpose (20-20-20) fertilizer, or side-dress with granular bulb fertilizer once a month.

- Deadheading will greatly increase the number and quality of flowers produced. Be careful not to damage the new, unopened buds when you remove spent flowers.

- After all the flowers have opened on the flower stalk, no more buds will be produced. At this point, remove the stalk by cutting it off, down to the next side shoot. A secondary flower stalk will appear from this point. Repeat when this stalk is finished. Most canna cultivars produce two, three or four secondary flower stalks, with each stalk becoming smaller until the entire main stalk has been removed. In most areas, this process will take the entire season, so you should have flowers until the fall.

- Cannas have very strong stems, so they don't require support or staking to remain upright even in fairly exposed locations. Some protection may be necessary if the location is extremely windy, to avoid tattered and ripped leaves.

How to lift cannas for storage

In cooler zones, lift cannas at the end of the season and store them over the winter. After the first frost in the fall has blackened the foliage or the foliage begins to wither, cut it back to 10–15 cm. Then gently dig up the rhizome and dry it off. Do not wash the rhizomes! Dust bulbs with soil and bulb dust to prevent the development of disease. Store in moist, sterile horticultural sand, vermiculite or peat moss, in a cool (3–10°C), fairly dark location. Canna rhizomes must not dry out during storage. If the rhizome and the surrounding storage medium begin to feel dry, sprinkle lightly with water. That said, do not allow the medium to remain wet, or the bulbs will rot. Canna cultivars with large, stocky rhizomes store much more successfully than those with long, stringy rhizomes. • Six to eight weeks before date of average last spring frost in your area, remove the rhizomes from the storage medium, split as described below and plant up for indoor forcing. Transplant into the garden when all risk of frost has passed and the days are warm. Allow cannas to harden off gradually before transplanting.

How to split cannas

Canna rhizomes are best split in the spring. Splitting cannas in spring gives them the entire growing season to recover and grow; there is also greater risk of disease and desiccation problems if you split them in the fall. Dig up the individual plants from the garden or remove the rhizomes from storage, being careful not to damage the rhizomes. Brush the soil from the roots. Cut the rhizomes into sections using a sharp knife. Ensure that each section has at least one good root and at least one eye (growing point). Remove any rotten pieces of plant, damaged foliage or large leaves. Let the cut surface dry in the open air for at least 24 hours before planting to prevent the development of fungal diseases. Plant the rhizome pieces in individual pots, using good-quality potting soil; water and place in a warm, sunny spot until they are well rooted.

Canna foliage is striking used in mixed flowerbeds

Cannas as Perennials

In milder climates, it is not cold that threatens cannas left in the ground over winter. Wet, rainy conditions may also cause cannas to die.

If you live in an area where the winters are very rainy (Zones 7 or warmer), plant cannas in a raised flowerbed or mounded location with good drainage. When foliage withers in the fall, cut it back to just a few centimetres above ground. This treatment prevents water from sitting in the stem area and causing rot.

Cover the planting area with a waterproof tarp. Covering the soil will prevent rain and snow from soaking through to the rhizome. Fasten a sheet of chicken wire over the tarp to keep it from blowing around. Then mulch the area with a generous layer of bark, partially composted leaf matter, straw or other rough garden compost. The mulch should be light and airy, not heavy and wet, and should be at least 15 cm deep.

In mid spring, when the soil is warm and all danger of frost has passed, remove the tarp and replace the mulch. Because the mulch will have decomposed somewhat over the winter, it will be shallower and the new canna shoots should emerge through it easily. The mulch will add some protection and condition the soil for the coming growing season. If slugs and snails are a problem, sprinkle slug pellets in the area before the new growth emerges.

Cannas left in the ground require dividing and revitalizing every three to five years to prevent weak growth and poor flowering (see method on page 104).

TIPS

• Choose rhizomes that are fat, firm and healthy with at least one eye. A good-quality canna rhizome has three eyes (dormant buds).

• Add a shovelful of compost or well-composted manure with some granular bulb fertilizer mixed in before putting cannas in the ground.

• Once your cannas begin to bloom, avoid overhead watering. The water may damage the petals.

• Overwinter canna rhizomes in several small containers, such as paper bags or plastic buckets, to prevent the spread of diseases that may develop in storage. This method also allows you to store and label different cultivars separately.

• Dormant cannas are difficult to identify. Use a permanent marker to write the variety name on a plastic or metal label with a hole in it. Using thin wire or string, tie the label to the leaf remnants on the rhizome. Tie it tightly: the stems will shrivel and shrink during storage. Or store several rhizomes of the same cultivar in a single container and label clearly.

• If your cannas develop scorched leaves shortly after they have been moved outside, the night temperatures in your area are probably too cool for the plants. The leaves haven't been frozen, but cool temperatures or chilling winds have caused injury. Cannas do not tolerate temperatures below 7°C well, especially when they are first moved outdoors. Fortunately, cannas recover once the heat returns. Keep them well watered and give them a bit of fertilizer; they will perk up quickly.

Canna seeds are hard, black and small, about the size of a pea. They resemble bullets or shot, hence the common name Indian shot plant.

Canna *cultivar* Wine 'n' Roses

Canna *cultivar 'Shining Pink'*

- To create a strong colour impact, plant several smaller hybrid cannas about 30 cm apart, allowing at least 45 cm between the cannas and other plants in the garden.
- For an appealing change, use cannas instead of dracaena in large planters.
- If you prefer to avoid the trouble of lifting and dividing cannas each year, treat the bulbs as annuals and allow the plants to remain in the garden until fall clean-up. Starting with new bulbs each spring allows you to experiment with many more colours and varieties.
- Canna leaves decay easily in the compost heap, but the foliage can be quite bulky. If you would like to speed the process up, simply chop or shred the leaves before adding them to the pile.
- If you are growing cannas only for their foliage, remove the main flower stalk right to the foliage to prevent the development of additional flower stalks. The plant will then use its energy to produce foliage.

The Big Issue

Beginning on page 109, we have listed some of the common cultivars for each of the canna groups. But when it comes to cannas, the cultivar name does not always identify the plant the consumer is actually buying. Take 'King Humbert', for example. This cultivar name is often used in the greenhouse trade to describe any red-flowered canna with dark leaves. Similarly, 'Black Knight' may be used to describe any dark-leaved canna with dark-red flowers. Confusion in the trade may also occur between older varieties and newer, similar-looking varieties. For instance, 'Rosamond Coles' is sometimes incorrectly sold as 'Lucifer', a newer, superior cultivar. And the name 'Primrose Yellow' is used loosely in the trade to describe any dwarf yellow canna, because of the true cultivar's great reputation. Growers depend on name recognition and reputation to appeal to buyers, so popular cultivars quickly become common names—despite that their desirable qualities may in fact be rather uncommon!

The flowering period of cannas varies among species and cultivars. Under good conditions, cannas begin to bloom about midsummer. Flowering will continue into the fall, until the first frost. In hot climates, high summer temperatures can stop flowering. In cooler climates, low temperatures or light levels will cause cannas to stall—preventing growth and flowering. If the weather is very cool, flowering can be delayed by up to three to four weeks. Each flower lasts about three days; it will then fall to the ground or shrivel up on the stem. New hybrids have been bred for early, continuous flowering and self-cleaning—spent flowers drop from the stem. Flowers of older cultivars tend to remain on the stem.

IN THE GARDEN

• Cannas make superb focal points in any garden. They look magnificent positioned among large, round rocks and against chunky sections near gazebos or decks. They are also beautiful located at or near the edge of ponds, provided the soil is well drained.

• Shorter cannas look great massed in flowerbeds or along borders, and are the best choice for planters and containers. They look excellent mixed in planters and used as background plants or central feature plants in the pot. They are gorgeous in a group at the peak of a mounded flowerbed.

• Taller, more upright cannas are extremely attractive used to accentuate vertical architectural lines in contemporary gardens. (Smaller varieties in the same situation complement horizontal lines.) Taller varieties also look superb placed behind lower-growing annuals and perennials.

Canna *cultivar 'King Humbert' in the Hole's show garden*

Canna *cultivar 'Pink Princess'*

TRY THESE!

There are more than 100 varieties of canna lilies available commercially. Choose cannas by deciding what you would like the final size of your plants to be, where you are going to plant them and how you are going to use them in your garden. Then pick the flower colour and foliage you like best. Cannas are usually sold as short (less than 1 m tall), medium (2–3 m tall) and tall (over 2 m tall) varieties.

There is no formal classification system for canna lilies. They are typically divided into four main groups: tall, brown-leaved varieties; tall, green-leaved varieties; dwarf, brown-leaved varieties; and dwarf, green-leaved varieties (the final height of dwarf varieties is 50–80 cm). We have also included a few novelty varieties that are very attractive, if difficult to obtain, and have noted some recent hybrids.

Canna *cultivar 'Wyoming'*

Group 1 • *Tall, brown-leaved varieties*

'King Humbert' • Orange-red flowers with dark leaves. Often listed under the name 'Roi Humbert' or 'Red King Humbert'.

'Wyoming' • Huge, soft-orange flowers. Final height 2.4 m. Probably the best known of the bronze-leaved cannas; widely available.

'Black Knight' • Large, dark crimson-red flowers and deep bluish-purple leaves. May be listed as 'Black Velvet' or 'Ambassador'. Widely available but stock is often not true to type. The true 'Black Knight' cultivar is one of the deepest red-flowered cannas available.

Group 2 • Tall, green-leaved varieties

↜ **'City of Portland'** • Salmon-pink flowers flushed with yellow and matching thin yellow edge. An extremely reliable cultivar; produces lots of flowers. Not self-cleaning—finished flowers do not fall—deadhead regularly.

↜ **'Richard Wallace'** • Bright-yellow flowers with slightly frilled petals, some light-red spots in the flower throat; bright-green foliage. Very vigorous, reliable cultivar, although not as tall as other tall varieties; grows easily. May be listed as 'King Midas'.

↜ **'Rosamond Coles'** • Large red flowers with wide yellow edges and yellow spots in the flower throat. Vigorous, reliable cultivar; not self-cleaning.

↜ **'President'** • Bright scarlet-red flowers shaped like gladioli, with faint-yellow petal edges and some yellow in the flower throat. A classic cultivar with wide, bluish-green leaves. Reliable, grows easily.

Canna *cultivar 'Ingeborg'*

Group 3 • Dwarf, brown-leaved varieties

↜ **'Ingeborg'** • Salmon-pink, iris-like flowers and wavy, waxy bronze leaves. An older cultivar, developed by Wilhelm Pfitzer in the early twentieth century.

Group 4 • Dwarf, green-leaved varieties

↜ **'Orchid'** • Deep orchid-pink flowers with green leaves

↜ **'Lucifer'** • Bicolour red-and-yellow, iris-like flowers; width of yellow petal margin sometimes varies. One of the best canna cultivars; produces numerous flowers; very vigorous, reliable. May be listed as 'Dwarf Lucifer'; widely available.

↜ **'Primrose Yellow'** • Yellow flowers with pink dots on petals. May be listed as 'Pfitzer's Primrose Yellow'.

Canna *cultivar 'Lucifer'*

Novelty Varieties

↬ **'Bengal Tiger'** • Orange flowers with beautiful, distinctly striped green-and-white leaves, with very thin purple edges. Grows 1–1.5 m. May be listed as 'Striata', 'Striatum', 'Pretoria' or 'Panache'; may be difficult to obtain.

↬ **'Phasion'** • Large bright-orange flowers. Especially attractive foliage: dark purple, veined with pink, green, gold and orange.

↬ **'Stuttgart'** • Small apricot flowers and long, slender, pale-green leaves. Leaves are variegated with irregular silver and white markings. Best grown in light shade to avoid scorching the leaves; ensure this cultivar receives adequate water. Final height up to 2 m. May be unstable—sometimes reverts to plain green form.

Canna *cultivar 'Bengal Tiger'*

Hybrid Varieties

Breeders have recently developed many wonderful new hybrids, vastly superior in flower size, flower production and garden performance. These cultivars flower early and have relatively short (about 75 cm) growth habits. New varieties also have better vigour, greater weather tolerance and larger, longer-lasting flowers in an astonishing array of colours. The flowers are self-cleaning.

↬ North Star series • Short or medium plants with green foliage. Six cultivars in a range of flower colours, including white, yellow, creamy white, dark red, coral pink and deep red. May be difficult to save bulbs over winter.

↬ Shining series • New series with large, self-cleaning flowers. Great garden performance in areas with hot summers.

↬ Liberty series • Nine cultivars in a beautiful range of flower colours, including red-yellow bicolour, pale cantaloupe-orange, deep coral-rose, pale creamy-yellow, soft pink, light rose with cream splashes, bright red, bright yellow and raspberry pink. Foliage colour varies from green to burgundy to bronze.

Water Cannas

Water cannas derive from *Canna glauca* and are less well known than *C. indica* hybrids, although the two species are closely related. Water cannas tend to have a willowy growth habit and look very graceful. Unlike most cannas, which require full sun and rich, well-drained soil, water cannas can be grown as marginal aquatics beside ponds or as bog plants in plastic baskets around the edge of a garden pool. They will survive with up to 15 cm of water above the rhizome. Water cannas grow best in warm water, particularly in shallow pools that warm up quickly, but they must be planted in full sun. In areas with cold winters, water cannas must be lifted and stored at the end of the summer, but in milder climates (Zone 7 and above), they will survive outdoors as perennials.

glory of the snow

Type
True bulb

Planting season
Fall

Blooming season
Early spring

Hardiness
Zones 3–9

How many
Start with 25 bulbs, in a drift or informal cluster

Golden Rules
- Best used in informal settings—a tiny gem!
- Plant in full sun or partial shade
- Provide moist, well-drained soil

Chionodoxas

Chionodoxa spp.

If I had to choose just one rock garden bulb, I would be tempted to pick chionodoxa, one of the prettiest little bulbs available. Despite their Mediterranean origins, these bulbs are extremely hardy—they will thrive in Zone 3. As soon as there is a hint of warmth in the sun, chionodoxas burst into bloom, lighting up borders, rock gardens, meadows and woodland plantings with their large, bright flowers.

Once these undemanding little bulbs in are the ground, they require next to no care. They die down a few weeks after blooming and disappear until next spring—no untidy foliage to deal with!

Chionodoxa *is a Greek name:* chion *means snow and* doxa *means glory. The Greeks gave this name to the plant because, in its natural settings in the eastern Mediterranean, it flowered at the edges of melting mountain snowdrifts.*

PLANTING

- Plant as soon as possible in the fall, to ensure the bulbs are well rooted.
- Plant 8–10 cm deep and 6–8 cm apart. Chionodoxas are most effective planted closely in informal clumps or drifts of 50 to 100 bulbs. Although they spread rapidly, they have a narrow growth habit—you don't have to worry about them crowding out other plants.
- Chionodoxas thrive in full sun to part shade.
- These bulbs grow best in moist, well-drained soil but will tolerate a range of soil conditions.

GROWING

- Chionodoxas propagate by self-seeding and bulblets. If you want to move or thin clumps, do so just after the leaves wither.
- Chionodoxas readily self-sow. New plants will flower in two to three years from seed.

Chionodoxa causes more confusion in classification than any other bulb. Swiss botanist Edmund Bossier was the first to discover Chionodoxa luciliae. It was later discovered by another botanist, Edward Whittall, who classified it as C. gigantea. *Neither knew the other had given the plant a different name, and the bulb became well established in gardens under the name* C. gigantea. *The name* C. luciliae *eventually became attached to a different species, today called* C. siehei. C. siehei *is still the most common species to be found in garden centres, but it is also typically still mislabeled and sold as* C. luciliae, *indicating* C. gigantea. *The confusing identification is seldom a problem for home gardeners, but it can cause retailers and commercial growers a real headache! At the bulb stage it is impossible to tell which species is which.*

Chionodoxa sardensis *and* C. forbesii *(pictured here) are both well suited to naturalizing*

TIPS

• For an immediate massed effect, plant the bulbs a bit closer, but be prepared to split up crowded clumps after a few years.

• Chionodoxas will tolerate summer drought conditions as long as the location in which they are planted stays reasonably cool. Plant them among trees, shrubs and herbaceous perennials.

• Chionodoxas will not thrive in locations that are both hot and dry, nor will they survive the winter in locations where the drainage is poor and soil conditions are wet and cold.

IN THE GARDEN

• Chionodoxas look great tucked in along a stony bank or near a rocky ledge. They are also beautiful planted in drifts in woodland gardens or in mixed perennial flowerbeds. They are most effective in elevated beds, especially rock gardens, where they may be viewed up close. They also look wonderful alongside small shrubs such as daphne and dwarf evergreens.

• Try planting chionodoxas in combination with other species. Pretty spring-flowering bulbs that bloom at the same time as chionodoxa include *Eranthis hiemalis, Galanthus* spp., *Scilla siberica, Puschkinia scilloides, Tulipa kaufmanniana, Tulipa tarda* and *Tulipa turkestanica*. Spring-flowering perennials that look beautiful planted among chionodoxas include creeping phlox, vitaliana, primrose, adonis, candytuft, drabas, hepatica, trilliums and *Gentiana acaulis*.

TRY THESE!

Chionodoxa forbesii
(C. siehei; incorrectly listed as C. luciliae or C. gigantea)

Common names ✒ snow gloss
Height ✒ 12–15 cm
Blooming season ✒ Early spring
Hardiness ✒ Zones 3–8

Perhaps the best-known chionodoxa species, *C. forbesii* is native to Turkey. **Flowers** ✒ It produces up to 15 star-shaped lavender-blue flowers shading to white at the centre. The flowers face outward and are produced on one-sided racemes. This species typically flowers very early in the spring (February to March)—it is one of the first little bulbs to come into bloom. It naturalizes readily in the garden or lawn.

✒ **'Alba'** • White-flowered cultivar

✒ **'Blue Giant'** • Extra-large lavender-blue flowers with white centres

✒ **'Pink Giant'** • Extra-large light-pink flowers with white centres

✒ **'Rosea'** • Deep-pink blooms

Chionodoxa luciliae *'Alba'*

Chionodoxa luciliae
(C. gigantea)

Common names ✒ glory of the snow
Height ✒ 10–12 cm
Blooming season ✒ Early spring
Hardiness ✒ Zones 3–8

Flowers ✒ This species produces 1 to 4 large, pale lavender-blue, upward-facing flowers per raceme. Blooms are produced close to the foliage.

✒ **'Alba'** • Produces 2 to 4 large, upward-facing white flowers per raceme

Chionodoxa sardensis

Common names ✒ Sardenian glory of the snow
Height ✒ 8–10 cm
Blooming season ✒ Early spring
Hardiness ✒ Zones 5–9

If you can find the bulbs, you must try this outstanding species. A good-sized patch of this little gem looks just gorgeous. **Flowers** ✒ This species produces bright, outward-facing, gentian-blue flowers, deeper in colour than *C. luciliae* but lacking the white patch in the flower centre. *C. sardensis* usually produces 8 or more flowers per bulb. **Requirements** ✒ *C. sardensis* is native to Turkey but not as hardy as *C. forbesii*. If you garden in Zone 4, you may be able to overwinter this bulb in a sheltered area protected with mulch.

Chionodoxa luciliae

*autumn crocus,
meadow saffron*

Colchicums
Colchicum spp.

Type
Corm

Planting season
Late summer to early autumn

Blooming season
Late summer to early autumn

Hardiness
Zones 4–9

How many
Start with 3 to 5 corms; naturalizes readily

Spring-flowering species are so numerous that the fall-flowering bulbs often get overlooked. But just look at what we're missing! Colchicums produce large, goblet-shaped pink or purple flowers in the fall, when most flowers have finished. And colchicums in the garden will thrive for many years with virtually no care—not even watering.

Colchicums bloom on bare stems, unaccompanied by foliage. The following spring, the corm produces 3 to 5 glossy, strap-shaped leaves, typically 15 to 20 cm long and 20 to 30 cm high. In early summer, the leaves turn yellow and die. Then between late August and early November (usually in September or October), long, tight flower buds emerge and the flowers bloom, 10 to 15 cm high, a final splash of colour before winter.

Golden Rules

• Provide full sun to light shade, but not too hot

• Plant in moist, rich, deeply prepared, well-drained soil

• Allow adequate space for large, spreading leaves to grow and die back on their own

Colchicum speciosum *'Waterlily'*

Colchicum belongs to family Liliaceae, the same family as tulips. True autumn crocuses, on the other hand, belong to Iridaceae, the iris family.

Planting

- Plant as soon as possible after purchasing. Colchicums begin to flower shortly after transplanting. If the corms are left in a warm location for any length of time, flowers will emerge—even in the display boxes in garden centres.
- Plant 10 to 15 cm deep, 15 cm apart.
- A sunny (but not hot), fairly sheltered location is ideal. Locations that are lightly shaded or receive dappled sunlight are also suitable.
- Colchicums grow best in lighter, looser soils, rich in nutrients, with good tilth. They do not tolerate lime soils.
- Water as needed to maintain an even moisture level. In most areas, rainfall will suffice.
- Colchicums require little fertilizer when planted in rich soil. They are best fertilized by allowing fallen leaves to rot; you can also mulch colchicums with leaf mould or compost. Add a handful of granular bulb fertilizer when you plant the corms.

The Big Issue

The common names for colchicum are terrible misnomers. Colchicum may be listed as meadow saffron or autumn crocus, but it is not related to the crocus family. It is poisonous, not edible like the saffron-producing crocus, and is botanically distinct from the true fall-flowering crocuses. To avoid confusion, avoid these common names when talking about colchicum.

Colchicum autumnale *'Album'*

Tessellation refers to checkered patterning. The petals of many colchicums exhibit subtle tessellation; it is one of the unique characteristics of these bulbs. Tessellated varieties typically flower later, blooming in late autumn and early winter. They also tend to produce larger flowers and are more susceptible to being spoiled by inclement weather. Thanks to an upsurge of interest in colchicums, plant breeders are working on new tessellated varieties: 'Conquest' and 'Princess Astrid' are particularly gorgeous. Unfortunately, both are difficult to obtain.

GROWING

- Once established, each corm increases annually, like a daffodil bulb. Divide the clumps when they begin to look crowded. This is best done at or just after flowering. That way you won't damage the flowers, it's easy to locate the bulbs and you don't interrupt the active growth of the leaves. Carefully lift the entire clump, gently brush off the soil and separate the individual corms. Enrich the soil where you are going to replant the corms by adding compost, well-rotted manure or a handful of granular bulb fertilizer (or a mixture of all three). Replant immediately, placing the corms about 15 cm apart. Place the corms randomly, creating a natural-looking drift.

TIPS

- Never rake off fallen leaves where colchicums are emerging; instead, allow the flowers to come up through the leaves. The fallen leaves provide a lovely contrast for the flowers and help support the flower stems.

- If you have planted your colchicums too deep or too close together, simply dig them up during their dormant period and reposition them.

- Colchicums are poisonous and unpalatable to most pests, including rodents and deer.

- If you have only a few bulbs, try planting them near the front of the flowerbed. If you have a large number of bulbs, plant them in a mass so you can enjoy a carpet of mauve in the autumn.

Colchicum speciosum *'Waterlily' (foreground)*, C. autumnale *'Album' (midground)*, Crocus speciosus *(background)*

Colchicum giganteum 'Lilac Wonder'

Colchicums make lovely miniature cutflowers. Cut when the goblet of the flowers is fully formed, but before the petals have opened up. Place in a vase with floral preservative. The blooms should last about a week.

In the Garden

- Grow colchicums in woodland gardens, in front of shrubs and under taller deciduous trees that do not compete aggressively for moisture. Plant in clumps and drifts in garden corners, meadows, naturalized gardens or open spots in mixed perennial flowerbeds.

- Colchicums have very large leaves. A clump of corms produces a large volume of foliage in the spring, which can leave a hole in your garden after the leaves die back. Set the corms back in the flowerbed, in front of low deciduous shrubs or behind spring-flowering perennials near the front of the border. The dying leaves will be hidden in the spring and the flowers will stand out in the autumn because the other plants in the border will be finished blooming.

- The large leaves of colchicums may look untidy but the plants can be neatly set among low perennial ground-covers such as creeping jenny, veronica or thyme. They are beautiful interplanted with species like *Anemone nemorosa* or woodland ferns, which provide support and set off the flowers. Other successful combinations include creeping veronicas, phlox, low-growing junipers, fall-blooming gentians, bluegrass, vinca or wintergreen. Colchicums look stunning interplanted with hostas.

- Colchicums are well suited to naturalizing. They can be left in the garden for years without special care. However, they will not naturalize in frost-free zones. Colchicums require *vernalization* (see page 12) to propagate.

Colchicum bulb

TRY THESE!

Colchicum blooms range from pure white through light shades of lavender to pur-plish-rose. There is one exception: *C. luteum* flowers are yellow. Pastel-coloured variet-ies seem to jump out from among the fallen leaves and brown tones in the autumn garden. Darker-flowered varieties tend to blend subtly with the background.

Colchicum agrippinum

Height ➷ 10 cm

Hardiness ➷ Zone 5

C. agrippinum is an older, cherished hybrid of *C. autumnale* and one of the most distinctive colchicum species. **Flowers** ➷ The blooms have tessel-lated violet-pink petals. The flowers are funnel-shaped, with narrow leaves early in the spring, and tend to re-semble stars when they are fully open. *C. agrippinum* flowers in early Septem-ber. Blooms are immediately followed by the emergence of small, narrow, strap-shaped blue-green leaves. Each corm produces one or two flowers. **Requirements** ➷ This species prefers well-drained soils and dry, sunny, warm microclimates. It spreads readily and forms dense clumps if grown in the right location. Regrettably, this species is not widely available and may take some perseverance to find.

Colchicum autumnale

Height ➷ 8–12 cm

Hardiness ➷ Zones 4–8

This widely available species is one of the first to flower, typically blooming in early September. It is also quick to naturalize. *C. autumnale* tends to be a hardy, reliable species, which makes it easy to grow. **Flowers** ➷ It produces a succession of 1 to 6 small laven-der-rose flowers; the flowers of the cultivars are larger and prettier. **Re-quirements** ➷ This species is found naturally in meadows and tolerates a range of moisture conditions. It prefers moist, very fertile soil. It stands up poorly to heavy wind and rain, so it is best planted in a sheltered location among perennial groundcovers for support.

➷ **'Alboplenum'** • A rare cultivar with large white double flowers and pink tinges—resembles a white water lily

➷ **'Album'** • Produces abundant small, snow-white flowers; increases rapidly

➷ **'Plenum'** • Features large rosy-pink double flowers. Also listed as *C. autumnale* 'Roseum Plenum' and *C. autumnale* 'Pleniflorum'

Colchicum autumnale *'Album'*

Colchicum bivonae
(C. sibthorpii, C. bowlesianum)

Height ᘓ 15–20 cm
Hardiness ᘓ Zones 5–6

A robust species with tessellated petals, *C. bivonae* is the parent of many of today's hybrids and an outstanding species on its own. **Flowers** ᘓ Each corm produces up to 15 large flowers that emerge over several weeks, from late August through late September. Flowers reach 20 cm. The lightly fragrant flowers are bright rosy-violet with white throats and are much larger than *C. autumnale*. The petals are overlaid with conspicuous darker-purple tessellations. Each corm usually produces 2 flowers. **Requirements** ᘓ *C. bivonae* prefers a sunny location in a sheltered spot, with well-drained soil that is not too dry. This species may be difficult to find.

Colchicum bornmuelleri

Colchicum bornmuelleri
(C. speciosum var. bornmuelleri)

Height ᘓ 12–15 cm
Hardiness ᘓ Zone 5

Flowers ᘓ This cultivar flowers in late September and early October. The fragrant, funnel-shaped lilac-rose flowers have conspicuous white centres and green flower tubes. Each corm produces 1 to 6 blooms. **Requirements** ᘓ *C. bornmuelleri* tolerates light shade.

Colchicum byzantinum
(C. autumnale var. majus, C. autumnale var. major)

Height ᘓ 10–15 cm
Hardiness ᘓ Zones 5–6

This is one of the most prolific species, both in number of flowers produced and in rate of spread. **Flowers** ᘓ The corms of this species are especially large; each produces up to 20 fragrant purplish-pink flowers, similar in form to *C. autumnale* but slightly larger. It is not uncommon for several flowers to open in a bunch. **Requirements** ᘓ The leaves of this cultivar are large but attractive, something to keep in mind when choosing a spot in your garden. *C. byzantinum* flowers in early September and produces no seed. It is presumed to be a hybrid of *C. autumnale* and has been around since the sixteenth century.

ᘓ **C. byzantinum album** • Has sturdy white flowers with feathered purple tones on the petal tips

Colchicum cilicicum

Colchicum cilicicum
(C. balansae var. macrophyllum, C. byzantinum var. cilicicum)

Height ᛣ 10–12 cm
Hardiness ᛣ Zones 5–6

Native to southern Turkey, this species is found naturally growing in rocky, mountainous areas. **Flowers** ᛣ *C. cilicicum* typically flowers in late September, slightly later than *C. byzantinum*, a species to which it is closely related. It produces light violet-purple, star-like flowers with a slight honey-like fragrance. The flowers have shorter flower tubes that stand up better to windy and rainy conditions than those of other colchicum species. This species produces leaves immediately after it finishes flowering instead of the following spring. **Requirements** ᛣ *C. cilicicum* prefers an open, sunny location in the garden with deep, well-drained soil that doesn't get too dry. It is not a good choice for gardeners who live in areas with short fall seasons, because the corm may not complete its growing cycle.

ᛣ *C. cilicicum* var. *'purpureum'* •
Produces numerous beautiful, fragrant deep rosy-purple flowers

Colchicum giganteum

Height ᛣ 10–15 cm
Hardiness ᛣ Zone 5

Flowers ᛣ This species produces numerous large, fragrant, funnel-shaped violet flowers with long petals and a lighter centre. Compared to other species, *C. giganteum* flowers quite late. This species spreads well.

Colchicum giganteum

Colchicum speciosum

Height ᛣ 10–15 cm
Hardiness ᛣ Zones 4–8

Native to northern Turkey and Iran, this is one of the best varieties for growing in the home garden, especially for less-experienced gardeners. **Flowers** ᛣ Each corm typically produces 1 to 3 purplish-pink, globe-shaped flowers up to 30 cm tall. Flowers appear in September; they are larger and more weather resistant than those of *C. autumnale*. The flower tubes are especially strong, holding the flowers well above the ground. **Requirements** ᛣ This species prefers dappled shade and well-drained soil rich in organic matter. However, it also grows beautifully in a sunnier location with consistent moisture. The leaves of this species are quite large, something to keep in mind when choosing a spot in the garden. Commonly known as showy colchicum.

↬ **C. speciosum var. bornmuelleri** • Features purple flowers with white throats and a pink blush on the outer petals

↬ **'Album'** • Produces white flowers that resemble tiny tulips. Fairly tough and very prolific—one of the best varieties for growing in shade.

↬ **'Autumn Queen'** • Features rose-purple, checkered flowers. Flowers especially early, typically in late August or early September.

↬ **'Violet Queen'** • Has purple flowers with purple-and-white-veined centres. Bright-orange anthers in the centre of each flower contrast beautifully with the petals. Especially pretty grown near plants with silver-coloured leaves.

↬ **'Waterlily'** • One of the most common colchicum varieties; easy to grow. Tolerates a wide range of soils, but grows best in humus-rich soils in a sunny location. Flowers double, lilac-pink, each producing more than twenty petals. Each corm produces a succession of blooms; several often open simultaneously. The large, heavy flowers may trail on the ground; autumn rains often splash them with mud.

Colchicum 'Lilac Wonder'

Height ↬ 15–20 cm
Hardiness ↬ Zones 4–8

Flowers ↬ This cultivar typically flowers in October and produces large, slender, violet flowers.

Colchicum 'The Giant' (C. 'Giant')

Height ↬ 20–25 cm
Hardiness ↬ Zone 4

This cultivar is the result of a cross between *C. giganteum* and *C. bornmuelleri*. **Flowers** ↬ 'The Giant' produces large violet flowers with white bases that grow up to 25 cm tall on sturdy stems. **Requirements** ↬ It is a vigorous variety that multiplies quickly when planted in rich soil. 'The Giant' blooms in late September and early October.

Bulbocodium vernum
(Colchicum bulbocodium)

Common name ↬ spring saffron

Height ↬ 10 cm

Hardiness ↬ Zone 4

Recently reclassified as *Bulbocodium vernum*, this bulb no longer belongs with the colchicums. Unlike colchicums, it blooms in late winter or early spring. This bulb is very worthwhile—one of our special favourites. **Flowers** ↬ A low-growing plant with 1–3 goblet-shaped, lavender-pink, star-like blooms—similar to colchicum. Leaves may or may not be present when blooms appear. **Requirements** ↬ Plant 7 cm deep and space 10 cm in well-drained, preferably sandy soil. Best planted in clumps of at least 5 bulbs. Use for rock gardens, woodland gardens or naturalizing.

Crocuses

Crocus spp.

Type
Corm

Planting season
Fall

Blooming season
Early spring or mid autumn

Hardiness
Zones 3–8

How many
En masse—at least 100 corms

Golden Rules
- Plant in full sun
- Plant in sandy, well-drained soil
- Allow the foliage to die back naturally

Most people think crocuses bloom early in the spring for two or three weeks. But did you know there are also fall-flowering crocuses? There are, and they're absolutely beautiful!

Crocuses are the most colourful and most widely grown of the early-spring bulbs. Spring-flowering varieties are among the first bulbs to emerge after the snow melts, often flowering while the snow is still on the ground. They can persist in the garden for years with virtually no care because they are marvellous naturalizers. Fall-flowering varieties flower in early to mid fall, and the leaves emerge the following spring to replenish the bulb below. And crocuses are tough! Spring and fall varieties alike cope easily with bouts of frost and snow. By planting several patches of both spring- and fall-flowering varieties, you can produce a gentle 'bookend' effect in the garden, beginning and ending the season with these lovely, tiny gems.

Crocus vernus *'Pickwick'*

PLANTING

- Plant the bulbs as early as possible in the fall. This is particularly important if you are planting fall-flowering varieties.

- Plant in large, informal drifts. Crocuses are tiny, so for the best effect, grow in groups of 100 or more.

- Full sun. Crocuses require a sunny location, although they will tolerate light shade. Sun encourages the flowers of the crocuses to open wide.

- Well-drained, slightly sandy soil. Crocuses will tolerate a range of soil types, provided they are well drained; the corms will rot in wet, heavy soil. Dutch crocuses prefer well-fertilized soil rich in compost, while species crocuses prefer leaner soils and less fertilizer.

- Plant 10 cm deep. Corms at this depth are less likely to be eaten by rodents or to work themselves up to the surface.

- Space 3–5 cm apart.

All crocuses have narrow, green, sword-shaped leaves with a signature silvery-grey stripe down the upper side of the leaf. This trait distinguishes the fall-flowering Crocus *varieties from colchicum, commonly—and wrongly—called autumn crocus. Fall-flowering crocuses also self-sow and spread much more readily than colchicum.*

Crocus chrysanthus
'Prins Claus'

Crocus chrysanthus 'Snow Bunting'

*Crocuses are native
to the Mediterranean
Basin, from Spain to
Turkey. In their natural
habitat, they have
adapted to baking heat
in the summer and
plenty of rain in the
autumn, winter and
early spring.*

GROWING

- Crocuses require a good supply of moisture in the spring—usually provided by melting snow and spring rain. Water needs may be reduced during the summer—see chart opposite.

- Crocuses may need revitalizing every few years. A poor show of flowers is a common indication that the corms need respacing. Divide crocuses in the early fall, about the time you would plant new crocus corms. Dig up the clump and separate the corms, removing any diseased or damaged ones. Replant the corms at their original spacing, and transplant the smaller corms to another area of your garden or give them to other gardeners. If the planting area has become hard and compacted, mix in some coarse sand and leaf mould.

- Mice love to eat crocus corms. They can easily devour an entire bed of crocuses over the winter. Birds, especially sparrows, may also be pests. They peck off the flowers and flower buds, and have a definite preference for yellow-flowering varieties.

Specific Crocus Needs

Crocuses grow in a range of habitats, so some species will be better suited to particular garden conditions than others. We have divided crocuses into three rough groups according to their cultural requirements. Note there is some overlap in the growing requirements of each group.

Crocus chrysanthus
'*Goldilocks*'

Group 1: *Crocus biflorus* (SF), *C. cartwrightianus* (AF), *C. ochroleucus* (AF)

- Well-drained, relatively coarse soils
- Sunny location
- Plentiful moisture in the fall, in early winter and through the completion of their active growth cycle
- Long, dry conditions during summer dormancy
- Excellent tolerance of very cold winter temperatures

Group 2: *Crocus ancyrensis* (SF), *C. angustifolius* (SF), *C. chrysanthus* (SF), *C. etruscus* (SF), *C. flavus* (SF), *C. korolkowii* (SF), *C. sieberi* (SF), *C. sativus* (AF), *C. serotinus* (AF), *C. versicolor* (SF)

- Well-drained soil
- Sunny location
- Good tolerance of moisture during summer dormancy, allowing them to grow easily in an open garden
- The best group for cultivation in the home garden: these species have the best tolerance of variable conditions

Group 3: *Crocus tommasinianus* (SF), *C. vernus* (SF)

- Consistent moisture/intermittent rainfall throughout the year, peaking in autumn and winter (soil seldom dries out completely)
- Warm, dry summer not required, making these species especially suitable for areas with rainy summers
- Will tolerate some shade and actually prefer some shade from the hot summer sun.
- *Crocus speciosus* (AF), *C. kotschyanus* (AF) fall into this group but also require a sheltered location with well-drained soil that retains moisture.

SF = spring flowering
AF = autumn flowering

Because crocuses bloom before most other plants, it is common to see bees collecting food from crocus flowers. Wild bees begin feeding when daytime temperatures rise above 11 or 12 °C.

Tips

- You can double the blooming period of crocuses in your garden by planting the same varieties in two different exposures, one warm and sheltered, the other cool and exposed. The bulbs planted in cooler, more exposed locations will bloom two or three weeks later than the variety planted in a warm, sheltered location.

- Crocus corms that have been in the garden for at least one season will flower earlier than newly planted bulbs.

- The smaller-flowering crocuses propagate readily. When the leaves have almost died back, you will see seed capsules just above the soil surface. The capsules open as they mature and the seeds are scattered by wind and rain. Within two or three years, seeds that find a suitable home will form corms large enough to produce more crocuses.

Crocus flowers open only on sunny days. They remain closed on cloudy and rainy days, and close up at night.

- Perhaps the easiest crocus to grow is *Crocus tommasinianus*. It flowers very early in the season and is an aggressive colonizer—great for naturalized gardens!

Crocus chrysanthus *'Ard Schenk'*

Crocus vernus *'Remembrance'* and C. vernus *'Pickwick'*

IN THE GARDEN

- Plant crocuses in clumps in corners, at the edges of mixed flowerbeds, around trees or near small shrubs.

- Crocuses are ideal for growing among dwarf alpines in a sunny rockery. For rock gardens, try *Crocus chrysanthus* (both species and cultivars).

- Try planting crocuses in layers among other bulbs: they flower very early in the season and produce little foliage, so they won't interfere with later-emerging bulbs. Plant the crocus corms in the top layer above deeper-planted bulbs such as tulip, narcissus or hyacinth. Plant numerous corms for best effect. The results are beautiful: the early flush of crocus flowers will soon be followed by the emergence of other flowering bulbs.

- To camouflage the dying foliage, plant low-growing, open groundcovers over crocus corms; try *Phlox subulata*, *Arenaria* spp., *Dianthus* spp., thyme, creeping veronica, creeping penstemon and *Vinca minor*. Or try planting clusters of cool-season, early-flowering annuals, such as pansies, violas or low-growing snapdragons, among clumps of crocuses. Deeply planted crocuses won't be disturbed when the annuals are transplanted into the garden.

- When planting crocuses with early-flowering perennials, choose smaller plants such as pulmonaria, hellebore, hepatica and pulsatilla. Several species of *Primula* will work nicely, including *P. marginata*, *P. pruhonicensis* (Wanda types), *P. varis*, *P. elatior* and *P. denticulata*. Try similar companion plantings with fall-flowering crocuses. The bronze or deep-burgundy leaves of ajugas contrast beautifully with *C. speciosus*. Other dark-leaved, low-growing perennials also look stunning.

- Naturalized crocuses will grow well for years in a lawn or meadow planting. If you want them to naturalize successfully in the lawn, you must be prepared not to cut your lawn for several weeks after flowering has finished. Gently scatter the corms across the grass and plant them where they fall. Use 125 to 150 corms per square metre. (See pages 297 to 299 for more details on naturalizing.)

TRY THESE!

We have divided our discussion be-tween spring-flowering and autumn-flowering species.

Spring-flowering crocuses

Spring-flowering crocuses are typically divided into two groups: the spe-cies and their cultivars, and the larger Dutch hybrids. Most gardeners are familiar with the Dutch crocuses. The most widely available crocuses are the large-flowering hybrids and the *C. chrysanthus* cultivars. Most people don't grow the other species because they can be difficult to obtain. We have listed some of them below. Many of the species are regularly sold in mixtures.

Crocus ancyrensis

Common names ⚘ golden bunch crocus, yellow bunch crocus, ankara crocus
Height ⚘ 5–8 cm
Hardiness ⚘ Zones 3–9

This very pretty little crocus blooms in January and February in warmer areas, and is one of the first crocuses to emerge in cooler areas. It seems to burst into bloom almost as soon as the snow melts. **Flowers** ⚘ This species produces golden-yellow flowers in very early spring. Each corm produces several blooms in succession, for an extended show.

Crocus ancyrensis

Crocus angustifolius
(C. susianus)

Common names ⚘ cloth-of-gold crocus
Height ⚘ 5–8 cm
Hardiness ⚘ Zones 7–9

This is a very early-blooming species.
Flowers ⚘ It has pretty two-tone flowers whose inner petals are golden-yellow and outer petals are deep purple with brownish-purple stripes. **Requirements** ⚘ *C. angus-tifolius* is much less hardy than most other crocuses.

Crocus biflorus

Common names ⚘ Scotch crocus
Height ⚘ 5–8 cm
Hardiness ⚘ Zones 4–9

This species has several cultivars. Its height is variable. **Flowers** ⚘ The flowers are usually white with blue or purplish tones on the outer petals. Blooms typically appear in March. The leaves are medium green with a white vertical stripe.
Requirements ⚘ This species prefers coarse, well-drained, poor or moderately fertile soil in a sunny location. *C. biflorus* is an excellent choice for rock gardens.

Many *C. biflorus* hybrids are found under *C. chrysanthus* because it is the dominant parent. We have listed them under *C. biflorus* because they are hybrids of both species.

⚘ **C. biflorus alexandri** • Flowers are nearly white inside; outer petals are deep purple. Excellent rock garden crocus.

⚘ **C. biflorus weldenii 'Fairy'** • Flowers are almost white inside, deep blue-grey on the outer petals, but species is variable. Excellent choice for rock gardens and raised beds. May be difficult to find.

Crocus biflorus *'Miss Vain'*

ᔥ **'Argenteus'** • White flowers with brownish-purple stripes on the outer petals

ᔥ **'Fairy'** • Soft lilac-blue petals with brownish purple stripes on the outer surface

ᔥ **'Miss Vain'** • Ivory-white variety whose outer petals are spotted light blue on the base

Crocus chrysanthus

Common names ᔥ snow crocus, botanical crocus
Height ᔥ 8–10 cm
Hardiness ᔥ Zones 3–9

Originating in southeastern Europe and southern Turkey, the varieties in this group are among the earliest crocuses to bloom and make excellent choices for naturalizing in turf, rock gardens and borders. **Flowers** ᔥ Although this species has small corms, it produces numerous clustered, bicolour flowers. The blooms have a sweet honey scent. **Requirements** ᔥ Most varieties are small and delicate, and prefer an open, sunny site in the garden and coarse, well-drained, poor to moderately fertile soil.

There are currently approximately 35 known cultivars of *C. chrysanthus*, developed over the last century. These hybrids owe their origin to both *C. chrysanthus* and *C. biflorus*.

ᔥ **'Ard Schenk'** • White flowers with bronze-yellow centres

ᔥ **'Blue Pearl'** • Features bicolour flowers whose petals are dark blue on the outside and light blue on the inside

ᔥ **'Cream Beauty'** • Pale-yellow flowers with a bronze-green base. One of the most vigorous varieties.

ᔥ **'Dorothy'** • Light-yellow flowers with bronze-coloured stripes. This is the most common *C. chrysanthus* cultivar.

ᔥ **'Fuscotinctus'** • Yellow flowers whose outer petals are entirely striped with purple

ᔥ **'Gypsy Girl'** • Golden-yellow flowers with purplish-brown striped and feathered outer petals

ᔥ **'Goldilocks'** • Deep-yellow flowers with a purple-brown base

ᔥ **'Herald'** • Bicolour flowers whose petals are feathered plum on purple on the outside and golden-yellow on the inside

ᔥ **'Ladykiller'** • Stunning two-tone purple and white flowers. Outer petals are purple-violet with white margins; inner petals are pale lilac.

Crocus chrysanthus
'Cream Beauty'

Crocus chrysanthus *Princess Beatrix*

ﾐ **'Moonlight'** • Pale lemon-yellow flowers

ﾐ **'Prince Claus'** • Beautiful bicolour flowers whose petals are mauve-blue on the outside and white on the inside. Plant tightly for best effect. Sometimes listed as 'Prins Claus'.

ﾐ **'Princess Beatrix'** • Clear sky-blue flowers with a golden-yellow base

ﾐ **'Saturnus'** • Deep-yellow flowers with purple stripes on the outside of the petals

ﾐ **'Snow Bunting'** • Pure icy-white flowers

ﾐ **'Zwanenburg's Bronze'** • Very pretty brown flowers with yellow inner petals and yellow stripes on the outer petals

Crocus etruscus 'Zwanenburg'
Height ﾐ 5–8 cm
Hardiness ﾐ Zones 5–8

This species flowers early in the spring, usually in February and March. **Flowers** ﾐ It has pretty pinkish-violet inner petals and outer petals feathered with deep-violet tones; the leaves are dark green with a white vertical stripe. **Requirements** ﾐ These crocuses grow well in rock gardens, preferring coarse, well-drained, poor to moderately fertile soils in a sunny location.

Crocus flavus
(C. aureus, C. luteus)
Common name ﾐ yellow crocus
Height ﾐ 8–10 cm
Hardiness ﾐ Zones 3–9

C. flavus tends to flower in later spring, blooming in March and April in warmer areas and in early May in cooler zones. **Flowers** ﾐ This species produces five or six large, fragrant bright-yellow flowers. It is a great naturalizer and one of the best choices for planting into lawns: the bright-yellow flowers contrast well against dark-green grass.

Crocus flavus

Crocus korolkowii

Common name ⚘ celandine crocus
Height ⚘ 5–8 cm
Hardiness ⚘ Zones 4–9

This pretty species flowers very early in the season. It is native to northern Afghanistan. **Flowers** ⚘ *C. korolkowii* produces clusters of three to five fragrant golden-yellow flowers whose outer petals are brushed with deep-bronze tones.

Crocus sieberi

Height ⚘ 8 cm
Hardiness ⚘ Zones 3–8

Native to the Balkans, the crocuses in this group are well suited to growing in rock gardens. **Flowers** ⚘ The flowers are light blue with yellow centres and bright-orange pistils. The cultivars tend to flower about three weeks later than the species form. **Requirements** ⚘ *C. sieberi* prefers coarse, well-drained, poor to moderately fertile soil.

⚘ *C. sieberi sublimis* **'Tricolour'** • Deep lilac-purple flowers with a white central zone

⚘ **'Bowles White'** • Large white flowers with deep-orange throats

⚘ **'Firefly'** • Light reddish-violet flowers with clear-yellow centres

⚘ **'Violet Queen'** • Beautiful deep-mauve flowers. An excellent variety for rock gardens: the smaller flowers and overall size of the plant put this species on the scale of many alpines.

Crocus sieberi sublimis *'Tricolour'*

Crocus tommasinianus

Common names ⚘ tommie crocus, tommies
Height ⚘ 7–8 cm
Hardiness ⚘ Zones 3–8

The blooms of this free-flowering species appear early in the spring: in February to March in warmer zones, and as soon as the snow melts in cooler regions. In areas with very mild winters, it may even flower in January. **Flowers** ⚘ The species flowers are pale lavender. **Requirements** ⚘ *C. tommasinianus* prefers coarse, well-drained, poor to moderately fertile soils, but will tolerate heavier soils. It grows in less than perfect conditions, including partial shade. It is also one of the most profusely self-seeding species, and its leaves die down rapidly after the flowers are finished. Its spontaneous self-propagation tendencies make it an excellent naturalizer, particularly in turf.

⚘ **'Albus'** • Pure-white form

⚘ **'Lilac Beauty'** • Lavender-purple flowers with silvery undersides

⚘ **'Ruby Giant'** • Numerous large, brilliant ruby-purple flowers

⚘ **'Whitewell Purple'** • Very good naturalizer with showy purple flowers

Crocus vernus 'Purpureus Grandiflora'

Crocus vernus

Common names ᔭ Dutch crocus, hybrid crocus, large-flowering crocus, spring crocus
Height ᔭ 15 cm
Hardiness ᔭ Zone 4

This group is by the far the most important of the crocuses. The species originates in the mountainous areas of Europe, in an area encompassing the Pyrenees east through Poland and Russia and as far south as Sicily and Yugoslavia. Note that "Dutch crocus" is a name used by commercial growers to refer to large-flowering crocuses; the trade typically divides this group according to colour rather than variety. **Flowers** ᔭ Excellent for growing in lawns or containers, these crocuses flower later than C. chrysanthus and have much larger flowers; indeed, the flowers are the largest of any species crocus. They tend to form clumps rather than randomly self-sowing, and are particularly attractive because

of their large flowers and blasts of colour. **Requirements** ᔭ C. vernus cultivars multiply quickly: their numbers double about every three years. These cultivars are the best choice if you must plant late in the fall; they tolerate delayed planting better than other crocuses. They are also the best choice for indoor forcing.

ᔭ **'Flower Record'** • Large, shiny violet-mauve flowers

ᔭ **'Grand Maitre'** • Purple flowers with a silvery shine; profuse bloomer, blooming early to mid season

ᔭ **'Joan of Arc'** • Large, pure-white flowers. Sometimes listed as 'Jeanne d'Arc'.

ᔭ **'King of the Striped'** • Large purple flowers with lighter purple stripes, early to mid season

ᔭ **'Mammoth Yellow'** • Large golden-yellow flowers. An old-garden variety—cultivated since the seventeenth century; sometimes listed as 'Yellow Mammoth'.

ᔓ **'Pickwick'** • Very pretty, medium-sized striped violet-purple flowers with a grey-white background

ᔓ **'Purpureus Grandiflora'** • Violet-purple flowers with darker-purple base

ᔓ **'Remembrance'** • Large violet-blue flowers with darker-purple base and silvery blush; early-flowering variety

Crocus versicolor **'Picturatus'**
Height ᔓ 5 cm
Hardiness ᔓ Zones 5–9

This dainty, pretty species is very easy to grow. In the last century, forms of this crocus were readily available, but most have disappeared from cultivation. Fortunately, 'Picturatus' is still generally available. **Flowers** ᔓ This cultivar produces white flowers with darker violet-purple veins.

Crocus vernus *'Flower Record'*

Autumn-flowering crocuses

These crocuses are not widely cultivated. Many gardeners are not familiar with them, and the fall weather must be fairly good to enjoy them. The transplanted corms produce an almost-instant garden: they may burst into bloom only days after planting. Always transplant fall crocuses as early as you can. If they are planted too late, after growth has begun, the first crop of flowers will be poor or possibly non-existent; however, you should get flowers the following autumn. Fall-flowering crocuses produce leaves in the spring. This foliage gradually dies back, replenishing the bulb, which then remains dormant through the summer and flowers in the fall.

Crocus cartwrightianus
Height ᔓ 5 cm
Hardiness ᔓ Zones 6–8

This tiny crocus is the white form of the wild saffron crocus. It flowers in September and October, and is well suited to alpine gardens. **Flowers** ᔓ It has white to deep-lilac flowers with bright-red stigmas. **Requirements** ᔓ *C. cartwrightianus* requires full sun and a growing medium of equal parts of soil, leaf mould and coarse sand. It needs a dry summer dormancy period. This species is uncommon—may be difficult to find.

Crocus sativus

Crocus ochroleucus
Height ᔾ 7–10 cm
Hardiness ᔾ Zones 5–9

C. ochroleucus is suitable for naturalizing in turf and grows well in coarse, well-drained soils with poor to moderate fertility. It is also a good choice for gardens with high amounts of leaf mould and sand in the soil. **Flowers** ᔾ It has creamy-white flowers with a yellow base, and flowers in October and November, sometimes as late as early December. **Requirements** ᔾ *C. ochroleucus* requires full sun and a summer with relatively warm, dry conditions during dormancy. This species is uncommon—may be difficult to find.

Crocus pulchellus
Height ᔾ 5 cm
Hardiness ᔾ Zones 3–8

C. pulchellus is another rapidly spreading species suitable for naturalizing in turf. **Flowers** ᔾ It is a very fine, small, dainty crocus that produces very pale-lavender flowers with bright-orange throats and white stamens. The petals are delicately veined with darker lilac. **Requirements** ᔾ This species prefers coarse, well-drained, poor to moderately fertile soil in a sunny location. This species is uncommon and may be difficult to find.

Crocus sativus
Common names ᔾ saffron crocus
Height ᔾ 7–10 cm
Hardiness ᔾ Zone 4

This is a particularly attractive crocus; it is also one of the oldest cultivated crocus species and is mentioned in the Song of Solomon. The ancient Greeks used it in perfumes, as medicine and for performing magic in religious ceremonies. **Flowers** ᔾ This species has reddish-violet flowers with conspicuous dark-violet veins and branched, bright orange-red stigmas. The stigmas are used to dye wool, and to add flavour and colour to food. **Requirements** ᔾ *C. sativus* prefers a degree of fall warmth and sunshine that cannot be relied on in all areas. Most saffron crocuses are grown in warm climates. But don't hesitate to give it a try even if you live in a cooler zone—just be sure to plant it in a warm, sheltered part of the garden. This species can be unreliable.

Crocus speciosus *'Album'*

Crocus speciosus

Common names ↬ showy crocus, autumn crocus

Height ↬ 15 cm

Hardiness ↬ Zone 4

C. speciosus is the most reliable and popular of the fall-flowering species. It is one of the easiest crocuses to grow, naturalizes rapidly and has nicely scented flowers. It typically begins flowering in late September and continues through October; some cultivars will bloom as late as November. It grows in full sun or dappled shade, in borders or in grass, and is stunning grown in woodland gardens in a tapestry with other small woodland bulbs. **Flowers** ↬ Species flowers are dark violet-blue; cultivar colours vary from silver-lavender to deep violet-blue. Flowers bear bright orange-red stigmas. This is one of the bluest crocuses, and the petals display a network of attractive deep-blue veins. The flowers tend to lie flat within days of appearing, as if the stems are weak, particularly if it has been very windy and rainy. But this tendency shouldn't prevent you from planting a few. They're really pretty, and they look lovelier each year! **Requirements** ↬ *C. speciosus* prefers coarse, well-drained, poor to moderately fertile soil.

↬ **'Album'** • Snowy-white flowers with bright-orange stigmas

↬ **'Atchinsonii'** • Lavender-purple flowers that are somewhat larger than species flowers

↬ **'Artabir'** • Light-blue flowers with darker-blue stripes

↬ **'Cassiope'** • Large-flowering cultivar with bright-blue flowers

↬ **'Conqueror'** • Bright sky-blue flowers

Crocus zonatus
(*C. kotschyanus*)

Height ↬ 10 cm

Hardiness ↬ Zones 3–8

This is a vigorous variety that naturalizes quickly, growing best in coarse, well-drained soil with poor to moderate fertility. It is a good choice for gardens with large amounts of leaf mould and sand in the soil. *C. zonatus* blooms in late September and early October. **Flowers** ↬ It has long, tubular pale-lilac flowers with yellow throats. **Requirements** ↬ *C. zonatus* requires relatively warm, dry conditions during its summer dormancy and needs full sun to grow well.

Crocus zonatus

Type
  Tuberous root

Planting season
  Spring

Blooming season
  Late spring through frost

Hardiness
  Zones 9–11 (Zone 8 with protection)

How many
  Start with 2 or 3 roots

Golden Rules
- Plant in full sun
- Feed regularly with all-purpose fertilizer
- Water consistently and abundantly

Dahlias

Dahlia rosea

Dahlias thrive on attention. They require constant care and sustenance to grow successfully, but respond to nurturing better than almost any other plant.

The dahlia is a relative latecomer to the garden. The first varieties were developed in the 1800s and initially did not enjoy widespread popularity. Today, dahlias come in an enormous range of sizes, growth habits, flower colours and flower types. The flowers range from tiny to an amazing 45 cm in diameter, and plant heights range from 40 to 180 cm. As with roses, there are no true-blue dahlias, but almost every other flower colour exists, from pastel-pink, mauve and white to maroon, scarlet and gold. Dahlias may be bicoloured, tricoloured, specked, striped or spotted, and the foliage ranges from green and olive to deep brownish-maroon and burgundy-black. Dahlias are also among the few bulbs that thrive during cool, rainy summers. The flowers remain beautiful even after extended wet weather. With such an array of possibilities, it's no wonder so many gardeners are willing to devote a little TLC to these gorgeous plants!

Peony-flowering dahlia 'Poeme Bronze'

Dahlias are native to Mexico and Central America, especially Guatemala. The native Mexicans grew dahlias in their gardens before the Spanish arrived. Early Spanish explorers tried to eat the dahlia tubers, mistakenly thinking they were a form of exotic potato-like vegetable.

Gallery dahlia 'Art Deco'

PLANTING

- Plant tubers about a week before the date of average last spring frost for your area, provided the soil has warmed up.
- Transplant growing plants outdoors only after all danger of frost has passed. Dahlias are extremely sensitive to frost.
- Full sun, including at least two hours of morning sun. Of all the bulbous plants, dahlias are the least tolerant of shade. In areas with very hot summers, however, dahlias grow best in a location with some shade in the afternoon; the plants do not tolerate very hot or dry conditions.
- Rich, moist, well-drained neutral soil. Dahlias require soil with excellent tilth and abundant organic matter. Dig the area deeply to loosen the soil below the tubers, where the roots will grow, to encourage a large, deep root system.
- Mix a granular bulb fertilizer into the soil right under the tubers, where the roots will grow. After transplanting, apply water-soluble 10-52-10 fertilizer once a week for three weeks, and then switch to 20-20-20.

The Big Issue

There's a common belief in gardening that dahlias are easy to grow. What might be more correct to say is that dahlias grow easily if they receive proper care and growing conditions. Although dahlias respond to attention more quickly and consistently than almost any other plant, they also suffer much more significantly from neglect or improper care.

*Semi-cactus dahlia
'Good Earth'*

- Space large varieties 90 cm apart, medium varieties about 75 cm apart and small varieties about 60 cm apart. Dwarf bedding varieties should be spaced 30 cm apart. Some gardeners who grow dahlias for flower shows space their plants as much as 120 cm apart.

- Dahlias that grow over 45 cm may require staking, particularly the larger-flowered varieties. Green bamboo stakes are a great choice. Set the stakes in the ground when you plant the roots to ensure that the stake is well positioned and that you don't inadvertently injure the root placing the stake later. Tomato cages also work well; position them around the tubers right after planting. The foliage will quickly engulf the metal cage. Another alternative is to plant tall varieties in a sheltered location out of the wind and among shrubs, which will support the plants as well as protect them. (Be sure the shrubs do not shade the dahlias.)

How to transplant dahlia tubers into the garden

Dig a hole 15–20 cm deep. Set the tuberous root into the hole horizontally, spreading any roots apart radiating outward from the tuber. If the root is a single tuber, set it in the hole at a 60° angle. Make sure the eyes are pointing upwards. The eyes should be sitting 8–15 cm below the soil surface. Add granular bulb food. If you are growing a large variety, place a supporting stake so that the tuber is just touching it. Cover the tuberous root with about 5 cm of good-quality potting soil mixed with well-rotted manure, compost or peat moss. Water in well. As the

Ball dahlia 'Eveline'

The Mexican name for dahlia is acocotli, which means water pipe or water cane. In their natural habitat, dahlias grow on volcanic soils that are naturally well supplied with water. They were used by hunters and travellers for hauling water or as a water source.

Dahlia flower bud

Some dahlias are available from garden centres in seed packs or as bedding plants. They're called seed dahlias and are actually a different species: Dahlia pinnata. *Seed dahlias reach 30–40 cm high and tend to bloom earlier than the tuberous types. Seed dahlias form small tubers by the end of the growing season, but the tubers are usually too small to store successfully over winter.*

shoots emerge, cover them with another 5 cm of soil mixture; water in well. Repeat until the hole is level with the ground. Build a slight ridge around the edge of the hole, to create a trough to hold water. If the shoot has produced leaves that will be covered by soil, pinch them off, being careful not to injure the main stem.

GROWING

In Europe, the name of this plant is pronounced DAW-lia, while in North America, it's pronounced DAY-lia.

- Dahlias require consistent care throughout the growing season. Dahlias grow best when cultural practices allow them to maintain an active state of growth without check from the time the plant first begins to grow until it finishes flowering in the fall. Flower production is directly related to the health of the plant. If the plant is stressed at any point during its growth cycle—by lack of water, inadequate fertilizer, low nutrient levels or poor soil—the stems and shoots become woody, and the plant enters semi-dormancy. No amount of water or fertilizer will return it to fully active growth.

- During the first month of growth, pinch out the tip of each new plant shoot. Pinching diverts growth to the shoots in the leaf axils, producing a stockier, healthier plant. Pinch tall varieties when the main shoots have four leaves, small varieties when the shoots have six leaves.

- Prune dahlias until they are 40–45 cm tall. If you are growing very tall varieties, allow only four to six stems to grow for best results. On medium-height varieties, leave eight to ten stems, and on smaller varieties, leave ten to twelve stems.

Waterlily dahlia 'Le Castel'

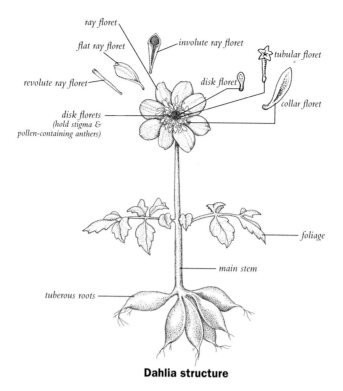

ray floret

flat ray floret

involute ray floret

tubular floret

revolute ray floret

disk floret

collar floret

disk florets
(hold stigma &
pollen-containing anthers)

foliage

main stem

tuberous roots

Dahlia structure

- Dahlias require at least 3 cm of water per week. When they reach their final size, this requirement doubles. Water thoroughly once or twice a week. During extended dry periods, dahlias may need water three times a week. Apply water directly to the roots using a soaker hose or flood nozzle, rather than overhead sprinkling.

- In areas with hot summers, dahlias must be mulched to grow well. Mulch helps conserve water, keeps the roots cool, minimizes weeding and reduces soil compaction. Apply 3–5 cm of coarse mulch such as bark or light hemp.

- Provide plentiful high-quality all-purpose (20-20-20) fertilizer throughout the active growing season. Dahlias are very heavy feeders. You can increase the recommended feeding rates by 50 percent without risk. For extra nutrition, plant dahlias in rich, well-composted soil.

- Deadhead regularly. Removing the dead and dying flowers encourages continual flower production, prolongs the flowering period and increases the number of blooms produced.

- Avoid disturbing the shallow root systems and feeder roots by pulling out weeds while they are still small and limiting soil tillage to the surface once the dahlia plants have matured.

- After you lift the bulbs, add coarse sand and fine, sandy gravel to the planting area to lighten and break up the soil. You can also add at least 5 cm of compost, peat moss or well-composted manure every year to enrich the soil.

• Use a cotton blanket, towel or sheet to protect dahlias from a couple of degrees of frost. If the temperatures stay cold for two or three days, leave the covering over the plants; they will be fine.

How to lift dahlia tubers

After the first light frost has blackened the foliage, leave the roots for a few days to absorb what moisture and nutrients they can from the top growth. These extra few days will also help the roots begin to cure. (If the weather is likely to remain cold, cover the plants with a heavy blanket, night and day if necessary.) When the temperature is above freezing (on a sunny day, if possible), cut the stalks off about 10 cm above the base of the plant. Using a spade or garden fork, carefully dig up the roots. Be careful not to damage the tubers: injured tubers will not store successfully. • Lift the root up and then let it drop, bottom side down, hard enough to knock off most of the soil. Leave any remaining soil. Do not wash the roots! There will be a clump of six to eight tubers, each of which will grow into a separate, identical dahlia next year; do not separate the clump. Invert root clumps with large, hollow stem stubs to prevent moisture from collecting inside. Tag the clump by fastening a wire label through the stem and place the clump in a flat in the sun for a few hours to dry. Store the flats in a cool (2–7°C), dark, humid location to cure for a few more days. Pack the cured clumps in a large box or bucket filled with damp peat moss and vermiculite, and store. • The root clumps are susceptible to drying out; check the tubers a few times during the winter for signs of shrivelling or withering. If the tubers start to dry out, remove them from the peat mix, mist and tuck back into the mix. Four to six week before the date of average last spring frost for your area, remove the clumps from the mix, split into individual tubers and plant in high-quality potting soil, 1 tuber per 15-cm pot. Moisten the peat mix about two weeks before you plant up the tubers, to encourage the development of new buds. Each root should have at least one strong, healthy eye.

Gallery dahlia 'Art Nouveau'

*Gallery dahlia
'Berliner Kleene'*

*Peony-flowering dahlia
'Rosamunde'*

Tips

- On average, dahlias take 8 to 12 weeks to begin blooming. In areas with very hot summers, plant dahlias in mid to late June to avoid the intense midsummer heat; the flowers will develop in the fall. In areas with shorter summers, start dahlias indoors.

- Create a large soil basin around the dahlia planting. The basin allows you to give the plants a large volume of water that will slowly sink down to the roots.

- If stressed, dahlias suffer from stunting, signalled by hardened stem tissues and poor, undersized growth. Stunted plants may partially recover if you cut off the hardened growth and provide consistent, abundant water and fertilizer.

- Plant dahlias among your tulips. Force the bulbs in pots and then transplant them into your garden when the tulips have finished blooming. About this time, the tulip foliage becomes unsightly, but the large, lush growth of the dahlias will hide the fading tulips.

- Some varieties of dahlias are notoriously reluctant to produce good tubers. If the tubers you dig up in the fall are very small and underdeveloped, don't bother keeping them. They will not survive the winter.

- Dahlias usually produce three flower buds per stem. The centre bud is usually the plumpest, particularly on the larger-flowered varieties. To produce the largest, showiest flowers, remove the side buds before the flowers start forming. To grow very large flowers, limit each plant to no more than four blooms.

- If you have had trouble keeping dahlia tubers from drying out over the winter, try placing the tubers in a large, clear, heavy-duty plastic bag filled with vermiculite. Don't let the tubers dry out before placing them into the bag. Keep the clumps of tubers separated in the bag. That way, if one rots, then it won't infect the others right away. Leave the bag open to allow air circulation, which will help prevent disease. Finally, place the most valuable tubers towards the bottom of the bag, because the tubers close to the top may dry out a bit more than those deeper in the bag.

Single-flowering dahlia 'White Sneezy'

Decorative dahlia 'Babylon Purple'

In the Garden

- Dahlias look great in small groups among shrubs, in borders, in containers, as backgrounds to flowerbeds or against a fence or wall.

- Tall dahlia varieties can make a beautiful, fast-growing annual hedge. Use a single variety to create a stunning mass of flowers and colour.

- Medium-sized varieties look great placed amid shrubs, while shorter varieties make excellent mixed borders or container displays.

- Dahlias make an excellent addition to the perennial garden. Orange- and red-flowered perennials that bloom in late summer are hard to find, but these two colours are prominent among dahlias.

- Dahlias are underused in the landscape. Most flowering shrubs do not produce any flowers after mid summer. But tall-growing dahlias look beautiful tucked in among shrubs, and their blooms will last until fall. The green foliage of the shrubs sets off the blooms beautifully!

Genus **Dahlia**, *made up of about 25 species, is part of the aster family (Asteraceae/ Compositeae).*

TRY THESE!

Because of the considerable degree of breeding that goes on and the large number of new varieties whose characteristics overlap, the classification of dahlias changes regularly. They may be grouped in many different ways, depending on the grower, the wholesaler or the retailer. For example, dahlias may be classified by the size of the flower:

Giant	Blooms 25 cm-plus in diameter
Large	Blooms 20–25 cm in diameter
Medium	Blooms 15–20 cm in diameter
Small	Blooms 10–15 cm in diameter
Miniature	Blooms 10 cm in diameter
Bedding	Blooms 5 cm in diameter.

Although these categories are unofficial, you may see them used in articles and other literature.

HEIGHT GROUPING

You may also see dahlias classified by plant height. This isn't the best way to group dahlias, because it doesn't indicate flower size or type, and height depends on growing conditions. However, height ranges help consumers make better-informed decisions about how to use varieties in the garden and where to plant them.

• **Tall varieties:** Final height is 120 cm-plus. These dahlias can be used in tall borders or as feature plants. They generally require staking or other support, such as planting among shrubs or against a fence, especially if the variety produces large flowers—provide a sheltered location.

• **Medium varieties:** Final height is 90–120 cm. These dahlias also look good in borders—the effect is like that of a summer-flowering shrub. These varieties usually require support.

• **Small varieties:** Final height is 60–90 cm. These dahlias are great for small borders, especially to edge a driveway or walkway. The shorter members of this group can be grown in containers. They generally do not require support, unless the variety has particularly large flowers or the plants are grown in an exposed location.

• **Compact varieties:** Final height is 30–60 cm. The dahlias can be used like tall bedding plants. They are especially attractive in outdoor planters and containers, or as short borders.

Divisions

Dahlias are most commonly organized by flower characteristics such as flower shape and petal pattern. There are no internationally defined classifications, so although the major groupings are generally the same, they vary between breeders and countries. We have based our discussion below on the classifications of the Netherlands Flowerbulb Association.

Division 1
Single-flowering dahlia

Division 2
Anemone-flowering dahlia

Division 3
Collarette dahlia

Division 4
Waterlily dahlia

Division 5
Decorative dahlia

Division 6
Ball dahlia

Division 7
Pompom dahlia

Division 8
Cactus dahlia

Division 9
Semi-cactus dahlia

Division 10
Peony-flowering dahlia

Division 11
Mignon dahlia

Division 12
Topmix dahlia

Division 1 • Single-flowering dahlias

Traits ↬ A single ring of florets with a central group of disc florets
Height ↬ 40–60 cm

The simplest dahlias fall into this group. Flowers typically have a single or double row of 8–10 petals. These dahlias are excellent in borders and gardens.

Orchid dahlias are a subgroup of the single-flowering division and are the result of recent breeding. The flowers are star-shaped, with open centres and petals that curve backward at the tips.

Division 2 • Anemone-flowering dahlias

Traits ↬ One or more rings of florets and a central group of tubular florets; also listed as pincushion dahlias
Height ↬ 60–90 cm

The flowers of anemone dahlias resemble a pincushion.

Division 3 • Collarette dahlias

Traits ↬ A single outer ring of flat florets, an inner ring of collar florets and a central group of disc florets
Height ↬ 75–120 cm

The central tubular florets frequently contrast with the outer petals, creating some really striking flowers.

Division 4 • Waterlily dahlias

Traits ↬ Fully double florets with a flattened shape and slightly curved margins
Height ↬ 120 cm

Various dahlia forms have been more or less in vogue over the years, and today's most fashionable forms are the waterlily dahlias. They are fairly similar to the decorative types; the biggest difference is the shape of the petals. Waterlily petals are wider than those of decorative dahlias, giving them a flatter appearance. The blooms of waterlily dahlias closely resemble those of true water lilies, hence the name.

Waterlily dahlia 'Sympathy'

Division 5 • Decorative dahlias

Traits ∾ Fully double, flat flowers with broad, blunt-ended florets
Height ∾ 150 cm

This is the largest, most common group of dahlias, with the largest number of varieties. It also produces some of the largest flowers, including the subgroup 'Dinnerplate' dahlias, on some of the tallest plants. Many of the varieties bred for exhibition come from this group. The flowers are truly spectacular, but they require extra care. Because of their large flowers and tall growth habits, these dahlias may be susceptible to damage from wind and exposed locations in the garden. Plant in a sheltered spot. They usually also require support, because the extra-large blooms are so huge that the stems literally fall over from the weight. Try tucking these varieties among smaller shrubs.

The decorative division may be separated into two groups, formal and informal. The main difference is the arrangement of the petals and the petal ends. Informal varieties tend to have more loosely arranged petals, with less uniform petal tips.

Decorative dahlia 'New Orleans'

Ball dahlia 'Eveline'

Division 6 • Ball dahlias

Traits ∾ Fully double, ball-shaped blooms of (often flat) florets with blunt or round ends
Height ∾ 120 cm

The flowers in this division resemble those in the pompom category. The main difference is that the flowers are larger—greater than 9 cm in diameter. Miniature dahlias, which are actually ball dahlia varieties whose flowers are 5–9 cm in diameter, are also placed in this division.

Division 7 • Pompom dahlias
(Drumstick dahlias)

Traits ∾ Fully double, globe-shaped involute florets with blunt or round ends
Height ∾ 80–120 cm

The flowers in this group are perfectly rounded and have short, very neat, very uniform petals that look so perfect you may wonder whether they're real. These flowers are usually no larger than 5 cm across. (If they are larger, they are classified in Division 6.) These plants bloom prolifically; their strong stems can easily support up to 15 flowers. These varieties also tend to bloom earlier than the larger-flowered types.

Anemone-flowering dahlia 'Riverdance'

Division 8 • Cactus dahlias

Traits ❧ Fully double involute florets with narrow or pointed ends
Height ❧ 150 cm

The cactus dahlias have been the most consistently popular division over the years. The petals curl back upon themselves to form long tubes, giving the flowers an attractive, spiky appearance that appeals to many gardeners. Their growth habit and unusual flowers also make them one of the best dahlias for display in the garden and use as cutflowers.

There are two subgroups of cactus types: laciniated and incurved. On laciniated varieties, the petals tend to be narrow, irregular and jagged. On incurved varieties, the petals are bent or curved inward toward the centre of the flower.

Division 9 • Semi-cactus dahlias

Traits ❧ Fully double, pointed florets that are involute for half their length or less
Height ❧ 150 cm

The dahlias in this group make excellent cutflowers and look fantastic in flower gardens. The main difference between the varieties in this group and Division 9 is that these flowers are less spiky.

Division 10 • Peony-flowering dahlias

Traits ❧ Fully double florets with round ends
Height ❧ 100 cm

These dahlias have two or more rows of petals, and the centre of the flower is open.

Division 11 • Mignon dahlias

Traits ❧ Small flowers, 6–10 cm
Height ❧ 50 cm

With their shorter height and smaller flowers, mignon dahlias tolerate windy, exposed conditions better than the larger-flowered varieties. They make particularly good choices for pots and containers.

Division 12 • Topmix dahlias

Traits ❧ Small flowers, 3–5 cm
Height ❧ 35 cm

These dahlias are well suited to container planting with their compact growth habit and smaller flowers.

Topmix dahlia 'Red'

Dahlianova type 'Provence'

OTHER DAHLIAS

Some newer groups are officially recognized but fall outside the standard divisions. These plants are the result of recent hybridizing and are widely available at garden centres.

Dahlianova Types

These are smaller plants that produce fully double flowers in almost every colour. They grow to 20–30 cm. The tubers are smaller and denser than those of typical dahlias. They are best suited to small garden spaces and container growing.

Gallery Types

These dahlias include varieties from both the cactus-flowering division and the decorative dahlias. The most notable characteristic of this group is their final height, 30–35 cm, considerably shorter than typical varieties from these divisions. This group has some truly beautiful varieties that are outstanding grown in pots on a deck or patio.

Impression Types

These dahlias are collarette types, best suited for pots and containers on decks, balconies and patios. The final height of this group is variable, but they are significantly shorter than the traditional collarette dahlias. Final plant height reaches 30–50 cm.

Elephant Ears

Bearing huge leaves that resemble the ears of elephants, Colocasia
and Alocasia *have become extremely popular in northern gardens.
They are closely related genera of large, herbaceous wetland plants
native to the tropical climates of the South Pacific and Asia. In fact,
until recently, they were grouped as a single genus because they have
so much in common. However, each genus prefers somewhat different
care and conditions, so we have discussed them separately.*

These plants are just enormous! Colocasia *typically reaches one to
two metres in a single season, although in warmer zones it may hit
three metres.* Alocasia *grows even larger, reaching heights of 3.5 to
4.5 metres with a spread of 2 to 3 metres. The leaves reach 50 to
120 centimetres in length, growing on metre-long petioles. The bulbs
are slow to break dormancy, but once the leaves emerge the plants
take off rapidly, provided they are growing in the right conditions. In
general, larger bulbs produce larger plants.*

Colocasia *and* Alocasia *are both wonderful choices for extra-large
containers or hot, sheltered areas, lending a lush, tropical ambiance
to the garden. They are also surprisingly easy to grow. The keys to
success are warmth, moist soil and a consistent water supply—neither
species tolerates drying out. Try at least one of these beautiful plants
and we guarantee it will be the talk of your garden this season!*

Genera *Alocasia* and *Colocasia* are
both members of the arum family, Araceae.

giant taro, giant elephant ear, pai, ape

Type
Tuber

Planting season
Spring

Blooming season
n/a

Hardiness
Zones 10–11 (Zones 8–9 with protection)

How many
Start with 1 tuber

Golden Rules
- Provide abundant water
- Plant in a warm, shady or partially shady location
- Enrich the planting area with compost or other organic matter

Upright Elephant Ear

Alocasia macrorrhiza

If you're looking for a big, beautiful bulb to add daz-zle to your garden, elephant ear is a spectacular choice. Alocasia macrorrhiza *is grown not for its flow-ers but for its gorgeous arrow-shaped leaves and lush skyward habit. In fact, the flower—which resembles a large jack-in-the-pulpit—is rarely seen in cultivated varieties. But this plant's size is unrivalled: it routinely reaches two metres and may stretch to more than twice that height under optimum conditions.* Alocasia *prefers a sheltered, shady location—it doesn't enjoy full sun. However, it needs warm shade, so choose partial rather than full shade if your area is cool.*

Sometimes called ape, this bulb may look big and tough but ultimately it's tender. In most zones, Alo-casia *must be lifted at the end of the season and stored until warm temperatures return. Breaking dormancy requires some coaxing, but once it gets started this elephant ear will amaze you with its sumptuous foliage and vigorous growth.*

Attractive seeds/fruit remain after Alocasia *has finished flowering*

As the plants become dormant, the leaves die off and leave a brown husk over the tuber. If you remove the husk, you will see rings underneath. Each ring is a scar from the leaf that was produced at that spot. The rings are a good indication of how many leaves the plant produced the previous growing season.

PLANTING

- Start indoors in late winter, 6 to 8 weeks before transplanting outdoors. Plant outside after the soil has warmed and all danger of frost has passed. Growth is checked at temperatures below 15°C.
- Partial shade; will tolerate full shade. When grown in more shade, the leaf stalks tend to elongate to 2 to 3 times their usual height.
- Planting depth should be twice the height of the bulb.
- Plant in a sheltered location: strong winds will shred the large leaves.
- Moist well-drained soil, rich in organic matter. *Alocasia* grows well in most soil types provided the plant gets abundant water.
- Add plenty of organic matter or compost to the planting area. You can also mix a good granular bulb fertilizer into the surrounding soil (about 250 mL per bulb).
- Water thoroughly at planting and then not again until the soil begins to dry. Once new growth emerges, keep soil moist.

GROWING

- Once the leaves emerge, ensure the soil stays wet.
- Fertilize newly emerged plants every 2 weeks with 20-20-20 diluted to half the directed rate. Once the plants are well established and growing rapidly, increase fertilizer to the directed rate and feed every 2 weeks. *Alocasia* is a heavy feeder.

How to lift *Alocasia*

About a month before the average date of first fall frost in your area, stop watering. Dormancy is triggered by a lack of water. The leaves will start to wither and die. (You can also cut off the foliage without waiting for dormancy to set in.) Dig up the tuber and place it in a cool, dry location, such as a heated garage or basement, to cure for a few weeks. (In areas with warmer falls, the bulbs can be dried in open shade, provided the temperature does not drop below 1°C.) The leaves or foliage remnants will soon dry and fall off, and the bulb will look dry and shriveled. Any clinging soil and roots should also dry up and fall off. Store the tuber by hanging it in a well-ventilated sack in a dry, cool (about 10°C) place until late winter. The tubers should be kept as dry as possible during the dormant period. Multiple tubers overwinter better than individual bulbs (especially smaller ones, which have a greater tendency to desiccate), so leave clumps of bulbs together.

TIPS

- When growing elephant ear in a container, note that container size may limit growth. The plant grows rapidly until the roots fill the container; at that point, the top growth slows significantly and appears to stop. The plant doesn't die; it simply stops increasing. Transplant it to a larger pot or into the garden, and watch it take off again.
- *Alocasia* cannot tolerate hot, bright sun and needs humidity. Mist the plant regularly during periods of low humidity.

- *Alocasia* likes abundant moisture but does not tolerate flooding. It will grow for only a short time in shallow standing water before the bulb begins to rot.

- *Alocasia* increases by forming offsets at the base of each tuber. Each offset produces its own plant, which means that a single tuber can quickly increase to a clump. A single tuber may produce 4 or 5 offsets in a season if growing conditions are optimum. Leave offsets attached to the mother tuber when you lift the plant in the fall; twist them off and replant them separately the following spring.

- While the plants are growing actively, the stalks grow larger with each new leaf. In tropical areas, the stalks may reach 10 cm in diameter. If the plant is struggling in its location, it will begin to go dormant and each new leaf will be progressively smaller. The growth of the plant will continue to slow down until it receives the appropriate conditions. Once proper conditions are restored, the plant comes back quickly.

In the Garden

- Upright elephant ear is an outstanding, exotic feature plant. Its strongly vertical growth habit and fan-like leaves suit formal gardens more than *Colocasia* does. This elephant ear grows extremely well next to water features, in water gardens and near small streams.

- Elephant ear looks gorgeous planted in extra-large containers. Be sure to provide sufficient space to grow— containers must be at least 60 cm in diameter.

- Elephant ear grows well in almost any garden border as long as there is adequate moisture and room for the roots to run underground. The plants don't compete well for space underground but will easily win any above-ground battle for light and space.

Try these!

There are more than 70 *Alocasia* cultivars, which are selected for either their edible tubers or their tropical-looking ornamental foliage.

- **'Black Velvet'** • Black leaves with silver veins
- **'Variegata'** • Leaves are speckled with cream, grey-green and dark-green blotches

It was all hands on deck when we divided our overgrown Alocasia. The foliage was pruned and the clump was removed from the pot and sawed apart. Then the separated tubers were repotted.

Big-Leaf Elephant Ear

Colocasia esculenta

Colocasia antiquorum var. esculenta, Caladium esculentum

Other common names
taro, wild taro, dasheen, coco yam

Type
Tuber

Planting season
Spring

Blooming season
n/a

Hardiness
Zones 10–11 (Zones 8–9 with protection)

How many
Start with 1 tuber

Golden Rules
• Provide abundant water

• Plant in a warm, partially shady location

• Enrich the planting area with compost or other organic matter

Elephant ear is an eye-catching plant, perfect for expansive gardens and large, decorative containers. With its arching, spreading growth habit and wide, drooping leaves, Colocasia is an excellent choice for the gardener who wants something big and gorgeous.

Colocasia *rarely flowers in cultivation, but then again, it hardly needs to. With good care and the right conditions, it will reach at least two metres in a single growing season, and spread as wide as it is tall. It grows vigorously from tubers and offsets, and will thrive in wet soil or on the margin of a pond. Colocasia loves heat and prefers stronger sun than its cousin Alocasia, so it's the best pick for northern gardeners. A tender bulb despite its robust habit, Colocasia must be lifted at the end of the season in most zones and stored through the winter. But as soon the warmth returns, this elephant ear will burst back into leaf to astound you with its vigour and flash.*

PLANTING

- Start indoors in late winter, 6 to 8 weeks before transplanting outdoors. Plant outside after the soil has warmed and all danger of frost has passed. Growth is checked at temperatures below 15°C.

- Partial shade. *Colocasia* will tolerate full sun if it has abundant water, but it may stall in a location that is baking hot and sunny all day.

- Planting depth should be twice the height of the bulb.

- Plant in a sheltered location: strong winds will shred the large leaves.

- Moist, well-drained soil, rich in organic matter. *Colocasia* prefers slightly acidic, moist or wet, heavier soils rich in organic matter.

- Add plenty of organic matter or compost to the planting area. You can also mix a granular bulb fertilizer into the surrounding soil (about 250 mL per bulb).

- Water thoroughly at planting and then not again until the soil begins to dry. Once new growth emerges, keep soil moist.

In Zones 8–11, where elephant ear is perennial, Colocasia *can become a serious weed. The Florida Exotic Pest Plant Council lists* Colocasia esculenta *(wild taro) as a Category I species, meaning it is known to disrupt native plant communities. In these zones,* Colocasia *should not be cultivated near wetlands where it could escape and establish a self-sustaining population.*

the science behind it

Hot Flowers!

Some members of the arum family (to which *Colocasia* belongs) produce flowers that can generate their own heat by burning their stored food, mainly fat. The air temperature may be only 4°C, but the flower temperature may rise to 46°C! The chemical that triggers the fat burning is salicylic acid, the substance found in aspirin. The flowers warm up to entice beetles, which are attracted to hot, rotting manure, to enter the reproductive structure. The beetles search the plants unsuccessfully but carry pollen with them and fertilize flowers as they move from plant to plant. It's an unusual reproductive strategy, but it works!

GROWING

• Once the leaves emerge, ensure the soil stays wet.

• Fertilize newly emerged plants every 2 to 3 weeks with 20-20-20 diluted to half the directed rate. Once the plants are well established and growing rapidly, increase fertilizer to the directed rate and feed every 2 to 3 weeks.

How to lift *Colocasia*

About a month before the average date of first fall frost in your area, stop watering. Dormancy is triggered by a lack of water. The leaves will start to wither and die. (You can also cut off the foliage without waiting for dormancy to set in.) Dig up the tuber and place it in a cool, dry location, such as a heated garage or basement, to cure for a few weeks. (In areas with warmer falls, the bulbs can be dried in open shade, provided the temperature does not drop below 1°C.) The leaves or foliage remnants will soon dry and fall off, and the bulb will look dry and shriveled. Any clinging soil and roots should also dry up and fall off. Store the tuber by hanging it in a well-ventilated sack in a dry, cool (about 10°C) place until late winter. The tubers should be kept as dry as possible during the dormant period. Multiple tubers overwinter better than individual bulbs (especially smaller ones, which have a greater tendency to desiccate), so leave clumps of bulbs together.

TIPS

- When growing big-leaf elephant ear in a container, note that container size may limit growth. The plant grows rapidly until the roots fill the container; at that point, the top growth slows significantly and appears to stop. The plant doesn't die; it simply stops increasing. Transplant it to a larger pot or into the garden, and watch it take off again.

- Some species of *Colocasia* produce offsets (sometimes called eddos) alongside the main tuber. They usually weigh 60–120 g. Leave them attached to the mother tuber when you lift the plant in the fall. Separate them in late winter and replant as desired.

- *Colocasia* roots readily from stem cuttings in water, especially in the spring and early summer.

Colocasia is native to swampy areas in southeastern Asia, Polynesia and Hawaii. It has been in cultivation for more than 6000 years as a food source and for ornamental purposes.

IN THE GARDEN

- With its huge leaves, elephant ear is an outstanding, exotic feature plant. It makes a very bold statement and is not suited to formal settings. Elephant ear looks gorgeous planted in extra-large containers, but be sure to provide sufficient space to grow: containers must be at least 60 cm in diameter.

- Elephant ear grows well in almost any garden border as long as there is adequate moisture and room for the roots to run underground. These plants don't compete well for space underground but will easily win any above-ground battle for light and space.

- *Colocasia* is a wetland plant and can be found growing in water up to 30 cm deep with its roots continually wet. It is an excellent choice for ponds, water gardens and water features.

- *Colocasia* is a favourite plant for indoor growing in solaria and greenhouses.

TRY THESE!

There are over 200 cultivars of *Colocasia*, most grown for ornamental purposes.

ᖇ **'Black Magic'** • Dark purple-black leaves up to 60 cm long. Less vigorous than the green-leaved varieties.

ᖇ **'Illustris'** • Green leaves up to 60 cm long with purple-black veins and purple petioles

Colocasia *'Black Magic'*

162

winterling

Type
Tuber

Planting season
Fall

Blooming season
Late winter to early spring

Hardiness
Zones 4–8 (Zone 3 with protection)

How many
Start with 25 tubers

Golden Rules
- Plant as early as possible
- Soak tubers for 24 hours and then plant immediately
- Keep the soil moist and cool

Winter Aconite
Eranthis spp.

Among the earliest of the spring-flowering bulbs is the tiny winter aconite. There can be no better promise of an end to winter than a flush of these dainty yellow flowers amid the late, lingering snow.

Winter aconite is a popular choice with gardeners in cold climates, and what's not to like? These tough little plants flower for weeks on end, self-seed readily and naturalize easily. Their flowers look like buttercups and are complemented by a collar of soft-green leaves. The flowers open in the sun and close on cloudy or overcast days, but even closed they're pretty, resembling big yellow beads. Give them a cool, moist spot in the garden and they'll put on a show for you each year, hurrying winter into spring.

Planting

- Plant as early as possible in the fall. If the bulbs are planted later than the end of September, they will not likely flower the first season. The bulbs are also tiny—about the size of a pea—and prone to desiccation.

- Plant about 5 cm deep; space 5–7 cm apart. In colder zones, plant 10–12 cm deep to insulate the bulbs.

- Partial shade. Winter aconite will grow in sun provided the location doesn't get too hot and dry over the summer.

- Moist, well-drained soil. Winter aconite prefers a loose, neutral to alkaline, moisture-retentive soil with lots of humus.

Growing

- The foliage must be allowed to die to replenish the bulb. However, it dies back quickly, before the rest of the garden is growing actively.

- Winter aconite prefers to be left undisturbed once it is established. Under ideal conditions, clumps of bulbs will form beautiful yellow drifts. If the clumps become overcrowded or you wish to move some bulbs, do so in the late spring, just as the leaves finish dying down. *Eranthis hyemalis* and *E. cilicica* also self-sow readily.

- Winter aconites need moist soil, even during the dormant period. They do not tolerate drying.

- Winter aconites are not heavy feeders and actually prefer not to be fertilized provided the soil is humus rich and moist.

Tips

- The tubers may look shriveled, like raisins, but this doesn't mean they have dried out. Unless the tubers are soft and withered, they are fine. Soak them for 24 hours in lukewarm water and then plant them immediately. You can also plump them up by putting them in moist peat moss or sand for a couple of days before planting.

- Some specialty mail-order companies dip their *Eranthis* bulbs in agricultural wax to keep them from drying out. This treatment increases the cost slightly, but if you've had limited success with these beautiful bulbs in the past, it's worth trying a few that have been protected in this manner.

Winter aconites are poisonous. All parts of the plant and the bulb are poisonous if eaten, and the bulbs may cause skin irritation in sensitive individuals.

- If hot, dry summer conditions are an issue in your garden, try mulching the planting area with well-rotted compost. *Eranthis cilicica* stands up best to drying conditions during the dormant summer months.
- For a quick blast of colour, plant these bulbs closely—about 3 cm apart. You may have to thin the patch due to crowding after a few years, but the gorgeous ground-cover effect is worth it.
- Winter aconite responds quickly to warming temperatures, so in zones where the winter weather is highly variable, plant the bulbs in an area of the garden that thaws slowly in the spring. This prevents the plants from emerging during a warm spell and being damaged when the weather turns cold again.

IN THE GARDEN

- Because the plants are so small, winter aconite is best suited to rock gardens or raised flowerbeds where the flowers are easily visible. They are very attractive planted at the front of perennial borders.
- Planted in large patches in a woodland garden, winter aconites give the appearance of a yellow blanket among the leafless trees. As the trees leaf out they provide some shade for the dormant bulbs during the hot summer months.
- Winter aconites look gorgeous planted near clumps of snowdrops because the two bulbs flower at about the same time. Don't interplant them, however, because the snowdrops tend to be bigger and will overgrow the aconites.

You can grow winter aconite from seed if you gather the mature seed pods before nature disperses them. The seed pods are very attractive, resembling tiny rosettes.

Eranthis hyemalis

TRY THESE!

Eranthis cilicica

Common names ᴧᴑ eranthis of Sicily, Sicilian winter aconite
Height ᴧᴑ 5–8 cm
Blooming season ᴧᴑ Early spring
Hardiness ᴧᴑ Zones 4–8 (Zone 3 with protection)

This species originates from southern Turkey. The plants have finely cut, bronze-toned leaves when they first emerge, turning green as the plant matures. **Flowers** ᴧᴑ The flowers are deep-yellow, buttercup-like, 1–2 cm across. **Requirements** ᴧᴑ This species prefers slightly more open, exposed locations than other species and will tolerate some drying out during dormancy.

Eranthis cilicica

Eranthis hyemalis

Common names ᴧᴑ common winter aconite, true winter aconite
Height ᴧᴑ 10 cm
Blooming season ᴧᴑ Early spring
Hardiness ᴧᴑ Zones 4–8 (Zone 3 with protection)

This species is native to southern Europe, from France to Bulgaria. In its native habitat, it flowers in January. **Flowers** ᴧᴑ • It produces large (2–3 cm), lemon-yellow flowers that resemble buttercups. **Requirements** ᴧᴑ This species prefers sheltered locations and tolerates shade. It is the most common winter aconite; it is also the most aggressive and naturalizes readily. As the clumps establish, they form a beautiful yellow groundcover in the late winter and early spring. This is the earliest-flowering *Eranthis* species.

Eranthis x tubergenii

Common name ᴧᴑ Guinea gold
Height ᴧᴑ 15 cm
Blooming season ᴧᴑ Early spring
Hardiness ᴧᴑ Zones 4–8 (Zone 3 with protection)

The largest of the winter aconites, this hybrid is slow to increase and flowers later than the species. The foliage has a strong bronze tinge. **Flowers** ᴧᴑ It produces very large, glossy golden-yellow flowers with a pretty, honey-like fragrance. The flowers are sterile and bloom for up to a month. The foliage dies down quickly. **Requirements** ᴧᴑ It is best located in well-drained alkaline soil beneath deciduous trees and shrubs. This hybrid prefers more sun than the species. This bulb may be hard to locate but is definitely worth trying if you find it.

Fritillaries

Fritillaria spp.

Type
True bulb

Planting season
Fall

Blooming season
Spring to mid summer

Hardiness
Variable: see individual species

How many
Large species: start with 3 bulbs; small species: start with 9–13 bulbs

Golden Rules

- Plant at least 10 cm deep or to 4 times the height of the bulb, whichever is greater

- Provide rich, open-textured, very well-drained soil

- Choose the location and prepare the soil for each species before purchasing and planting

Fritillaries have a reputation for being difficult, and some gardeners wonder whether these plants are worth the fuss. They certainly are! Some Fritillaria species are challenging, but the common varieties thrive with minimal care. The keys to growing these bulbs successfully are finding the right location and preparing the soil properly before you plant. And with more than 100 species to choose from, chances are that at least one fritillary will suit your garden.

Over the past half century, interest in fritillaries has grown significantly. Species that were lost are being rediscovered, and new cultivars are being introduced. Their unusual colours, distinctive forms and astonishingly large blooms are winning over gardeners around the world. Fritillaries may require a little extra effort, but their beauty makes it worthwhile.

Fritillaria meleagris *'Orion' (purple bloom) and* F. meleagris *'Alba' (white bloom)*

PLANTING

- Plant as early as possible in the fall. The bulbs dry out quickly, so buy them early and plant the same day as you purchase them.

- Handle fritillaries with care. Some varieties may sprout roots in the package. The roots are easily damaged and the bulbs are susceptible to bruising.

- Plant in coarse-textured, well-drained soil. The soil must be rich enough to retain an adequate moisture supply, but coarse enough to allow surplus water to drain away from the roots.

- All fritillaries (except *F. meleagris*) will benefit if you mix a large handful of grit into the soil 10–15 cm below the base of the bulb before transplanting. Grit or small gravel helps keep the bulb dry through the dormant months and promotes the development of roots in the fall before winter sets in.

- Plant deeply. Most problems with fritillaries are the result of shallow planting. Plant at least 10 cm deep to the top of the bulb—some species prefer depths as great as 25–45 cm.

Fritillaria meleagris *is a protected species, so the bulbs, seeds and flowers must not be collected from the wild. Bulbs available at garden centres have been commercially bred.*

The
Big Issue

Two factors determine whether fritillaries fail or succeed: desiccation and water management.

With fritillaries, planning really pays off. Prepare the planting area before you buy, buy the bulbs as early as possible in the season and plant them immediately after you buy them. Bulbs purchased early in the season are less likely to have dried out or sprouted roots in the package, making them much more likely to establish successfully in the ground.

Even more important is water management once the bulbs are planted. Unlike most plants, fritillaries don't depend on moisture near the surface: it's the moisture in the root zone that counts. For this reason, site preparation is critical to growing fritillaries successfully. The planting area must have excellent drainage not just at the surface (to allow water to pass to the roots) but well below the rooting area (to allow excess water to drain away).

If you want to grow these exquisite bulbs, be prepared to work hard to get them going. But once they're in the ground with the right conditions, fritillaries are tough and reliable.

Fritillaria pontica

The bulbs and flowers of Fritillaria imperialis *have an unpleasant, musky scent that deters deer, squirrels and other animals that tend to eat bulbs. Plant them away from windows, decks and outdoor seating areas.*

GROWING

Fritillaries have very particular growing needs. Check the species descriptions that follow for additional details.

- Apply granular bulb fertilizer in the early spring just as growth starts or lightly top-dress the growing area with compost.

- Do not over-water, especially during the summer dormancy period. Watering is necessary only during spring dry spells, especially if they occur before the bulbs flower.

- After flowering is finished, the flower stems can be removed. (*F. meleagris* is an exception—allow it to form seed pods and self-sow.) Allow the foliage to die down on its own.

- Divide fritillaries when the clump stops producing blooms. The best time to divide fritillaries is after the leaves have almost completely died down. Carefully dig up the clump and place it (with surrounding soil) on a large sheet of plastic. Gently break away the soil and select out individual bulbs. Discard any bulbs showing signs of damage or disease. Replant quickly.

- Once planted, fritillaries prefer to be left in place. If you must move them, it's best to leave them in the same place until they've flowered for at least two seasons.

- Fritillaries often take a year to settle in, so the flowers are usually better in the second year.

TIPS

- Never store fritillary bulbs. Plant newly purchased bulbs immediately after buying them. When you replant established bulbs, prepare the new location before you dig up the bulbs.

- The roots of fritillaries grow surprisingly deep. This adaptation is believed to protect the bulbs from fluctuating temperatures. When planting fritillaries, ensure that the soil below the bulbs is also coarse and well drained—don't plant these bulbs directly above a layer of clay.

- Never buy fritillary bulbs at the end of the season. They will be desiccated and damaged, and simply will not grow, no matter what you do.

- Fritillaries are best grown in locations protected from strong winds.

- Fritillaries grow best in gardens that are stable and relatively unchanging. They prefer to be left alone, undisturbed, to establish.

Fritillaria comes from the Latin fritillus, *which means dice box. The name refers to the flower shape or the checkered flower pattern.*

A Persian folktale tells of a beautiful queen who was unjustly accused of unfaithfulness. An angel took pity on her and changed her into the regal crown imperial fritillary, a flower that continues to weep (the drop of nectar suspended in each bloom) until the queen and her husband are once again united in love.

Emerging foliage of
Fritillaria imperialis

Fritillaria michailovskyi

In the Garden

Fritillaries dislike upheaval in the garden. Until they are well established, do not disturb the bulbs or the area around them. Most annual flowerbeds are too dynamic for fritillaries; instead, choose a location that is settled and relatively unchanging.

- Fritillaries grow very well among deciduous shrubs because they thrive on the stability the shrubs provide, the leaf matter they add to the soil and the dappled shade they lend. The shrubs also keep the soil drier and cooler during the summer months.

- Because of its height, *F. imperialis* is most attractive planted among perennials and in mixed shrub beds. It also makes an effective border or a striking feature plant in the garden, and looks great amid a sea of groundcovers or against a background of low evergreen shrubs.

- *F. meleagris* grows well at the front of mixed flower borders, in mixed perennial beds, in rock gardens and under deciduous trees and shrubs. It also naturalizes in grass or meadows. (Be sure to let the foliage mature and die down on its own to replenish the bulb.)

- *F. michailovskyi* is best used in shady rock gardens or in mixed flowerbeds with loose, coarse soil that is moist during the spring but dry and relatively cool in the summer.

- *F. persica* is a good choice for sunny perennial flowerbeds and borders. It looks great planted amid medium-height perennials or in front of larger deciduous shrubs.

- *F. pontica* is ideal for shady rock gardens and in mixed shrub beds among deciduous shrubs and trees.

Fritillaria imperialis *'Rubra Maxima'*

TRY THESE!

All fritillaries have six petals. The flowers are usually bell-shaped with straight sides, but in some species the petals flare outward. The fritillaries we recommend below are all comparatively easy to grow and readily available.

Fritillaria assyriaca

Height ↝ 30 cm
Blooming season ↝ Mid spring
Hardiness ↝ Zones 3–8

This little bulb is native to eastern Turkey and western Iran. It is pretty and unusual—definitely worth a try if you like something different. Ideal in a woodland garden! Plant in informal clumps of 3 to 5 bulbs. **Flowers** ↝ This species produces brownish-purple flowers with a metallic sheen, often subtly green-checked; the petal tip is yellow. The petals flare out at the ends. The foliage is also quite striking. Each bulb produces two broad, lance-shaped lower leaves and three or four thinner, lance-shaped leaves arranged alternately higher up the flower stem. The leaves have strong grey-green tones. **Requirements** ↝ *F. assyriaca* prefers a sunny location but likes very moist soil rich in organic matter. If you can provide both, it establishes well. The stems tend to be thin and weak; the weight of three or four blooms may cause the stems to arch over, pulling the flowers to the ground if they aren't in a sheltered location.

Fritillaria imperialis

Common names ↷ crown imperial fritillary
Height ↷ 100–120 cm
Blooming season ↷ Early to mid summer
Hardiness ↷ Zones 4–8

By far the best-known member of the fritillary family, this species was also one of the earliest bulbs to be cultivated. It may reach 2 m or more under ideal conditions. **Flowers** ↷ A large number of lush green leaves develop along the flower stem up to the top of the stem where a large, showy cluster of up to six bell-shaped flowers develops. Each flower develops a large drop of glistening nectar that is suspended from inside the flower bell like a teardrop. This drop of nectar is a favourite of bees and humming-birds. Above the flowers, a crown of shiny, narrower leaves develops. The flowers can bloom for up to a month. **Requirements** ↷ Plant this species deeply: 25–45 cm to the base of the bulb. *F. imperialis* needs a location where the soil drains quickly and

thoroughly. The bulb tends to catch moisture on its top, causing rot. To prevent this, mix sharp sand or small gravel into the soil and tip the bulb slightly on its side when planting. This species prefers sun or light shade. In warm zones, some shade may be necessary if the sun is too hot. This species is a heavy feeder. Mix in some granular fertilizer or bulb booster around the base of the plants right after they emerge and again after they finish flowering. Use granular rather than liquid fertilizer because this fritillary does not like to be wet.

↷ **'Aurora'** • Orange-red flowers

↷ **'Lutea'** • Bright-yellow flowers

↷ **'Lutea Maxima'** • Very large, lemon-yellow flowers; taller cultivar

↷ **'Rubra'** • Deep vermilion-red flowers

↷ **'Rubra Maxima'** • Very large, deep vermilion-red flowers; taller cultivar

↷ **'The Premier'** • Orange-red flowers

Fritillaria imperialis *'Lutea Maxima'*

Fritillaria meleagris

Common names ᚬ checkered fritillary, snake's-head, leopard lily, guinea-hen fritillary, snake's-head lily, drooping tulip, death bell, leper's bell
Height ᚬ 25 cm
Blooming season ᚬ Mid spring to early summer
Hardiness ᚬ Zones 3–8

This is a fairly versatile species provided it receives adequate moisture. Once in the ground, it thrives if left undisturbed; it self-seeds readily. Of the 'easy to grow' fritillaries, this one is the easiest. **Flowers** ᚬ The flowers are large, pendent bells with square shoulders, ranging from white or cream to pink, mauve or dark purple. The petals are *tessellated* (see page 118). **Requirements** ᚬ This species prefers moist, well-drained locations in full sun to partial shade; the bulbs will die in very dry gardens. Plant in informal groups of at least 13, 10 cm deep. Before planting the bulbs, mix coarse peat moss and other organic matter into the soil to help retain moisture.

ᚬ **'Alba'** • White flowers with subtle checkered pattern on the outer petals. Forms vary in purity, from icy-white to creamy to muddy. Like most albino plants, 'Alba' is shorter and less vigorous than the parent species.

ᚬ **'Aphrodite'** • Creamy-white cultivar with deep-green veining on petals

ᚬ **'Charon'** • One of the darkest cultivars; the deep-purple flowers are so dark that the checkered pattern is sometimes difficult to discern

ᚬ **'Jupiter'** • Deep-red flowers with lighter tessellation

ᚬ **'Orion'** • Rich violet-purple flowers with pale lilac-mauve tessellation

ᚬ **'Saturnus'** • Dark-red flowers with pale lilac-red tessellation

Fritillaria michailovskyi

Common names ᚬ Michail's flower, Michail's fritillary
Height ᚬ 18–20 cm
Blooming season ᚬ Late spring to early summer
Hardiness ᚬ Zones 4–8

This unusual fritillary is not difficult to grow but is slow to increase. Plant in clumps of 3 to 5, 15 cm deep.
Flowers ᚬ The bottom two-thirds of the flower is deep maroon. The top third and outer petal edge is bright golden-yellow. The flowers are usually borne singly on each flower stem, rarely in pairs. **Requirements** ᚬ This species grows in full sun to partial shade, provided it doesn't get too hot. It does not tolerate wet winter conditions. Ideal soil is a loose, gritty, peaty, well-drained loam that gets cold in the winter and then stays cool and dry in the summer, when the bulbs are dormant.

Fritillaria michailovskyi

Fritillaria persica

Common names ∽ Persian fritillaria, fritillary of Persia
Height ∽ 75 cm
Blooming season ∽ Early to mid summer
Hardiness ∽ Zones 4–8

Persian fritillaries are native to Cyprus, Turkey, Iran and Syria, where they are found growing on rocky hillsides. This species does not like to be pampered. Its cultural requirements are similar to those of *F. imperialis*; the species do well planted together. **Flowers** ∽ The flowers are a beautiful, shiny plum colour. They last for several weeks with the first blooms opening near the bottom of the stem and then gradually working their way up. **Requirements** ∽ This species does not tolerate late spring frosts, so plant 25–45 cm deep. It prefers coarse, well-drained soils, rich in compost; the soil should not dry out over the summer dormant period. Provide a sheltered spot in the garden, because the stems are tall and fairly thin, and can be easily knocked over in exposed windy locations. This species does not tolerate shade.

Fritillaria persica

Fritillaria pontica

Fritillaria pontica

Height ∽ 20–40 cm
Blooming season ∽ Late spring to early summer
Hardiness ∽ Zones 4–8

This fritillary is not well known or easy to obtain, but it is beautiful and easy to grow, so if you find it, it's well worth planting. It is native to the mountains of Albania as far west as Bulgaria and into northern Greece and western Turkey. **Flowers** ∽ The flowers are green with brown-and-orange spots on the petal backs. Each flower stem has a whorl of three leaves on the tip set above two or three bell-shaped flowers. The flowers have an unpleasant odour but it is not noticeable until you are close to them. **Requirements** ∽ This species grows in full to part shade in soil that is moist, cool and rich in organic matter. Hot, sunny conditions cause the flowers to wilt and die. The soil must be kept moist during the summer dormancy months. Plant in clumps of 3 to 5, 12 cm deep. This species self-seeds readily and the bulbs multiply quickly.

milkflower, pierce-
neige, procession
flower, snow bells,
snow piercers

Type
True bulb

Planting season
Fall

Blooming season
Late winter to very
early spring

Hardiness
Zones 3–8

How many
Start with 25 bulbs

Golden Rules

- Purchase and plant
  snowdrops as soon
  as they are available

- Keep the soil con-
  sistently moist and
  relatively cool

- Renew the patch
  every three or four
  years

Snowdrops
Galanthus spp.

Flipping through this book, you have probably noticed the many tender bulbs that require hot weather and loving care to thrive. Not so with snowdrops: they hate the heat! Snowdrops are tough little plants that thrive despite messy spring weather, late snow, cold rain and splattering mud.

In their natural habitat, snowdrops grow in clumps in deciduous forests, flowering before the trees leaf out. Each snowdrop leaf has a hard white tip that pushes easily through frozen soil and snow—in fact, snowdrops often bloom while the snow is still melting. Through summer and fall, they take advantage of the shade the trees provide—and here is the trick to establishing snowdrops in the garden. These bulbs need cool, consistently moist soil. Once they have the right conditions, snowdrops will reward you with an annual flush of dainty white blossoms, so early you'll hardly believe your eyes.

Galanthus nivalis

PLANTING

- Purchase and plant snowdrops as early as possible. The bulbs lack a protective tunic and are very prone to desiccation. They also produce roots very early in the fall.

- Before planting, soak the bulbs in tepid water for 24 hours. Plant immediately after soaking.

- Plant 10 cm deep; space 8–10 cm apart. Snowdrops tend to work themselves up to the soil surface if they are shallowly planted. Deep planting also helps to prevent bulbs from drying out during the summer dormant period.

- Partial shade. Snowdrops thrive in the dappled shade under deciduous trees or among herbaceous shrubs, but will not tolerate heavy shade.

- Snowdrops grow well in most soils as long as they are well drained, although they prefer neutral to slightly calcareous soils.

- A handful of bulb booster at planting time is all the fertilizer snowdrops require. They are not heavy feeders.

The Big Issue

Some North American retailers are adopting a practice that is already widely used in Europe. They're selling snowdrops 'green'—that is, growing in pots early in the spring, ready for transplanting. Buying growing snowdrops eliminates the problem of desiccation to which these bulbs are so prone; the plants establish much more readily than bulbs bought and planted in the fall. Selling snowdrops this way also allows retailers to carry less-common *Galanthus* varieties. The plants look like tiny bundles of green onions—watch for them!

GROWING

• Snowdrops need moist soil, even during their dormant period.

• Allow the foliage to die back naturally. One advantage of snowdrops is that their leaves die away by late spring, before the rest of the garden gets going.

• Under favourable conditions, snowdrops multiply very quickly. Plan to separate clumps every three to four years. Overcrowded bulbs flower less frequently and produce smaller flowers.

• The best time to divide snowdrops is just after the plants have finished flowering, before the leaves begin to turn yellow and die. Dig deep under the clump and gently shake off the soil. Carefully pull the bulbs apart. Be gentle to keep the foliage intact. (The foliage is needed to replenish the bulb's energy for next year's growth and flowers.) Replant the individual bulbs deep in the ground, 6–8 cm apart, ensuring that the entire white portion and 1 to 2 cm of the green portion of the leaves is buried. Build up the soil slightly around the stems for extra support. Remember, snowdrops are extremely susceptible to desiccation, so replant the bulbs immediately.

• Snowdrops also spread by self-seeding, but this is a slower reproductive process. The seed is ripe as soon as the seed pods turn golden. Like the bulbs, the seeds become desiccated quickly and are not viable once they dry out.

These bulbs were probably first introduced in England by Italian monks who used them for healing wounds. It was considered dangerous to pick snowdrops, because they were often found growing in churchyards—people believed they were a death omen.

Galanthus nivalis

Tips

- Snowdrops do not like heavy rain. The stems tend to flop and the flowers don't last if rain persists.

- Snowdrops do not tolerate hot, dry conditions. If this is an issue in your garden, plant *Galanthus elwesii* instead of *G. nivalis*; the former takes hot weather better than the latter.

- If you move clumps of actively growing snowdrops, be sure the white parts of the leaves are below soil level and the planting hole is sufficiently wide and deep for the roots to spread. Firm the soil well after transplanting to keep the bulbs from creeping upward.

The botanical name derives from the Latin gala *(milk) and* anthos *(flower), leading to the common name* milkflower.

Galanthus elwesii

Two old English common names for snowdrops are fair maids of February and Candlemas bells. It was believed that if a person picked a bowl of snow-drops and brought them to a house on Candle-mas (February 2), the home and everything in it would be purified.

Snowdrops are stunning planted en masse

Galanthus elwesii

In the Garden

- Nothing beats common snowdrops for dependability in mass plantings. Plant them in fairly tight, informal clumps of varying size for best effect. (Some gardeners also dot the surrounding area with individual bulbs for a more natural look.) Snowdrops look absolutely superb planted en masse in open woodland gardens.

- Snowdrops are a wonderful choice for any corner of the garden. Tuck them into little pockets of rock gardens, add them to raised beds or mixed perennial borders, and grow them in carpet-forming drifts under deciduous trees and shrubs.

- Snowdrops mix well with winter aconite, chionodoxa, leucojum and crocus. They also look great with hellebore, winter heather or pulmonaria.

- Snowdrops are excellent planted with hostas. They like similar conditions, but snowdrops flower weeks before the hostas begin to emerge. The hosta leaves obscure the dying foliage of the snowdrops and help keep the snowdrops cool and moist over the dormant period.

- Snowdrops can be naturalized in lawns, but the bulbs will spread more slowly than those planted in garden soil. The foliage must not be cut until it dies back on its own—about six weeks after the flowers emerge.

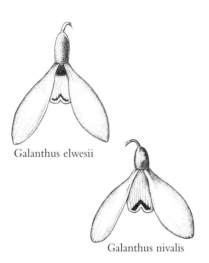

Galanthus elwesii

Galanthus nivalis

TRY THESE!

Galanthus elwesii

Common names ✍ giant snowdrop
Height ✍ 15–20 cm
Blooming season ✍ Early spring
Hardiness ✍ Zones 4–7

This species is found growing naturally in northern Greece and western Turkey. It has been overexploited in its native land, so when you purchase this species, be sure the bulbs have been produced from cultivated stock, not gathered from the wild. **Flowers** ✍ G. elwesii has comparatively large flowers (2.5 cm long) and broad, coarse, bluish-grey leaves. It is the best snowdrop species for cutflowers, because it's taller than the others. **Requirements** • This species is more heat tolerant than G. nivalis, but also less cold tolerant. The bulbs are about three times larger than those of G. nivalis.

Galanthus nivalis

Common names ✍ common snowdrop
Height ✍ 8–10 cm
Blooming season ✍ Early spring
Hardiness ✍ Zones 3–8 (Zone 2 with protection)

This is the most commonly grown species of snowdrops; it's also the most reliable. It is smaller and daintier than G. elwesii, and has greyish leaves. **Flowers** ✍ The flowers are bell-shaped and pendulous. They have a faint honey scent, more noticeable indoors than outside. **Requirements** ✍ These bulbs are about the size of a thumbnail and should be planted 6–8 cm apart and at least 8–10 cm deep. This species naturalizes very easily, especially in moist, nutrient-rich soils.

✍ **'Flore Pleno'** • Double white flowers resembling little white petticoats. Excellent for naturalizing but does not set seed. Commonly listed as 'Common Double Snowdrop'. This cultivar is lightly honey-scented.

Galanthus nivalis

sword lily, garden gladiolus

Type
corm

Planting season
Spring

Blooming season
Summer through early fall

Hardiness
Zones 9–11 (Zones 7–8 with protection)

How many
Start with 5 to 7 corms

Golden Rules
- Provide abundant water but do not allow to stand in wet soil
- Plant in full sun
- Use successive plantings to produce a constant flower display

Gladiolus

Gladiolus x *hortulanus*

Gladioli are easy to grow and are among the most popular summer-flowering bulbs. They come in a wide range of flower colours, in every shade but true blue. Glads are easy to hybridize, so new varieties are developed regularly as older ones decline in popularity. Botanists believe there are about 300 Gladiolus *species, but the flowers we plant in the garden are all hybrid varieties. Many of the well-known larger-flowered varieties were first hybridized in England and the Netherlands in the 1940s, making them some of the newer plants in our gardens.*

Gladioli are tender and cannot withstand temperatures below -10°C, so in colder zones they must be lifted in the fall and stored, or else treated as annuals. The corms store well, which makes it easy to enjoy your favourites year after year.

Gladiolus 'Florida'

Light-coloured glad varieties multiply faster than darker-flowered varieties.

PLANTING

- Plant as early as one month before the average last spring frost date, as soon as the ground can be worked.

- Full sun. Gladioli do best in an open, sunny location with no competition from shrubs and trees.

- Rich, well-drained soil, preferably a sandy loam. Gladioli are very forgiving and will grow satisfactorily in almost any type of garden soil, from almost pure sand to heavy loam. Any soil that produces good vegetable crops will produce good glads. Glads do not thrive in poorly drained soil.

- Plant large corms 10–15 cm deep, medium corms 8–10 cm deep and small corms 5–8 cm deep. If your soil is very light, plant 3 cm deeper. This depth will ensure the plants don't fall over as the flower spikes mature.

- Space corms 7–15 cm apart. Wider spacing produces firmer, higher-quality flower spikes.

- If your garden soil is fertile and has good tilth, there is no need to fertilize gladioli at the time of planting.

- Stake glads at planting time to reduce the risk of damage to the corm.

Gladiolus *is derived from the Latin word* gladius, *which means* sword. *The Romans thought gladiolus leaves resembled the short, pointed, double-edged swords that the gladiators used for cutting and stabbing. This is also the origin of the common name sword lily.*

Gladioli spikes exhibit negative geotropism. This means that if the cutflower spikes are laid flat rather then upright when they are stored or transported, the tips will curve up toward the sky. As a rule, North Americans prefer very straight, upright spikes, so glads are shipped with the stems standing up.

GROWING

- Ensure glads receive regular, ample water throughout the growing season. Glads can tolerate drought, but lack of water inhibits the growth of flower spikes, development of florets and development of new corms. The critical period for moisture is the first six to eight weeks of growth. During periods of dry weather, water thoroughly at least once a week, applying the equivalent of 3 cm of rainfall. Avoid light, frequent watering.

- Cultivate the planting area frequently, and kill weeds while they are small. Gladioli dislike compacted soil surfaces and competition from weeds.

Gladiolus *'High Seas'*

Choosing the Best Gladiolus Corms

A general rule with gladiolus corms is that the number of flower spikes produced and number of florets per spike depend on the size of the corm, increasing as the size of the corm increases. Glad corms are graded according to size based on their diameter in inches, as follows:

- Jumbo   5 cm or larger
- #1   3.75 cm or larger
- #2   3.2 to 3.75 cm
- #3   2.5 to 3.2 cm
- #4   1.9 to 2.5 cm
- #5   1.25 to 1.9 cm
- #6   under 1.25 cm.

The top four sizes (Jumbo, #1, #2 and #3) will produce flowers in the first growing season. The other sizes are too small to do so. Rather, during the growing season, they will produce leaves, collect energy and grow large enough to form flowers the following year. Larger corms also tend to flower earlier than smaller corms—there may be up to 5 days' difference between successive grades.

Thus, Jumbo and #1 corms produce higher-quality flower spikes earlier in the season. So when purchasing gladiolus corms, remember that more corms for less money does not necessarily mean you are getting the best value for your dollar!

- Apply a light mulch after the plants have emerged. Mulch creates a cooler environment for the roots and reduces the amount of moisture lost to evaporation. These conditions slow growth, lengthen the stem and flowerheads, and add distance between the buds, resulting in larger, more attractive flower spikes. Mulch will also help prevent the growth of weeds, which compete for valuable nutrients and moisture.

- Fertilize glads during flowering and after the flowers have finished. Apply a good-quality, water-soluble all-purpose fertilizer (20-20-20) as the flower spikes begin to develop, and continue fertilizing once a week for the rest of the season.

- If you do not remove the whole spike as a cutflower, deadhead individual florets as they fade. Deadheading allows the plant to put its energy into the remaining florets.

- Thrips are a major insect pest of glads. Thrips feed on the sap of glad leaves and flowers, and may overwinter on stored corms.

Gladiolus species are native to Eastern Europe, Asia and Africa. Modern garden glads derive from species native to South Africa. The first South African species was bought to Europe in the mid 1700s by Dutch and English ships that were trading with India. Cape Town was a major stop for these ships to pick up fresh water and supplies for their crews.

How to lift gladiolus corms

After flowering, remove the flower spikes to prevent seed pods from developing. Apply one dose of fertilizer and, if the ground is dry, water well. Allow the foliage to turn brown (this may take 4 to 6 weeks). If the ripening period is cut short by frost, dig up the corms promptly—before the first hard freeze. Using a spade or garden fork, loosen the soil near the base of the plant. Pull gently on the foliage to remove the stem, with corm still attached, from the ground. Shake off any loose soil. With shears or scissors, cut off the old foliage to 3 cm above the corm. (Do not twist or snap the tops off as this will damage the corms, leaving a small hole in the top.) Dry the excavated corms in the sun for a few hours and then move them to a frost-proof location such as a heated shed, garage or basement. The curing location must have good air circulation and a cool, but not cold, temperature. Cure the corms for a few weeks to prevent breakdown in storage; do not allow the corms to freeze. • When the corms are ready to be stored, the stems and old corms will come off easily by hand. Discard the old corms. You will notice a clean scar on the new corm. Gently rub off any other debris or dirt, but do not wash the corms! Remove any loose husks, leaving wrapper husks intact. Sort and label the corms, and then store them until spring in well-ventilated area in a paper bag, loose-weave basket, mesh bag, small box, wooden flat or old nylon stocking. The optimum temperature for storage is 4–5°C, but the corms will tolerate storage temperatures as high as 10°C and as low as 2°C. Discard any corms that dry out over the winter; plant remaining corms.

Corms are storehouses for food. After the plant has used the food supply, the corm withers and dies, and a new corm forms on top of the old one.

Sometimes tiny cormels form around the base of the new corm. These will have to grow for at least two more years to be large enough to produce flowers.

How to save cormels

When you lift the corm at the end of the season, you will notice that tiny cormels have formed around it; they are the main propagation method for certain glad varieties. Lift the cormels with the corm, but allow some soil to adhere to them: cormels dry out much more quickly than the larger corm. Separate and store the cormels over the winter in slightly moist peat moss. Check on them regularly to ensure they are not drying out—they should feel firm and plump—and are not beginning to sprout. If the cormels begin to sprout and you cannot plant them outside, transplant them into flats or pots using a good all-purpose potting soil. • In the spring, as soon as the ground can be worked, plant the cormels outside. (If they seem dry and hard when you are ready to transplant them, soak them in tepid water for two to five days, until they're just ready to sprout.) Plant about 5 cm deep and 2–5 cm apart (they can be sown like garden peas), and provide regular water and fertilizer. These cormels will not grow any larger, but about six weeks after the new shoots develop, the cormels will be replaced by new corms. This new crop of corms is known as virgin corms; they will vary considerably in size. Many of the new corms will be large enough to produce flowers the following year; others will require another growing season before they reach flowering size. Lift the virgin corms at the end of the season and replant the following spring.

Gladioulus nanus 'Charm'

Although glads are not normally fragrant, they are the most widely grown outdoor cutflower. Spikes should be picked in their prime, before the florets begin to open, for a vase life of up to two weeks. Cut glads during the cooler part of the day—early morning or late evening. Leave the stem as long as possible, cutting at a slant. Unless you are treating your corms as annuals, leave at least four leaves on the plant to support corm development. Immerse spikes in water immediately to prevent the flowers from wilting and keep in a cool, shady location.

TIPS

• An easy way to speed growth is to set glad corms in a tray of water in a warm indoor location. When the new shoots reach several centimetres, transplant the corms into the garden, ensuring the base of the bulb is planted to the appropriate depth.

• When you plant large-flowering varieties, initially cover the bulbs with 5 cm of soil. Cover the emerging shoot with additional soil until the soil reaches ground level. When the shoots reach 20 cm, hill soil around the base of the plant for added support.

• Overhead watering is not recommended: it causes spotting on the petals and splashes soil on the leaves, which can promote soil-borne diseases. Be sure the hose nozzle is close to soil level when you water, or use drip irrigation or a soaker hose.

• Glads can provide flowers for up to three months if you plant corms in succession, from the time the ground thaws until early July. Simply plant corms at one- to two-week intervals. Time your final planting so that the flowers are finished by the average date of the first killing frost in the fall; use early-flowering varieties for the late plantings. (Time from planting to flowering ranges from 55 to 90 days; the average time is 80–85 days.) If you try succession planting, buy all your glads early in the season to ensure the best selection of high-quality corms. Choose fat, firm corms free of blemishes, nicks and disease.

- Beware of bargains that sound too good to be true: they usually are. Corms with a diameter less than 2.5 cm are generally too small to produce a flower the first season and will require at least one season of growth before they are large enough to produce a flower spike.

IN THE GARDEN

- Because of their strongly vertical growth habit, gladioli can be easily tucked in the garden among other plants and then removed at the end of the season with minimal disturbance. They can be interplanted with perennials in spots where bulbs with a more spreading growth habit would not be suitable. The largest-flowering glads are best as cutflowers. Use medium and short glads in mixed flowerbeds.

- Use as background plantings or tucked in a group among perennials and in mixed flowerbeds. Gladioli are excellent for landscape plantings. They look great planted towards the back of informal and mixed flowerbeds, around the base of evergreen shrubs and against walls or fences. Because of their majestic, upright growth habit, gladioli are outstanding used as a feature or accent planting.

- Glads also look great in an informal drift—use at least half a dozen bulbs per variety for best effect. Or mix them with other tall perennials that will support the spikes.

- Try a clump of glads in a perennial border!

Gladioli add a strong vertical dimension to the garden design

TRY THESE!

Glads are classified by flower size. The large-flowering gladioli are classified into three main groups: large-flowering, butterfly and primulinus. The smaller-flowering varieties are referred to as species gladioli.

The final size of the plants and flower spikes is directly related to the size of the corm. Corms are most productive during their first six years; as they become older, their vigour declines. For this reason, you should save cormels if you want to preserve a special variety or don't want to buy new corms every year.

Large-flowering gladioli

This is the largest and most important division, with the largest range of flower colours. Also known as the grandiflorus group, this division contains the majority of named garden cultivars, including the American hybrids subgroup. These glads typically flower from late spring to early fall, depending on when they are planted and whether the cultivar is early flowering or late flowering. These are the most vigorous of the glads and make great cutflowers. Each corm typically produces a single flower spike with up to 28 flower buds; up to 12 buds open at a time. The florets are somewhat triangular, with a diameter of up to 18 cm. Some cultivars produce multiple spikes, especially if the corm is very large, but this is not typical. These cultivars may grow to 1.2 m, and the flower spikes may reach 50 cm.

Butterfly gladioli

First introduced in 1951, these varieties have smaller flowers and overall smaller size than those in the large-flowering group. The flowers are usually two strongly contrasting colours and resemble butterflies, hence the name. They produce florets up to 10 cm in diameter,

often with a conspicuous blotch in the throat of each floret. The florets are densely arranged. These glads grow up to 1.2 m and make excellent cutflowers.

Primulinus gladioli

All cultivars in this group derive from the yellow-flowered *Gladiolus primulinus*, and the flowers still resemble the funnel-shaped, strongly hooded flowers of the wild species. The distinguishing characteristic of these varieties is the upper flower leaf that covers the pistils, stamens and other flower leaves like a little cap, making it difficult to see the flower centres. Primulinus glads typically flower from early to late summer. Each corm produces a single thin, whip-like stem 30–60 cm in length and up to 23 flower buds, up to 7 of which open at a time. The flowers are triangular, 3.5–8 cm in diameter, loosely arranged on the stem.

(above) Butterfly gladiolus 'Rhodes'; large-flowering gladiolus 'Don Juan' (opposite)

Species Glads

The gladioli in this group may be referred to as miniature glads or miniature hybrids. They are less commonly grown than the larger-flowered types and are closely related to the wild species. They have smaller flowers (up to 5 cm in diameter) and are shorter than the large-flowered types. The florets usually have frilled edges and are closely arranged on the spike. The foliage dies about six weeks after blooming is finished and can then be removed. In milder zones (Zones 7–11), these corms can be purchased and planted in the fall because they are hardy. In Zones 3–6, however, the corms are typically available in the spring and must be treated like annuals. These glads were initially used almost exclusively in greenhouses for forcing as cutflowers. More recently, however, they are becoming more popular as garden flowers.

Gladiolus colvillei

Gladiolus colvillei
Height ✃ 60 cm
Blooming season ✃ Late summer

These glads were named for Colville, their breeder, who produced his first hybrid in 1823. **Flowers** ✃ They produce very graceful, grass-like leaves and flower spikes topped with funnel-shaped flowers up to 5 cm wide.

Gladiolus nanus
Height ✃ 40 cm
Blooming season ✃ Summer

The most widely available division of the smaller-flowered glads. These glads produce flaring, star-shaped florets in a wide variety of bright colours and combinations, primarily in white, pink, rose, red and salmon tones; they are usually sold as mixes. Nanus glads are smaller overall than garden glads. They also mature earlier, flowering about 50 days from planting—a great choice if you live in an area with a short growing season. **Flowers** ✃ Each corm produces 2 or 3 flower spikes, each 22–35 cm in length. Each flower spike produces up to 7 flower buds, with 3 to 5 buds open at a time; the flowers are loosely arranged, 4–5 cm in diameter. Varieties in this group make excellent cutflowers and beautiful corsages.

✃ **'Charm'** • Beautiful purplish-red flowers with ivory-white throats

Gladiolus tubergenii
Height ᠕ 75 cm
Blooming season ᠕ Summer

These glads are hybrids whose origins are not definitely known. They resemble the hybrids in the group G. *colvillei*, but the flowers are larger and the plants grow taller. **Flowers** ᠕ The flowers come in colours ranging from soft pink to a bright purplish-rose. The plants have narrow leaves and produce 2 to 4 flower stalks, with many side shoots. G. *tubergenii* grows well in the garden and makes good cutflowers.

Gladiolus communis byzantinus
Height ᠕ 40–50 cm
Blooming season ᠕ Late spring to early summer
Hardiness ᠕ Zones 6–10

This species is hardier than most other glads. **Flowers** ᠕ Its flowers are violet-red with white stripes, closely arranged toward the end of the flower spike. This glad grow wells in borders and rock gardens, and the blossoms make good cutflowers.

Gladiolus communis byzantinus

A glad old favourite

The Abyssinian gladiolus used to be listed as *Acidanthera bicolour* or *Acidanthera murieliae*. Recent taxonomic changes, however, have seen it reclassified as a glad: *Gladiolus callianthus*. These "new" glads look great planted in clusters in mixed borders, or near the house or deck where their beautiful scent can be enjoyed. This bulb comes into bloom after most bulbs have finished their season and makes a lovely cutflower. Unlike other glads, it will tolerate light shade but prefers a sunny location.

Gladiolus callianthus
(Acidanthera bicolour, A. murieliae, A. bicolour var. murielae)
Common names ᠕ Abyssinian gladiolus, acidanthera
Height ᠕ 60 cm
Blooming season ᠕ Late summer to early fall
Hardiness ᠕ Zones 9–11
(Zones 7–8 with protection)

These bulbs have a primrose-like fragrance. Their foliage is similar to that of the common gladiolus but more handsome. **Flowers** ᠕ The delicate, star-shaped flowers have 6 pure-white petals, 5–7.5 cm in diameter, with a prominent purple blotch in the centre. Up to 10 pendulous blooms are produced near the ends of 60-cm stems; some say they resemble lilies. **Requirements** ᠕ Plant in a warm, sunny fairly sheltered location, away from the wind, after all danger of frost has passed. Plant in well-drained soil, about 10 cm deep and 15 cm apart, in groups of 5 to 7 corms. Remove faded flowers to encourage branching and extend the flowering season.

common hyacinth,
Dutch hyacinth,
hyacinth of the east

Type
True bulb

Planting season
Fall

Blooming season
Spring

Hardiness
Zones 5–7 (Zone 4
with protection)

How many
Start with 3 to 5 bulbs

Golden Rules
- Provide moist, well-drained soil rich in organic matter
- Avoid hot, dry locations
- Never plant singly or in rows

Garden Hyacinths
Hyacinthus orientalis

Hyacinths are among the most popular spring-flowering bulbs, probably because of their lush, fragrant flowers. Each bulb produces 4 to 7 long, narrow leaves and spikes of large, dense, fully double blooms. The thick, waxy blossoms have a graceful elegance well suited to formal gardens, in colours ranging from red, yellow, orange and salmon to white, pink, purple and blue. These bulbs look their best mass-planted in clusters of a single cultivar. The growth habit is compact and strongly upright.

Hyacinths also have no rival when it comes to bulbs for indoor forcing, and the fragrance of the flowers will easily fill a room. If you live in a climate that is too cold for hyacinths in the garden, be sure to try forcing a few. They're well worth it!

'Splendid Cornelia'

The hyacinths pictured here have been forced indoors, but the bulbs are gaining popularity as cutflowers. They will last one to two weeks in the vase, depending on the cultivar and the warmth of the location—they prefer a cooler spot. The best time to cut the flower spike is when about half of the florets have opened.

PLANTING

- Plant hyacinths as early as possible in the fall. Hyacinths need 4 to 6 weeks to develop roots and establish themselves before the ground begins to freeze.
- Plant in groups of 3 to 5 bulbs of a single cultivar. Hyacinths planted singly look lonely and out of place; hyacinths planted in a row look stiff and unnatural.
- Full sun. Hyacinths will tolerate some shade. They will not thrive in a hot, dry location.
- Rich, well-drained soil. Hyacinths will tolerate a wide range of soils provided they are well drained; they dislike heavy soil.
- Plant 15–20 cm deep; space 6–8 cm apart. Plant deeper in Zone 4: the ground will help insulate the bulbs from the cold.
- Apply an all-purpose granular bulb fertilizer at planting time.
- Provide consistent moisture until the ground freezes.

Hyacinths were extremely popular during the seventeenth and eighteenth centuries, especially after the Dutch developed a double-flowering cultivar. Speculation on hyacinth bulbs was rampant. For years, hyacinths were objects of fascination for European gardeners, who searched for unusual flower colours, double flowers and large, full flowers. A single double-flowering bulb was known to sell for $300.

Hyacinths are native to the Mediterranean area and were first cultivated by the Greeks and Romans for their fragrance.

Hyacinth 'Blue Jacket'

GROWING

- Apply liquid starter fertilizer just as the new growing shoots appear in the spring.

- While the bulbs are growing actively, provide consistent moisture. Hyacinths prefer a drier soil during dormancy, so decrease watering in the summer.

- Mulch the soil to keep it cool and moist. If you live in Zone 4, mulch will also help insulate the bulbs from the winter cold.

- Deadheading prevents the formation of seedpods that divert energy from replenishing the bulb. To deadhead hyacinths, remove all the florets from the main flower stem as soon as they begin to look weary and before they dry. With one hand, loosely grasp the stem below the lowest florets. With the other hand, gently pull up along the stem to remove the florets. Then split the stem and open it flat. It will become the biggest leaf and help replenish the bulb.

- Allow the foliage to die back on its own.

- Slugs can be a problem when the hyacinth shoots are emerging in the spring, especially if the weather has been wet and rainy. Slugs find the hyacinth leaves palatable only at a very early stage. Once the leaves begin to unfurl, the slugs leave them alone. If slugs are a problem, scatter slug pellets around the shoots until the leaves have opened.

The Big Issue

Many bulbs have been incorrectly classified with hyacinths at one point in time—at one time 30 species were classified in genus *Hyacinthus*. As botanists learned more about these plants, it became evident that many so-called hyacinths were wrongly identified. Today, the genus has been reduced to a single species, *Hyacinthus orientalis*, the parent of all of modern hyacinths. The common names, however, have stuck.

For instance, *Hyacinthus amethystinus* has been reclassified to *Brimeura amethystine*, commonly called Spanish hyacinth or hyacinth of the Pyrenees. *H. candicans* has been reclassified to *Galtonia candicans*, commonly called summer hyacinth. *H. azureus* has been reclassified to *Muscari azureum*, commonly called azure grape hyacinth. *H. orientalis albulus* has been reclassified to *Bellevalia romana*, commonly called Roman hyacinth, while *H. princeps* has been reclassified to *Galtonia princeps*, commonly called summer hyacinth. And *H. ciliatus* has been reclassified to *Bellevalia ciliata*, *H. corymbosus* to *Polyxena corymbosa*, *H. dubius* to *Bellevalia dubia* and *H. lineatus* to *Hyacinthella lineata*.

The common names of many plants also include hyacinth. For example, *Camassia scilloides* is commonly called wild hyacinth; *Bletilla striata* is commonly called bletilla hyacinth. And bluebells, classified as *Hyacinthoides non-scripta* and *Hyacinthoides hispanica* are commonly called wood hyacinths (see pages 246–47 for more information). The genus *Hyacinthoides* itself means 'resembling hyacinth.' That's why we recommend you use the Latin name to refer to a plant—simply to ensure you get what you want.

Tips

- Although the bulbs are hardy to Zone 4, the flower spikes are sensitive to hard spring frosts. Plant hyacinths in a sheltered area or be prepared to protect the flowers if a harsh frost is expected.

- Hyacinth blooms are dense and large the first year, but in subsequent years the flowers gradually become longer and looser. If you don't like the looser, more open flowers, plan to replace your hyacinth bulbs every two or three years.

- Hyacinths are labelled by size. Smaller bulbs (size 15/16) are recommended for planting outdoors because the slightly smaller flowers are less susceptible to weather damage. Larger bulbs (size 18+) are better for indoor forcing. They are not recommended for garden planting because they produce flowers so heavy that the stems topple and make a poor display.

- Hyacinths do not like hot, humid conditions. Such weather can promote the development of grey mould on the dense, waxy flowers.

Double hyacinth 'Hollyhock'

In the eighteenth and nineteenth centuries, hyacinth flowers were used as decorations on women's fashions

• Small blemishes on the skin of a hyacinth bulb are nothing to worry about. Such spots are quite natural, especially with the varieties that produce darker-coloured and purple-toned bulbs. Handle the bulbs carefully as they can cause skin irritations in sensitive individuals.

IN THE GARDEN

• Hyacinths are very pretty used as accents along walkway edging, around lamp posts or near the front of a formal flowerbed. Hyacinths are best used in mixed flowerbeds and borders. They may also be used in larger, more formal rock gardens because of their stiff, stately growth habit.

• If hybrid hyacinths are allowed to naturalize, they will eventually revert back to their species form, which looks wilder. They gradually lose their thick, dense flowerheads, forming a few loosely arranged florets instead.

• Multi flowered hyacinths are excellent used for naturalizing in woodland gardens or planting among deciduous shrubs. Unlike the larger flowered, better-known hybrids, multi-flowered varieties do not deteriorate over the years; in fact, if left undisturbed in the garden, they improve each year.

In England, the Royal Horticultural Society awards the Award of Garden Merit, the society's symbol of excellence, to those plants that have outstanding garden value. Nine hyacinth cultivars have won this prestigious award. They are 'Anna Marie', 'Blue Jacket', 'Borah', 'City of Haarlem', 'Delft Blue', 'Gipsy Queen', 'L'Innocence', 'Ostara' and 'Pink Pearl'.

Dutch hyacinth

TRY THESE!

There are about 100 garden hyacinth cultivars currently in cultivation, but fewer than 25 of these represent 90 percent of the global production. We have highlighted the most significant and most common cultivars below. Hyacinths are normally classified as early, mid-season or late flowering, although the flowering periods overlap. Early refers to early April, mid-season to mid April, and late to late April and early May. Garden hyacinths reach 30–40 cm in height.

'Amethyst' • Lilac-blue flowers; late flowering

'Amsterdam' • Deep carmine-red flowers; mid-season flowering

'Anna Liza' • Blue flowers

'Anna Marie' • Bright-pink flowers; early flowering

'Atlantic' • Blue flowers

'Blue Jacket' • Deep-blue flowers stippled with purple

'Carnegie' • Pure-white flowers; late flowering

'City of Haarlem' • Bright primrose-yellow flowers; late flowering

'Delft Blue' • Porcelain-blue flowers; early flowering

'Fondant' • Pink flowers

'Gypsy Queen' • Salmon-orange flowers

'Hollyhock' • Deep-red double flowers

'Jan Bos' • Rich crimson-red flowers; early flowering

'Lady Derby' • Salmon-pink flowers; late flowering

'L'Innocence' • Pure-white flowers; mid-season flowering

'Marconi' • Deep rose-pink flowers; late flowering

'Ostara' • Deep violet-blue flowers; mid-season flowering

'Pink Pearl' • Brilliant bright-pink flowers, floret edges paler pink; early flowering

'Splendid Cornelia' • Blue flowers

'White Pearl' • Pure-white flowers; early flowering

Hyacinth 'City of Haarlem'

Hyacinth 'Pink Pearl'

flag iris, flags, flag
flower

Type
True bulb

Planting season
Fall

Blooming season
Spring

Hardiness
Zones 4–8 (Zone
3 with protection)

How many
Start with 5
to 13 bulbs

Golden Rules
• Plant in informal
clumps of a single
variety

• Provide a well-
drained, preferably
alkaline, location

• Add new bulbs to the
planting each year for
the first three or four
years to ensure flow-
ering each spring

Bulbous Irises
Iris spp.

When most people hear the word iris, they think of
the large perennial species, Iris germanica *(German
irises)* and Iris siberica *(Siberian irises), both grown
from rhizomes. The irises we're discussing here are
less well known and are referred to as bulbous irises.
These beautiful, underrated little species flower in the
late winter and early spring, and are normally found
in rock gardens or near the front of woodland borders.
Bulbous irises are sold in the fall alongside tulips and
daffodils, and if you haven't grown them before, you
may want to give them a try this year.*

*Irises are described as shy bulbs, meaning that they
flower only when the bulbs are mature. After they finish flowering, the mother bulbs break down, yielding
several smaller bulbs, none of which are large enough
to flower the following season. Leave these bulbs to
develop undisturbed (or replenish the clump by introducing a few fresh bulbs), and within a few years you'll
have a beautiful patch of irises blooming on their bare
stems to greet the returning sun.*

Iris reticulata *'Harmony'*

Iris reticulata *'George'*

Genus **Iris** *belongs to the iris family, Iridaceae. The name derives from the Greek word* **iridis***, meaning rainbow.*

Planting

- Plant 7–10 cm deep; space 6–10 cm apart.
- Full sun. *Iris danfordiae* and *I. reticulata* will tolerate partial shade, but *I. bucharica* will not.
- Light, well-drained, alkaline soil. Irises require dry soil during the summer dormant period. If the soil in your garden tends to stay wet, mix in some grit or coarse sand to improve the drainage.

Iris danfordiae

All iris flowers consist of three upright petals called standards and three petal-like sepals called falls, giving them a distinctive look.

Iris reticulata *'Clairette'*

GROWING

- The blooms emerge without leaves; once the flowers have faded, the leaves sprout. At this point, feed with high-potassium fertilizer.

- The foliage must die down on its own after the flowers are finished, to replenish the bulb.

- Irises need to dry out over the dormant summer months or the bulbs tend to rot. Group these bulbs with plants that have similar moisture needs.

- Irises prefer to be left undisturbed once they have been planted. Do not lift and divide or move irises for at least five years.

- Divide an established clump when flowering begins to diminish. Dig up the clump just after the leaves have died down, usually late summer. Separate and replant individual bulbs 6–10 cm apart. Smaller daughter bulbs take a few years to grow to flowering size, so introduce two or three fresh bulbs into each newly divided clump.

Greek mythology tells of the goddess Iridis, whose job it was to carry messages from the gods across a polychrome bridge that spanned the sky. A rainbow signalled that the gods were sending a private message to some mortal on earth.

Iris bucharica

Tips

• One of the reasons irises grow so well in rock gardens is that they tend to be left there to grow undisturbed. Rock gardens are also typically fairly open, sunny locations with well-drained neutral to alkaline soil.

• If your irises are located in a wetter part of the garden, the tendency to split into small, non-flowering-sized bulbs is increased. Small bulbs are also more prone to rotting. For these reasons, irises are often treated as annuals or short-lived perennials in areas with wet summers. To help ensure drier conditions during the summer, combine them with perennials that do not require watering or locate them in raised beds or the upper parts of rock gardens. If you are ambitious, you can also lift the bulbs after the leaves have died down and store them in paper bags in a warm, dry, dark location over the summer. Sprinkle them with water once a month and replant them in the garden in the fall.

In the Garden

• Irises are extremely well suited to rock and alpine gardens. They are also suited to woodland gardens and mixed flowerbeds, and grow well among shorter ornamental perennial grasses.

• *Iris bucharica* is a good choice planted with perennials and deciduous shrubs such as lavender and rosemary. Small shrubs help support the stems and take up any excess moisture in the planting area during the bulb's summer dormancy.

• *Iris reticulata* naturalizes well, *I. bucharica* more slowly and *I. danfordiae* poorly.

TRY THESE!

Iris bucharica
(I. orchioides)

Common names ぐ juno iris, scorpiris
Height ぐ 30–45 cm
Blooming season ぐ Mid spring
Hardiness ぐ Zones 5–9

This is probably the easiest juno iris to grow. It's an excellent choice for mixed flowerbeds, in borders and as a short-lived cutflower. The leaves resemble those of a small leek early in the spring; as they mature, they develop conspicuous white edges. **Flowers** ぐ This species has beautiful bicoloured ivory-white and golden-yellow blooms about 6 cm in diameter and fragrant. The flowers have three very small inner petals that project out and down, toward the base of the flower. Each bulb produces 2 or 3 flowers in the upper leaf axils. **Requirements** ぐ This iris requires light, well-drained soil, rich in humus to almost sandy. It prefers a warm, sheltered location in full sun. The bulbs are covered with a papery tunic and have very even, swollen, brittle, fleshy roots; take care when transplanting them because the roots are very fragile and break easily.

Iris bucharica

Iris danfordiae

Iris danfordiae

Common names ぐ Danford iris, reticulata iris, netted iris
Height ぐ 5–10 cm
Blooming season ぐ Late winter to early spring
Hardiness ぐ Zones 4–8 (Zone 3 with protection)

This pretty little iris grows in full sun to partial shade and is generally reliable. If planted in a shadier location, it will flower slightly later. It is an excellent choice for rock gardens and alpine gardens, and also grows well under deciduous trees and shrubs in woodland gardens. It is native to Turkey and was first introduced into cultivation in 1876. **Flowers** ぐ The fragrant flowers are a beautiful bright-yellow with brown flecks at the base of the outer petals. **Requirements** ぐ Some gardeners recommend planting this species fresh each year, since the bulb often dwindles after the first year and is unable to support a flower the following season. Flowering in the second year can be encouraged if you plant the bulbs a little deeper (up to 10 cm deep) and feed well with potassium-rich fertilizer right after flowering.

Iris reticulata

Common names ᛦ reticulated iris, dwarf iris, netted iris
Height ᛦ 5–10 cm
Blooming season ᛦ Late winter to early spring
Hardiness ᛦ Zones 4–8 (Zone 3 with protection)

This is by far the best known of the 'true bulb irises' and has the most cultivars. (Be sure to check the scientific name so you don't inadvertently buy *I. danfordiae*.) This iris is an excellent choice for rock and alpine gardens, and grows well in full-sun or partial-shade locations. **Flowers** ᛦ The flower are violet-purple with a yellow blotch on each petal and are very large relative to the overall plant size. Species *I. reticulata* is more commonly grown than the cultivars. All have a lovely fragrance similar to that of primroses. **Requirements** ᛦ The bulbs form thick clumps that eventually become crowded and require revitalizing. However, even in ideal conditions, this will take several years. *I. reticulata* and its cultivars may naturalize if they are planted in suitable conditions in Zones 4–7. The plant sometimes develops leaves at the same time as it is flowering, which diminishes the dramatic effect of the solitary flowers.

ᛦ **'Clairette'** • Bicolour, sky-blue and purple flowers

ᛦ **'Cantab'** • Light-blue flowers with lighter tips and dabs of yellow-orange and white on the outer petals

ᛦ **'George'** • Large two-tone purple flowers

ᛦ **'Harmony'** • Cornflower-blue flowers with royal-blue outer petals, a yellow ridge and white blotches on

Iris reticulata

each petal. This cultivar is a bit taller than the species, with a final height of 15 cm.

ᛦ **'J.S. Dyt'** • Violet-red flowers with dabs of orange on each outer petal; one of the later-flowering cultivars

ᛦ **'Joyce'** • Rich-blue flowers with orange-yellow marks in the centre of the outer petals

ᛦ **'Katharine Hodgkin'** • Unusual, pale creamy-yellow flowers with a golden-yellow blotch on each petal, overlaid with purple and blue veining. Very vigorous cultivar; thrives in open, sunny locations. One of the best dwarf irises; flowers regularly every year—a superb performer in the garden.

ᛦ **'Natascha'** • White flowers with a hint of blue on each petal and an orange ridge

ᛦ **' Purple Gem'** • Violet-purple flowers

grape hyacinth

Type
True bulb

Planting season
Fall

Blooming season
Spring

Hardiness
Zones 3–8

How many
Start with
13–15 bulbs

Golden Rules
- Plant in well-drained soil
- Choose location carefully: muscari self-sows readily
- Allow the foliage to die back on its own

Muscari

Muscari spp.

Grape hyacinths are the most common of the so-called little fall bulbs, and their bold blue flowers are truly breathtaking. Most species of muscari have tight, dark-blue flower spikes that resemble clusters of grapes—hence the common name. The flowers open gradually, extending not only the flowering period but also the pollination season.

These vigorous little bulbs are extremely versatile. They thrive in locations from full sun to part shade, and they have great longevity without requiring division. Muscari put on their best show in large, informal plantings. Be sure to save a spot in your garden for these bright heralds of spring!

*Despite the common name grape hyacinth, genus **Muscari** is distinct from the true hyacinths (genus **Hyacinthus**), although they are close relatives.*

PLANTING

- Plant 12–14 cm deep, 8 cm apart.
- Well-drained soil.
- Full sun to part shade.
- Unless the weather becomes exceptionally dry, supplementary watering is not necessary.
- After the flowers finish, feed lightly with an all-purpose fertilizer such as 20-20-20.

GROWING

- A distinct disadvantage of muscari is the dying foliage after the flowers have finished. To eliminate this problem, plant muscari among later-appearing perennials such as hostas or smaller deciduous shrubs.
- Muscari can be propagated by dividing the clumps of bulbs in midsummer, just after the leaves begin to turn yellow and wither, but before they have completely died down and disappeared.
- Some species of muscari form clumps of leaves in the fall. The bulbs will survive just fine over the winter, and new growth will emerge in the spring from these clumps without causing any harm to the plant.

Although rarely used as such, muscari flowers make excellent short-stemmed cutflowers. They are quite pretty and will last about a week in a vase. For best cutflower life, pick them in the morning when the temperatures are still cool and the flowers on the stem are half open.

Muscari botryoides

Tips

• If you want muscari in your garden but dislike its vigorous naturalizing tendencies, you can slow the process down. Choose *Muscari botryoides*, which is less invasive than other species but persists well year after year. Avoid *Muscari armeniacum*, which is the most vigorous naturalizer and multiplies rapidly from seed. Deadhead the plants after blooming to prevent self-sowing.

The name muscari comes from either the Greek word moschos *or the Latin word* muscus. *Both mean musk, referring to the scent of the flowers of some of the species.*

• Once it naturalizes, *Muscari armeniacum* is more prone to winter damage than the other species. Frost injury appears in the spring as brown tips on the ends of the leaves. The damage may be a little unsightly, but it does not harm the bulbs. The flowers are rarely affected and bloom normally.

• Grape hyacinths produce too much foliage to be suitable for outdoor containers.

In the Garden

- Muscari is excellent in mixed borders, in rock gardens, as a part of a woodland garden and under deciduous shrubs and trees. Muscari spreads rapidly, so keep this in mind when choosing a location.

- Muscari looks excellent combined with euphorbia, *Anemone sylvestris*, *Helleborus* spp., *Stachys* spp., and other low-growing perennial groundcovers such as early-flowering double fernleaf peonies, moor grass, fescue, adonis and heuchera.

- Grape hyacinths look pretty underplanted with early-flowering yellow daffodils and early red tulips. They also look excellent interplanted with yellow or white early to mid-season daffodils.

- Plant muscari in a long, winding pattern to create the effect of an undulating blue stream. Muscari also impresses when used to line the borders of paths and walkways in informal gardens.

- If you want to experiment with muscari, plant a few bulbs in a plastic flower pot and sink it into a border. The pot will limit the spread of daughter bulbs. Be sure to deadhead the flowers when the blooms are finished.

Muscari are resistant to rodents and deer.

Muscari botryoides '*Album*'

TRY THESE!

Although the common name grape hyacinth is used for all muscari, only *Muscari armeniacum* truly has the right to the name.

Muscari armeniacum

Muscari armeniacum

Common names ✧ grape hyacinth, Armenian grape hyacinth
Height ✧ 15–20 cm
Blooming season ✧ Mid spring
Hardiness ✧ Zones 2–8

This is the best known of the grape hyacinth species. **Flowers** ✧ Its flowers are usually dark blue or purple with a thin, constricted white mouth on each bell-shaped bloom; they have a beautiful musk fragrance. **Requirements** ✧ This species prefers full sun and is ideal for planting the front of mixed borders and in rock gardens. *M. armeniacum* is the most vigorous of the muscaris; in fact, it can be invasive.

✧ **'Blue Pearl'** • Clear-blue flowers

✧ **'Blue Spike'** • Light cobalt-blue double flowers with a lovely fragrance. Flowers are sterile, produced on dense spikes. Cultivar is slightly shorter than the species.

✧ **'Cantab'** • Has fragrant, light-blue flowers and blooms up to two weeks later than other varieties

✧ **'Fantasy Creation'** • The largest and showiest cultivar, it features fragrant, long-lasting, fully double blue flowers that fade to green. Blooms are sterile, so the plants devote their energy to the flowers. An excellent cultivar for indoor forcing.

Muscari azureum
(Hyacinthus azureus, Hyacinthella azurea, Pseudomuscari azureum)

Common names ᴄᴧ blue bottles, azure grape hyacinth
Height ᴄᴧ 10 cm
Blooming season ᴄᴧ Early spring
Hardiness ᴄᴧ Zones 3–7

If you can locate this hard-to-find species, purchase several bulbs. *M. azureum* is one of the earliest-flowering muscari, typically blooming in the early spring. If it is planted in a sheltered location in the garden, it will flower even earlier. **Flowers** ᴄᴧ The sweetly scented flowers are sky-blue with a darker stripe. The flowers are produced in tightly packed bunches; they are more bell-shaped and open more widely than traditional muscari, giving the blossoms a fluffier look. *M. azureum* self-sows readily, so a nice patch will form in a few years.

ᴄᴧ **'Album'** • A rare white cultivar

Muscari botryoides *'Album'*

Muscari botryoides

Common names ᴄᴧ common grape hyacinth
Height ᴄᴧ 15 cm
Blooming season ᴄᴧ Mid spring
Hardiness ᴄᴧ Zones 2–8

M. botryoides is compact with small foliage—an excellent muscari for rock gardens. This species is less invasive than some of the other species, but persists just as well in the garden. It is also one of the hardiest species. **Flowers** ᴄᴧ Its flowers are purple and fragrant. **Requirements** ᴄᴧ *M. botryoides* naturalizes slowly. Plant bulbs quite close together for the best effect. This species was the 'original' grape hyacinth for centuries, but it has been muscled out by the modern, more popular *M. armeniacum*. The species form may be difficult to find; the white cultivar is more popular and widely available.

ᴄᴧ **'Album'** • White-flowered cultivar, commonly called pearls of Spain or common white grape hyacinth. Flower clusters are narrower and more elongated than the flowers of *M. armeniacum*; the form is also daintier and neater, more compact. Its blooms have a unique sweet fragrance.

Muscari azureum

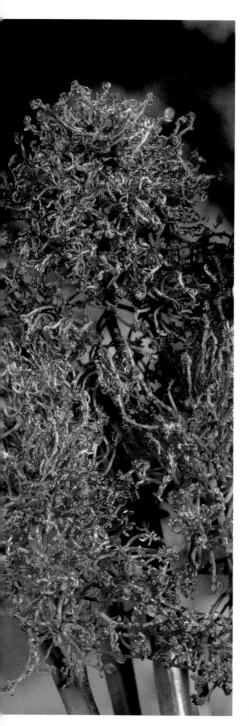

Muscari comosum
(Leopoldia comosa)

Common names ↶ tassel hyacinth, tassel grape hyacinth
Height ↶ 20–25 cm
Blooming season ↶ Late spring to early summer
Hardiness ↶ Zone 2

This species is rare compared to other muscari and has unusual, feathery flowers. **Flowers** ↶ At the top of the raceme grow tassel-like clusters of upward-facing, nearly round, bright violet-purple sterile flowers. Below grow the fertile flowers, which are olive-brown and urn-shaped.

Muscari comosum 'Plumosum'
(M. comosum 'Monstrosum', *M. plumosum)*

Common names ↶ feather hyacinth, plume hyacinth, feather grape hyacinth
Height ↶ 25–35 cm
Blooming season ↶ Late spring to early summer
Hardiness ↶ Zone 2

This cultivar is much more common than its parent species, *M. comosum*. **Flowers** ↶ The long-lasting, frilled violet flowers of 'Plumosum' are actually sterile branched purple flower stems; the true flowers appear lower on the flower stalk, a few weeks after the false blooms. Plant 'Plumosum' at the front of a mixed shrub or herbaceous perennial border or in a large rock garden. For best effect, plant several bulbs together to create an unusual focal point. 'Plumosum' makes a great cutflower.

Muscari comosum *'Plumosum'*

Muscari latifolium

Common names ఌ bicolour muscari, giant grape hyacinth, one-leaf hyacinth
Height ఌ 20–25 cm
Blooming season ఌ Mid to late spring
Hardiness ఌ Zones 3–5

Native to the mountain pine forests of Turkey, this attractive species is gaining in popularity. It is well suited to mixed perennial beds, larger rock gardens or borders. **Flowers** ఌ *M. latifolium* produces attractive, broad, deep-green leaves and beautiful bicoloured blooms. Each flower spike is made up of two different kinds of flowers. At the top of each spike are smaller, sterile light-blue flowers. Below them are fertile, dark purple-blue flowers. Combined, they form a beautiful and unusual contrast. **Requirements** ఌ This species prefers cooler zones.

Muscari neglectum
(M. racemosum)

Common names ఌ common grape hyacinth, musk hyacinth
Height ఌ 15–25 cm
Blooming season ఌ Mid to late spring
Hardiness ఌ Zone 3

This species is not always readily available, but if you can find it, you'll enjoy it. **Flowers** ఌ It produces deep bluish-black, urn-shaped flowers with their distinct white-ridged rim. **Requirements** ఌ *M. neglectum* grows easily in any well-drained soil and prefers a partially shaded location.

Muscari latifolium

daffodil, jonquil

Type
True bulb

Planting season
Late summer or early fall

Blooming season
Spring

Hardiness
Zones 3–8

How many
Start with 9 to 13 bulbs

Golden Rules
- Plant as early as possible
- Plant only in well-drained soil
- Watch moisture requirements carefully: heavy during the spring, minimal during the summer, light but consistent during the fall

Narcissus

Narcissus spp.

My favourite heralds of spring are yellow daffodils, and many gardeners must feel the same way. After tulips, narcissus is the world's most popular spring-flowering bulb.

Gardeners appreciate two features of these bulbs aside from their beauty: their hardiness and their versatility. Nearly all varieties of narcissus are winter hardy to Zone 3. As long as the bulbs are planted sufficiently early and sufficiently deep, narcissus will withstand harsh winters and rebloom happily year after year. Narcissus also multiplies on its own, although you'll see the most flowers in the second and third springs after planting. With a little planning and minimal effort, you can create a beautiful, low-maintenance narcissus bed to complement almost any garden—and with hundreds of varieties to choose from, enjoy an incredible range of flower shapes, sizes and colours, too!

Trumpet daffodil 'Spellbinder'

Planting

- Plant narcissus bulbs as early as possible in the fall to ensure they develop a strong root system before the ground freezes. Narcissus roots grow better in cool soil, so plant when the ground temperature is below 15°C. This is typically when the trees begin to lose their leaves—around the date of the first killing frost.

- Full sun to part shade. Narcissus requires at least a half day of sun to produce flowers.

- Well-drained soil. The bulbs will rot in wet, boggy conditions. Narcissus prefers slightly acidic soils, so if your soil is very alkaline, add garden sulphur.

- Plant large bulbs 15 to 20 cm deep, small bulbs 10 to 15 cm deep. Space to about twice the bulb width.

- Water thoroughly immediately after planting. Ensure that the soil stays evenly moist until the ground freezes for the winter (in milder regions, until the rainy season).

- Mix in some granular bulb food at the time of planting.

Narcissus cultivars developed prior to 1940 are designated as heirloom daffodils. But the term is typically used broadly to refer to species, cultivar or natural hybrids in existence before 1940. Many of today's daffodils have been cultivated since the late 1500s. Gardeners grow heirloom varieties for both sentimental and practical reasons—these bulbs are reliable, relatively carefree, and resistant to pests and diseases.

Choosing the Best Narcissus Bulbs

Because daffodils are true bulbs, the size of the bulb is directly related to the number and size of blooms produced. That is, the bigger the bulb, the bigger and more abundant the blooms. But note that bulb size varies from cultivar to cultivar, so size is relative to the variety or species.

Commercial growers refer to the size or grade of narcissus cultivar bulbs based on their noses: DNI, DNII or DNIII. The DN stands for double-nose, although it's a little misleading because the Roman numeral following DN does not refer to the number of noses. Here's how to read the designations.

• DNI bulbs are the largest of the three categories. They are described as number-one grade double-nose; they may also be referred to as mother bulbs or exhibition size. DNI bulbs feature three noses, or offsets, and usually produce three or more blooms.

• DNII bulbs are number-two grade double-nose; they may also be referred to as top size or bedding size. They have two noses and produce two or more blooms.

• DNIII bulbs are described as number-three grade rounds; they are usually listed as landscape or naturalizing size. They have one nose and produce one or more blooms.

Got it? Good, because there's more to sizing than the number of noses.

Bulb diameters are measured in centimetres. Bulbs are sorted by their size using machines with long slots, rather like large-holed sieves. The grade of bulbs, then, relates to their diameter. For Division 1, 2, 4 and 11 bulbs, the diameter of a DNI bulb is 6–7.5 cm; of a DNII, 5–6 cm; and of a DNIII, 4–5.5 cm. For Division 3, 5, 6, 7, 8 and 9 bulbs, the diameter of a DNI bulb is 5–6 cm; of a DNII, 4.5–5 cm; and of a DNIII, 3.5–5 cm. Note that DNIII rounds come in several sizes. The largest rounds, #3 size, produce large, uniform flowers—they're your best buying choice at this size.

When you buy miniature and species narcissus, the size varies widely, so select firm, healthy, blemish-free bulbs. In all cases, the quality of the bulb is essential: a healthy bulb is the key to success.

GROWING

- During the spring growing season, daffodils require about 3 cm of moisture every week. Water regularly in the spring until the flowers have finished, and then water the foliage for another three weeks.

- Deadhead daffodils when they have finished blooming.

- Never remove or cut the foliage until the leaves have turned yellow, usually six to eight weeks after the flowers have finished. Yellowing foliage signals that the bulbs are entering dormancy.

- The best time to divide or move narcissus is when the foliage turns yellow and starts to collapse. Try to dig around the planting to minimize damage to the bulbs and roots. Remove dirt by gently shaking the bulbs. If some of the bulbs are firmly attached, do not break them apart. Thin out undersized and injured bulbs, and replant the largest and healthiest. If you must store the bulbs for later planting, do not wash them. Allow them to dry and store them in a dry, dark, cool (17–20°C) location with good air movement.

- Fertilize twice per season: once after flowering and again in the fall as roots develop. Give narcissus bulbs you want to naturalize a shot of 20-20-20 just after they finish flowering. In the fall apply a granular bulb booster. Top-dress the planting area regularly with good compost.

Double daffodil 'Tahiti'

First-year narcissus bulbs often bloom a week or two later than the same variety of established bulbs planted in the same location. This happens because the summers in England and Holland, where most commercial daffodil bulbs are grown and produced, are cooler and the bulbs mature later in the season; as a result, the blooms the following spring are also later. The bulbs come into line with local conditions over the summer and produce flowers at the same time the following spring.

Large-cupped daffodil 'Ice Follies' planted with drumstick primula

TIPS

- In areas with harsher winters, mulch narcissus bulbs the first year to insulate against the cold and help the soil retain moisture.

- For the best growth, build up the spot where you're planting narcissus by adding humus-rich soil, compost or sand. This slightly mounded area offers great moisture-retaining capability during dry periods and excellent drainage during wet periods, two crucial elements for growing great daffodils. You can raise the soil 15 to 20 cm above the surrounding site.

- Companion plants perform an important function with narcissus: they absorb excess water during the summer, which is when dormant bulbs need less water. Companion plants also help hide dying foliage.

- Divide large-flowered daffodils every three or four years to ensure they continue to bloom profusely.

- If your garden has heavy clay soil, follow the shallower depth recommendation; if your soil is very sandy, follow the deeper recommendation.

- Never plant narcissus in an area of the garden that has automatic irrigation.

Species daffodils propagate primarily by seed. The seeds are produced in the ovary, or seed pod, which is the swelling immediately behind the petals. After the flower is finished, the seed pod often swells without producing any seed. Insects or wind sometimes pollinates the flowers, but it's rare. If pollination occurs, a few seeds may form inside the ovary. But remember, if you want to grow daffodils from seed, it's a long wait. It can take more than five years for a plant produced from seed to bloom.

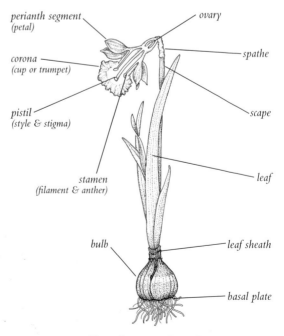

perianth segment (petal)

ovary

corona (cup or trumpet)

spathe

pistil (style & stigma)

scape

stamen (filament & anther)

leaf

bulb

leaf sheath

basal plate

Narcissus structure

Large-cupped daffodil 'Carlton'

Cyclamineus daffodil 'Peeping Tom'

IN THE GARDEN

- Narcissus is incredibly versatile in the garden. These bulbs are excellent for woodland gardens, meadow gardens and rock gardens; they also grow well in mixed flowerbeds, in mixed perennial borders and under deciduous trees and shrubs. Some varieties are suitable for indoor forcing, and many are great for container growing in milder zones.

- To hide the dying foliage, plant narcissus among taller perennials or annuals. Because narcissus bulbs are planted relatively deep, you can plant most perennials and ground-covers right over the bulbs. In the spring, plant bedding plants around the bulbs; the annuals start to bloom as the daffodils finish.

- Choose companion plants for narcissus carefully. Tall, deep-rooting plants such as delphiniums, obedient plants, baby's breath, gas plants and peonies may discourage daffodils. Shallow-rooting, lower-growing perennials such as mother of thyme, stonecrop, veronica, mortemisia, spiraea, dianthus, most alpines, or hens and chicks are excellent choices.

- If you plant narcissus under deciduous trees, choose species with taproots, such as oak, rather than species with shallow, spreading roots, such as poplar or maple. Shallow-rooted species may interfere with the bulbs. Avoid planting near evergreens—the soil there is too dry.

- Dwarf or miniature daffodils are loose terms for rock narcissus. *Dwarf* refers to the overall plant height, generally 15 cm or less. *Miniature* refers to flower size, generally 4 cm or less in diameter. Both are excellent choices for rock gardens and small spaces, and some varieties are also suitable for indoor forcing. The smaller hybrid daffodils are usually larger than the species narcissus. They are referred to as *small* rather than miniature daffodils. By grouping them this way, all cultivars smaller than the standard garden narcissus can be included, even though they are larger than true miniatures.

How to Naturalize Narcissus

If you want to naturalize narcissus, you must choose a variety that is suitable for naturalizing and plant the bulbs in the right location. Plant the bulbs in drifts, using varieties with similar growth habits and flower colours. You will need at least 50 bulbs per variety. (See page 299 for a list of daffodils for naturalizing.)

The location must have excellent drainage and should receive full sun for at least half the day. (Early-blooming daffodils can be planted near the edge of a wooded area, because they will flower before the leaves develop on the trees.) South- or west-facing hillsides or slopes are excellent choices. If you're naturalizing a lawn, pick an area where the grass can be left uncut until the narcissus leaves have matured and turned yellow—about the beginning of July.

If you're starting from scratch, dig the planting area down at least 30 cm. If you have heavy clay soil, now is the time to amend it. Spread a thin layer of horticultural sand over the soil, and then sprinkle the area with granular bulb fertilizer. Place the bulbs and cover with top-quality garden soil. Water thoroughly and ensure the soil stays moist until freeze-up.

To create a natural-looking drift, scatter a handful of large pebbles over the planting area, and set a bulb where a pebble has landed. Be careful that the pebbles aren't scattered too widely—if they are too far apart, the planting will lack focus. To add visual interest and mimic natural growth, set a few bulbs outside the drift.

In sodded or grassy areas, naturalizing requires a little more work. Use a wide spade to cut two spade lengths to a point, like two-thirds of a triangle. Lift the turf out of the way. Continue removing soil until you reach 20 cm depth. Spread a thin base of sand and set 5 to 7 bulbs in the hole. Mix more sand, peat moss and a handful of granular bulb fertilizer; barely cover the bulbs with this mixture. Replace any soil and the original turf. Continue this process until you've covered the desired area.

If your bulbs don't emerge the following spring, the turf may be too dense. This problem can be fixed by plugging the hole above the bulb with good compost or potting soil when planting instead of simply replacing the turf. The grass will eventually regrow over the plug, but in the meantime the bulbs will become well established and will have no difficulty emerging through the grass.

To fertilize naturalized bulbs, sprinkle granular bulb food around the emerging shoots and water it in.

Once established, the bulbs will take care of themselves for years. Some of the older, reliable cultivars can be left for thirty years or longer without revitalizing. The key is to put in the effort at planting time. Plant your bulbs deep in a sunny, well-drained spot, and you can leave them undisturbed for many years to come.

Try these!

There are more than 60 distinct species of daffodils and thousands of hybrids, and new varieties are introduced every year. Despite similarities in colour and shape, narcissus flowers vary from one cultivar to the next. They are classified into divisions based on this variation and their botanical relationships, as shown below.

These classifications were set by the Netherlands Flowerbulb Association, the world authority on bulbs and classification. The definitions are rather technical, but we have followed the Association's presentation to ensure clarity and accuracy.

Narcissus flowers are described by specific terms, which may be unfamiliar to some gardeners. The *perianth* refers to the flower parts surrounding the trumpet; the term *perianth segments* refers to the outer petals. The *corona* refers to the central flower part; it is synonymous with trumpet or cup, depending on the hybrid, and refers to the inner petals. See the structural illustration (p. 218) and the glossary (pp. 301–02) for more detailed explanations.

We list the most significant cultivars at the end of each division description. Cultivars marked with an asterisk (★) are recommended for indoor forcing. Cultivars marked with a dagger (†) have smaller flowers and stems, and produce more than one flower per stem.

Division 1 • Trumpet daffodil cultivars

Traits ✣ Single flower per stem; corona as long as or longer than the perianth segments

Height ✣ 35–50 cm

Colours ✣ Yellow, white, bicolour

Blooming season ✣ March to May

The daffodils in this division are best suited to growing areas in Canada and the northern and mid-western United States. They produce the best show when planted in groups to create focal points in the garden. The cultivars in this group tend to bloom a little later in the spring.

✣ **'Arctic Gold'** • Yellow flowers★

✣ **'Ballade'** • Golden-yellow flowers★

✣ **'Brighton'** • Golden-yellow perianth with lemon-yellow trumpet★

✣ **'Dutch Master'** • Golden-yellow flowers★

✣ **'Exception'** • Yellow flowers★

✣ **'Foresight'** • White perianth with bright-yellow trumpet★

'Goblet' • Creamy-white perianth with yellow trumpet★

✣ **'Golden Harvest'** • Golden-yellow flowers★

✣ **'Gold Medal'** • Golden-yellow flowers★

✣ **'Las Vegas'** • White perianth with yellow trumpet★

'Little Gem' • Yellow flowers

✣ **'Magnet'** • White perianth with yellow trumpet★

✣ **'Mount Hood'** • Ivory-white flowers★

✣ **'Princewinner'** • Yellow flowers★

✣ **'Royal Gold'** • Yellow flowers★

✣ **'Spellbinder'** • Canary-yellow perianth with pale-yellow trumpet★

✣ **'Standard Value'** • Yellow flowers★

✣ **'Unsurpassable'** • Canary-yellow perianth with golden-yellow trumpet★

Trumpet daffodil 'Mount Hood'

Large-cupped daffodil 'Ice Follies'

Division 2 • Large-cupped daffodil cultivars

Traits ᔕ Single flower per stem; corona more than a third the length but less than equal to the length of the perianth segments
Height ᔕ 30–50 cm
Colours ᔕ Yellow, white, bicolour
Blooming season ᔕ March to May
One of the largest, most widely grown groups of daffodils, these cultivars are suitable for a wide range of uses, including focal points in flowerbeds, naturalizing, indoor forcing and floral shows.

ᔕ **'Accent'** • White perianth with pink cup★

ᔕ **'California'** • Yellow perianth with yellow cup

ᔕ **'Camelot'** • Yellow perianth with yellow cup

ᔕ **'Carlton'** • Canary-yellow perianth with golden-yellow cup★

ᔕ **'Flower Record'** • White perianth with yellow and red cup★

ᔕ **'Fortissimo'** • Yellow perianth with orange cup★

ᔕ **'Fortune'** • Canary-yellow perianth with orange cup★

ᔕ **'Gigantic Star'** • Canary-yellow flowers★

ᔕ **'Ice Follies'** • White perianth with canary-yellow cup★

ᔕ **'Johan Strauss'** • White perianth with yellow cup★

ᔕ **'Juanita'** • Canary-yellow perianth with bright-orange cup★

ᔕ **'Salome'** • White perianth with salmon-coloured cup★

ᔕ **'Scarlet O'Hara'** • Bright-yellow perianth with luminous-orange cup★

ᔕ **'Slim Whitman'** • White-yellow perianth with orange cup★

ᔕ **'Yellow Sun'** • Canary-yellow perianth with yellow cup★

Division 3 • Small-cupped daffodil cultivars

Traits ✍ Single flower per stem; corona no more than a third the length of the perianth segments
Height ✍ 25–50 cm
Colours ✍ White and yellow, bicolour
Blooming season ✍ March to May

These cultivars are excellent if you want to create long-term plantings. They are relatively carefree and excellent for naturalizing. These daffodils are also very attractive planted in groups as a focal point in mixed flowerbeds. They tend to flower later in the spring.

✍ **'Aflame'** • White perianth with orange and yellow cup

✍ **'Amor'** • White-yellow perianth with orange cup

✍ **'Barrett Browning'** • White perianth with bright-orange cup★

✍ **'Birma'** • Clear-yellow perianth with orange cup

✍ **'Edna Earl'** • White perianth with orange-red cup

Small-cupped daffodil 'Barrett Browning'

Division 4 •
Double daffodil cultivars

Traits ‿ One or more flowers per stem, with doubling of either the perianth segments or the corona, or both
Height ‿ 30–40 cm
Colours ‿ Yellow, white, red
Blooming season ‿ April to May

These cultivars are wonderful used as features in mixed flowerbeds—they are best enjoyed when viewed up close. They also make excellent cutflowers. Because of their large, heavy flowerheads, these daffodils should be planted in a sheltered location to prevent damage from strong wind and heavy rain.

‿ **'Abba'** • White perianth with yellow centres†

‿ **'Acropolis'** • White perianth with red centres

‿ **'Bridal Crown'** • White perianth with yellow centres†

‿ **'Cheerfulness'** • White perianth with yellow centres†

‿ **'Dick Wilden'** • Golden-yellow flowers†

‿ **'Double Fashion'** • Yellow perianth with red centres†

‿ **'Golden Ducat'** • Golden-yellow flowers†

‿ **'Ice King'** • White perianth with white and yellow centres

‿ **'Irene Copeland'** • White perianth with yellow centres

‿ **'Manly'** • Yellow perianth with orange centres†

‿ **'Pencrebar'** • Yellow flowers

‿ **'Rip van Winkle'** • Yellow flowers

‿ **'Tahiti'** • Golden-yellow perianth with golden-yellow and vermilion centres†

‿ **'Texas'** • Lemon-yellow perianth with yellow and orange centres†

‿ **'Von Sion'** • Lemon-yellow flowers†

‿ **'White Lion'** • Ivory-white perianth with pale-yellow centres

‿ **'Yellow Cheerfulness'** • Yellow flowers

Double daffodil 'Ice King'

Triandrus daffodil 'Hawera'

Division 5 • Triandrus daffodil cultivars

Common names ✲ angels' tears
Traits ✲ Characteristics of *Narcissus triandrus* are clearly evident; usually two or more pendent flowers per stem; perianth segments are reflexed
Height ✲ 25–30 cm
Colours ✲ White, yellow
Blooming season ✲ March to April

These daffodils make excellent perennials. They are also a good choice for container plantings, mixed flowerbeds, rock gardens and cutflowers. These cultivars tend to be fairly compact and low growing, and bloom later in the spring. Their petals are backswept, like the cyclamineus cultivars (Division 6), but the triandrus cultivars require drier conditions to grow successfully.

✲ **'Hawera'** • Golden-yellow flowers
✲ **'Ice Wings'** • White flowers
✲ **'Thalia'** • Pure-white flowers

Division 6 • Cyclamineus daffodil cultivars

Traits ✲ Characteristics of *Narcissus cyclamineus* are clearly evident; usually a single flower per stem; perianth segments significantly reflexed; flower at an acute angle to the stem, with a very short pedicel (neck)
Height ✲ 25–30 cm
Colour ✲ Yellow
Blooming season ✲ March to May

Cultivars in this group have been developed as a result of crosses with the wild species *Narcissus cyclamineus*, which is rarely cultivated. All sport the backswept perianth and bloom very early in the spring. These cultivars are shorter and tolerate more moisture than most daffodils, which makes them a good choice for growing in grassy areas.

The daffodils in this group create excellent long-term plantings. They are also well suited to rock gardens, mixed flowerbeds and container growing.

✲ **'February Gold'** • Golden-yellow flowers★
✲ **'Jack Snipe'** • Ivory-white perianth with yellow cup★
✲ **'Jenny'** • White flowers
✲ **'Jetfire'** • Yellow perianth with red cup
✲ **'Little Witch'** • Yellow flowers
✲ **'Peeping Tom'** • Lemon-yellow flowers★

Jonquilla daffodil 'Pipit'

Division 7 • Jonquilla and Apodanthus daffodil cultivars

Common names ✧ small jonquil
Traits ✧ Characteristics of section *Narcissus jonquilla* or *Narcissus apodanthus* clearly evident; one to five (rarely eight) flowers per stem; perianth segments are spreading or reflexed; corona is cup-shaped, funnel-shaped or flared, usually wider than it is long; flowers are usually fragrant
Height ✧ 25–35 cm
Colours ✧ Yellow, white and yellow, yellow and orange
Blooming season ✧ April to June

Do not confuse this group with the botanical *Narcissus pseudonarcissus,* which is also listed as common jonquil. Division 7 cultivars grow well in Zones 5 to 7, but are best suited to Zones 8 and 9.

The leaves of these cultivars are smaller than those of other daffodils, so the dying foliage is less noticeable. These daffodils make good long-term plantings, provided they experience hot summers; they must have a sunny location in the garden. They readily form clumps, and grow well in mixed flowerbeds, rock gardens and containers. They have a beautiful fragrance and make good cutflowers.

✧ **'Baby Moon'** • Golden-yellow flowers

✧ **'Dickcissel'** • Yellow perianth with white cup

✧ **'Hillstar'** • Yellow perianth with white cup

✧ **'Pipit'** • Yellow perianth with white cup

✧ **'Quail'** • Yellow flowers

✧ **'Sun Disc'** • Yellow flowers

✧ **'Suzy'** • Golden-yellow perianth with bright-orange cup

✧ **'Sweetness'** • Golden-yellow flowers

Division 8 • *Tazetta daffodil cultivars*

Traits ⌁ Characteristics of *Narcissus tazetta* clearly evident; usually three to twenty flowers per stout stem; perianth segments spreading, not reflexed; flowers fragrant

Height ⌁ 15–35 cm

Colours ⌁ White or yellow perianth; white, yellow or orange corona

Blooming season ⌁ March to April (paperwhites 3 to 5 weeks from planting)

The cultivars of this group derive from the species *Narcissus tazetta*. The true tazettas are not hardy in most of Canada and the northern United States, but make excellent long-term plantings in warm climates. Other cultivars in this group are hardy, vigorous and disease resistant, and grow well in the garden. All varieties in this division are sweetly perfumed, especially the paperwhites. They make excellent cutflowers, but some people find their strong scent overpowering.

⌁ **'Cragford'** • White perianth with vermilion-red cup★

⌁ **'Geranium'** • White perianth with orange cup

⌁ **'Grand Soleil d'Or'** • Golden-yellow perianth with orange cup★

⌁ **'Laurens Koster'** • White perianth with yellow cup

⌁ **'Minnow'** • Lemon-yellow perianth with golden-yellow cup; dwarf variety with small flowers

⌁ **'Scarlet Gem'** • Pale-yellow perianth with orange cup

This group also includes paperwhites, which are usually sold for indoor forcing although they can be planted outdoors in Zones 9 and 10. Paperwhites are native to Israel. In their natural habitat, the bulbs are dormant during the hot, dry summer; they flower in the cooler winter season— at roughly room temperature, which makes them easy to force indoors.

Common paperwhite cultivars include **'Bethlehem'**, **'Chinese Sacred Lily'**, **'Galilee'** ('Gallilea'), **'Israel'** ('Omri'), **'Jerusalem'** ('Sheleg'), **'Nazareth'** ('Yael') and **'Ziva'**— many of these names signal their Middle Eastern origins.

Tazetta daffodil 'Geranium'

Poeticus daffodil 'Actea'

other daffodils. They are also among the most fragrant daffodils. They make good long-term plantings; they naturalize well but multiply slowly. They look gorgeous planted among long grass and are good choices for mixed flowerbeds and borders, especially in cooler climates. The blooms make excellent cutflowers.

ᔰ **N. poeticus var. recurvus** • White and yellow perianth with orange cup

ᔰ **'Actea'** • Pure-white perianth and golden-yellow cup with bright-red edge

Division 10 • *Bulbocodium daffodil cultivars*

Common name ᔰ petticoat daffodils

Traits ᔰ Characteristics of *Narcissus bulbocodium* clearly evident; usually a single flower per stem; perianth segments insignificant compared to the dominant corona

Height ᔰ 15 cm

Colours ᔰ White and yellow

Blooming season ᔰ February to April

The cultivars in this group are all descended from the species *Narcissus bulbocodium*. The prominent corona is best described as megaphone-shaped, accompanied by dark-green, thread-like leaves. These daffodils naturalize well, although they spread only a few centimetres, and are well suited to gently sloped areas where water seeps through in the early spring. Because they tend to be very small, they are best located in areas where they won't compete with other plants.

These cultivars tend to be uncommon and are usually purchased through specialty mail-order catalogues, providing endless possibilities for the daffodil aficionado or collector.

Division 9 • *Poeticus daffodil cultivars*

Common names ᔰ poet's narcissus, pheasant's eye

Traits ᔰ Characteristics of *Narcissus poeticus* evident; usually a single flower per stem; perianth segments pure white; corona very short or disc-shaped, usually with a green or yellow centre and a red rim, but sometimes of a single colour; flowers usually fragrant

Height ᔰ 30–40 cm

Colours ᔰ White or yellow perianth; cup has an orange edge

Blooming season ᔰ April to May

This group is so valued because these cultivars bloom much later than most

Division 11 • Split corona narcissus

Traits ༈ There are two groups within this division.
GROUP A—Collar Daffodils: Corona segments are opposite the perianth segments; the corona segments usually occur in two whorls of three
GROUP B—Papillon Daffodils: Corona segments are alternate to the perianth segments; the corona segments usually occur in a single whorl of six
Height ༈ 40–50 cm
Colours ༈ Yellow, white, orange
Blooming season ༈ April to May

The flowers of this division are large and upward-facing, making them one of the best choices for mass plantings. They bloom fairly early. They also make good cutflowers and are among the nicest daffodils for floral arrangements. Papillon daffodils are sometimes called butterfly daffodils because the petals resemble a butterfly; collar daffodils are sometimes called orchid daffodils. The varieties in this division have been in production for years, but it is only recently that interest has really peaked, so they are now much more readily available.

༈ **'Cassata'** • Yellowish perianth with   lemon-yellow cup★

༈ **'Dolly Mollinger'** • Yellow perianth with orange cup

༈ **'Mondragon'** • Yellow perianth with orange cup

༈ **'Orangery'** • White perianth with bright-orange cup

༈ **'Palmares'** • White perianth with pink cup

༈ **'Papillon Blanc'** • White perianth and cup

༈ **'Valdrome'** • White perianth with yellow cup

Split corona daffodil 'Dolly Mollinger'

Division 12 • Other daffodil cultivars

This group includes those *Narcissus* cultivars that do not fit into the other divisions. Many are inter-division hybrids. These hybrids usually derive from a species crossed with a larger-flowered hybrid narcissus. The resulting cultivars have the compact size and attractive qualities of the species parent, and the vigour and resilience of the hybrid parent, making them excellent, easy-to-grow garden plants. When you buy these cultivars, it is useful to know the parentage, especially the species parent, to ensure you provide suitable growing conditions in your garden.

༈ **'Jumblie'** • Golden-yellow flowers

༈ **'Quince'** • Yellow flowers

༈ **'Tête-à-Tête'** • Lemon-yellow flowers★

Division 13 • Other daffodils

These are daffodils distinguished solely by botanical name; this division also includes species or wild daffodils. Botanically speaking, *Narcissus* is a difficult genus. Many recognized species are probably not true species; rather, they are likely cultivated plants that were first described hundreds of years ago and do not have exact counterparts in the wild. Many species have been vaguely defined, which makes distinguishing them challenging, and some are highly variable, which makes height measurements and flower descriptions imprecise. Use the following information only as a guideline.

Group A: Botanical Daffodils
Section *tapeinanthus*
Blooming season ✿ Fall
Leaves are glaucous (covered with waxy bloom), not always present on flowering bulbs. Flower is ascending, yellow; corona is absent or rudimentary. One to four flowers per rounded stem.

Section *serotini*
Blooming season ✿ Fall
Leaves are very narrow, not always present on flowering bulbs; glaucous. Perianth segments are pure white, usually twisted; corona is very short, may be yellow, orange or green. Flowers are fragrant, usually one or two per rounded stem.

Section *aurelia*
Blooming season ✿ Fall
Leaves are flat, not channelled, glaucous. Perianth segments are white; corona is rudimentary or absent. Flowers are fragrant, three to twelve per compressed stem.

Section *tazettae*
Blooming season ✿ Fall to spring
A widely variable group that contains several subspecies. Requires hot, sunny summers; grows poorly in colder climates. Leaves are flat or channelled, usually glaucous. Reaches 15–50 cm;
bears clusters of up to 20 small yellow-cupped flowers. Flowers white, yellow or bicoloured; fragrant. Three (rarely two) to twenty flowers per usually compressed stem.

Section *narcissus*
Blooming season ✿ Spring
Leaves are flat, not channelled, glaucous. Perianth segments are pure white. Corona is disc-shaped or very shallow, sometimes of a single colour, but usually with green base, yellow mid-zone and red or orange rim. Flowers are fragrant; usually a single flower (rarely two to four) per compressed stem.

Section *jonquilla*
Blooming season ✿ Spring
Leaves are narrow or semi-cylindrical, rush-like. Perianth segments are spreading or reflexed; corona is cup-shaped, usually wider than long. Flowers are yellow, never white; one to five (rarely eight) per rounded stem. Prefers sheltered spots and sandy soils. Makes a good cutflower; has a wonderful fragrance.

Section *apodanthi*
Blooming season ✿ Spring
Leaves are narrow, channelled, glaucous. Perianth segments are spreading or slightly reflexed; corona is

Narcissus bulbocodium

cup-shaped, funnel-shaped or flared, usually wider than it is long. Flowers are white or yellow, never bicoloured; a single flower or two to five per somewhat compressed stem.

Section *ganymedes*
Blooming season ✵ Spring
This section covers *N. triandrus*. Leaves are flat or semi-cylindrical. Perianth segments are reflexed; corona is cup-shaped (rarely bell-shaped). Flowers are pendent, white, yellow or bicoloured; a single flower or two to six per elliptical or cylindrical stem. Best suited to woodland gardens; prefers moist conditions when dormant.

Section *bulbocodium*
Blooming season ✵ Fall to spring
Leaves narrow, semi-cylindrical. Perianth segments are insignificant compared to dominant corona. Flowers are white or yellow; a single flower per rounded stem. Best suited to woodland gardens; prefers moist conditions when dormant. Other suitable locations include modest slopes where water can seep to the bulbs early in the season.

Section *pseudonarcissus*
Common names ✵ Lent lily, wild daffodil
Blooming season ✵ Spring
Leaves flat or channelled, usually glaucous. Perianth segments are usually spreading; corona is more or less cylindrical, often flared at mouth, yellow or white (never orange or red). Flowers are white, yellow or bicoloured; usually a single flower per roughly compressed, sometimes rounded stem. Best suited to woodland gardens; prefers moist conditions when dormant. This section is not widely available. Note that hybrids distinguished solely by botanical name are also assigned to this section.

Narcissus bulbocodium

Group B: Wild Daffodils

This group includes species that have not been crossed or selected. They are difficult to find and highly desired by collectors. There is some question about the number of individual species that exist. There are 26 commonly accepted species, not counting subspecies and varieties, but if we include cultivars of species, there are many hundreds more. We have listed the six most widely available.

Wild or species daffodils are among the smallest narcissus. In the wild they are found growing on slopes, which provide excellent natural drainage. Water drains readily during the spring rains, and exposed slopes dry out in the summer, preventing rot during dormancy. (Even the cultivars of narcissus species prefer to be planted in elevated locations.)

The key to growing them successfully is to simulate the climate of the mountains of southern Europe where they originate. If you don't have a sloped area in your garden, create raised beds or berms to simulate hilly conditions. Plant these species in well-drained soil, rich in compost, preferably in a spot with a south- or west-facing slope. Feed with water-soluble all-purpose fertilizer after the flowers have finished.

Narcissus bulbocodium

Common names ⚘ yellow hoop petticoat daffodils
Height ⚘ 15 cm
Colour ⚘ Golden-yellow
Blooming season ⚘ February to March

Flowers ⚘ This species bears unusual flowers with very narrow, pointed greenish-yellow perianth petals and a large, protruding cone-shaped cup. **Requirements** ⚘ It needs a sunny location and moisture-retentive soil to grow successfully. This species may naturalize but tends to increase slowly.

Narcissus canaliculatus

Height ⚘ 15 cm
Colour ⚘ White and yellow
Blooming season ⚘ March to April

Some authorities classify this species with Division 8. **Flowers** ⚘ Each stem produces up to six sweetly scented flowers; they have a white perianth with a yellow cup. The leaves often grow taller than the flowers. **Requirements** ⚘ To grow successfully year after year, these bulbs require hot, dry summer conditions to allow the bulbs to ripen properly and flower the next year. The bulbs should also be planted deeply to prevent them from splitting.

Narcissus cyclamineus

Height ⚘ 15 cm
Colour ⚘ golden-yellow
Blooming season ⚘ March to April

Flowers ⚘ This species produces a fully reflexed golden-yellow perianth with a narrow golden-yellow trumpet. It spreads quickly by self-seeding. It tolerates light shade and prefers a moist location with slightly acidic soil, which makes it a good choice for woodland gardens. It also tolerates naturalizing in thin grass, but is more prolific as a border.

Narcissus lobularis

Height ⚘ 20 cm
Colour ⚘ yellow
Blooming season ⚘ March to April

A low-growing species that produces a single flower per stem. **Flowers** ⚘ The trumpet-shaped flowers have a yellow perianth and yellow cup. **Requirements** ⚘ This species is tender—not suitable for areas with harsh winters.

Narcissus nanus

Height ⚘ 15 cm
Colour ⚘ yellow
Blooming season ⚘ March

This pretty little narcissus has short stems and small flowers with very large trumpets. **Flowers** ⚘ The flowers have a yellow perianth and yellow cup.

Narcissus odorus

Common names ⚘ campernelle jonquil
Height ⚘ 15 cm
Colour ⚘ yellow
Blooming season ⚘ March to April

An excellent narcissus for use in rock gardens. **Flowers** ⚘ The flowers have a yellow perianth and yellow cup. **Requirements** ⚘ It does not tolerate very dry soil conditions; keep it well watered.

Squills

'Squills' is an encompassing word used to describe a number of species of the lily family (Liliaceae). Technically, 'squill' refers to several early-flowering bulb species from genus Scilla. But the term has also been applied to other plants. Striped squill, for example, is actually the common name for species Puschkinia libanotica.

Puschkinia and Scilla are superficially similar. Both bulbs produce star-shaped white flowers with vertical blue stripes down the petals. Scillas tend to bloom earlier than puschkinias, and scilla flowers are attached individually along the flower stem, spread out and nodding, while puschkinia flowers are clustered close together near the top of the stem. The filaments are fused in Scilla to form a small tube, and the six petals are also fused at the base. Puschkinia and Scilla are closely related to each other—as well as to chionodoxa, treated separately on pages 112–15—you could call them first cousins!

But the confusion doesn't end there. Not all the Scilla species are called squills. One later-flowering species, Scilla campanulata (also known as S. hispanica), has the common name wood hyacinth. Another, Scilla nutans (also known as S. non-scripta), is commonly called English bluebells. These two have recently been reclassified under genus Hyacinthoides and are beginning to be listed separately. And just to add to the confusion, Scilla peruviana (see page 224) has the common name Cuban lily.

In this book, we decided to group these genera together but identify them distinctly. Most bulb companies and bulb catalogues list Puschkinia and Hyacinthoides with the squills, so that is where most people look for them. There are, however, enough significant differences to warrant the individual treatment of each genus.

Puschkinias

Puschkinia spp.

striped squill,
Lebanese squill,
Lebanon squill

Type
True bulb

Planting season
Fall

Blooming season
Mid spring

Hardiness
Zones 3–9

How many
Start with
25 to 50 bulbs

Golden Rules
- Plant as early as possible in the fall
- Plant in partial shade
- Provide moist, well-drained soil

If you want something beautiful but uncommon in your garden, try puschkinias. Commonly called striped squills, puschkinias are close relatives of scillas, yet many bulb books don't even list them. It's a shame because puschkinias produce lovely light-blue flowers with a dark stripe on each petal. They flower early in the season and die down quickly, leaving no mess behind them.

Puschkinias should appeal especially to gardeners in cold climates. These tiny beauties are very hardy, grow largely trouble-free and naturalize readily, increasing quickly to form informal drifts. Give these little bulbs a chance—you'll be charmed by their gentle elegance!

Puschkinia scilloides libanotica

Puschkinias were formerly classified as Scilla puschkinioides.

Rodents are not usually a problem with this species, except when the soil is freshly tilled and the scent of the bulbs is still present. They generally leave established clumps alone.

PLANTING

- Plant as early as possible in the fall. Puschkinias need time to root before winter.
- Plant in shade to partial shade.
- Plant 8 cm deep; space 4–5 cm apart.
- Well-drained soil. Puschkinias do not like to dry out, so choose a location that has good moisture retention.

GROWING

- Allow the foliage to die down on its own. Each bulb produces two small, strap-shaped leaves, which die down quickly after the flowers are finished.
- Puschkinias propagate by forming bulbils. The best time to move or thin crowded clumps is just after the leaves wither in the summer.

Puschkinias make excellent miniature cut flowers.

TIPS

- If the soil is sufficiently moist, puschkinias will self-seed.

- Puschkinias flower about the same time as Siberian squills and chionodoxas.

IN THE GARDEN

- Puschkinias are a wonderful addition to informal garden settings. Their drift-forming growth habit looks great in rock gardens, informal borders and woodland gardens, or under shrubs and trees.

This plant was named after Apollos Apollossow-itsch Mussin-Puschkin, a Russian count and avid plant collector.

- Puschkinias will tolerate slightly acid soils, so they make an excellent choice for interplanting with azaleas or rhododendrons. The puschkinias will flower and offer some beautiful colour before the azaleas and rhododendrons are in bloom.

Puschkinia libanotica

Puschkinia scilloides libanotica *'Alba'*

- Puschkinias look especially pretty planted in large, solid drifts or interplanted with other tiny bulbs that flower at about the same time, such as snowdrops, Siberian squills and chionodoxas.
- Puschkinias naturalize freely and are relatively undemanding once established. They're an excellent choice for naturalizing in lawns because they flower early and the leaves die down quickly.

TRY THESE!

Puschkinia scilloides
(P. hyacinthoides, P. libanotica,
P. scilloides var. hyacinthoides, P. scilloides var. libanotica)

Common names ✥ striped squill
Height ✥ 15–20 cm
Blooming season ✥ Early spring
Hardiness ✥ Zones 3–8

Flowers ✥ This species has small, lightly fragrant, bell-shaped pale-blue flowers with a darker greenish-blue stripe down the middle of each petal. The flowers are borne in dense clusters on upright racemes.

✥ ***Puschkinia scilloides* var. *libanotica* 'Alba'** • Small, white bell-shaped flowers in dense clusters. Definitely worth trying!

Squills

Scilla spp.

scillas, spring squills, blue squills

Type
True bulb

Planting season
Fall

Blooming season
Spring

Hardiness
Zones 1–10

How many
Start with at least 25 bulbs

Golden Rules
- Plant as early as possible
- Plant in sun to partial shade
- Best used in informal gardens, planted in large drifts

The early-flowering scillas deserve to be more popular. They are among the first flowers to bloom in the spring and are unfazed by cold or frost. They require little maintenance and are not fussy about soil or light conditions. The squills are also some of the few plants that produce true-blue flowers. Over the years, breeders have developed cultivars in white, pink and purple, but blue remains the favourite.

The broad, spreading foliage of scillas makes them an excellent choice in borders, edging and rock gardens. It's a useful adaptation because these low-growing bulbs bloom early in the season, when rain can spatter the pretty little flowers with mud. Scillas are also a good choice for planting in lawns because the foliage matures quickly and disappears. In short, scillas are wonderfully versatile plants, worthy of a spot in your garden.

Scilla siberica alba

Scilla peruviana *was discovered by Linnaeus. He thought it came from Peru, hence the name.*

Scilla siberica

Planting

• Plant as soon as possible after purchasing to ensure that the bulbs are well established before winter. The bulbs lack a protective tunic and are susceptible to drying out; they do not store well.

• Plant 8 cm deep; space 4–5 cm apart.

• Sun to part shade. Some species, such as *Scilla mischtschenkoana*, actually prefer shade. Scillas will not thrive in hot, dry conditions during the summer.

• Average to fertile soil with good drainage.

Growing

• Allow foliage to die back on its own.

• Scillas propagate by producing bulbils. They will also self-seed, but slowly. They naturalize well.

• The best time to move or thin crowded patches is just after the leaves wither in the summer.

Tips

• Scillas tend to be very inexpensive. A few dollars will usually buy a dozen or more bulbs.

Siberian squills were first introduced to North America in the 1830s. At the peak of their popularity in the early twentieth century, gardeners were encouraged to plant hundreds in every garden!

Scilla siberica

IN THE GARDEN

- Scilla are very hardy and reliable—particularly the Siberian squills   and offer great versatility in the garden. Try them in rock gardens, perennial borders, alpine gardens, stony banks, rocky ledges, mixed flowerbeds and woodland gardens, or under trees and shrubs.

- Scillas are an excellent choice when you want low masses of colour or if you want to fill a small corner of the garden. Because the plants are fairly tiny, they stand out best in elevated locations, where it is easy to observe the tiny flowers in detail.

- Siberian squills typically flower before leaves have emerged on deciduous trees and shrubs. They are well suited to areas that are sunny early in the spring but become shady as summer advances.

- Plant *Scilla mischtschenkoana* with winter aconite and snowdrops for a beautiful early-spring show! This species also looks very pretty grown under trees and deciduous shrubs in woodland settings.

Genus Scilla *belongs to the lily family, Liliaceae.*

Scilla siberica alba

Try these!

Scilla bifolia

Common names ↬ two-leaf squill, twin-leaf squill, blue star
Height ↬ 6–10 cm
Blooming season ↬ Spring
Hardiness ↬ Zones 4–8

This is an early-flowering species and is easy to grow and cultivate. It naturalizes superbly. **Flowers** ↬ Each bulb produces two linear leaves and a loose arrangement of up to ten individual blooms on one-sided racemes. The starry, upward-facing flowers are usually a beautiful, vivid blue, similar to the colour of gentians. **Requirements** ↬ Plant among short grass or shrubs in sun or partial shade.

↬ **S. bifolia robusta** • Purplish-blue flowers

↬ **'Rosea'** • Pink flowers

↬ **'Alba'** • White flowers

↬ **'Praecox'** • Vigorous, very showy, large blue flowers

Scilla bifolia

Scilla litardierei
(S. pratensis, S. amethystina)

Common names ↬ meadow squill
Height ↬ 15–25 cm
Blooming season ↬ Late spring or early summer
Hardiness ↬ Zones 4–8

This tiny squill is still commonly listed by its former names. It flowers somewhat later than the other early-flowering scillas. **Flowers** ↬ Each bulb produces up to 6 leaves and racemes of 15 to 30 deep lavender-blue, star-shaped blooms. **Requirements** ↬ This species prefers well-drained, moist soil in full sun or light shade. It prefers to be left to grow undisturbed once it has been planted. Plant in large drifts under trees or among shrubs in woodland gardens; allow the bulbs to naturalize.

Scilla litardierei

Scilla mischtschenkoana

Scilla mischtschenkoana
(S. tubergeniana, S. mischtschenkoana 'Tubergeniana')

Common name ✄ milk squill
Height ✄ 10–15 cm
Blooming season ✄ Early spring
Hardiness ✄ Zones 3–8 (Zone 2 with protection)

This is the only squill that has naturally white flowers, hence the common name. It is the first scilla to flower and has a longer flowering period than the others, and is one of the best for planting in semi-shady rock gardens. Each bulb produces racemes of 2 to 6, 2-cm blooms and up to 5 short, glossy, pale-green leaves. **Flowers** ✄ The flowers are pale blue to white, tinged with a darker-blue stripe on the outer side of each petal. The blooms are bell-shaped when they first open, eventually opening nearly flat in the full sun. The flowers open as soon as they emerge from the ground, often before the leaves. After the flowers open, the stems elongate and eventually grow 10–15 cm tall by the time flowering is complete. **Requirements** ✄ This species prefers a partially shady location, although it will tolerate full shade. It also tolerates drier soil conditions than other squills. This scilla is best left to grow and spread undisturbed until it forms a large clump.

Scilla peruviana

Common names ✄ Cuban lily, Peruvian jacinth
Height ✄ 15–25 cm
Blooming season ✄ Early summer
Hardiness ✄ Zones 7–10

This is the best scilla for warmer, southern areas. It is a very showy, tender species. Each plant produces up to 15 thick, broad, fleshy, sword-shaped green leaves. **Flowers** ✄ It forms large, fairly dense, conical 8-cm clusters of 50 to 100 star-shaped, lavender-blue flowers. It typically blooms in June. **Requirements** ✄ Unlike some of the earlier-flowering scillas, this species will not tolerate shade or cool temperatures. It needs a warm, sunny, preferably sheltered position; plant the bulbs close to the surface. *S. peruviana* is good for indoor forcing.

Scilla peruviana

Scilla siberica *(S. sibirica)*

Common names ᜪ Siberian squill,
spring squill
Height ᜪ 5–10 cm
Blooming season ᜪ Early spring
Hardiness ᜪ Zones 1–8

This is the most widely known and
available of all the squills; native to Si-
beria, it is exceptionally hardy. **Flowers** ᜪ This squill has beautiful, bright
true-blue flowers. **Requirements** ᜪ
Siberian squills grow best in rich, sandy soil, although they will tolerate a
fairly wide range of soil conditions as
long as the soil is well drained. These
squills prefer partial shade but grow in
full sun; the only locations they will
not tolerate are hot, dry spots.

Siberian squills are most effective
planted in informal patches or clusters
in woodland settings or among shrubs.
The plants may reach 15 cm and are
superb naturalizers. Each bulb produces three to four flowering stems with
three to five nodding, bell-shaped
flowers on each. These squills flower
at the same time as chionodoxas, and
look great combined with them in
the garden. Siberian squills are a great
choice for planting in mixed borders,
rock gardens and under trees and
shrubs in woodland gardens.

ᜪ ***S. siberica alba*** • White-flowering
form; grows to 10–12 cm. This form
is rare.

ᜪ ***S. siberica* var. *taurica*** • Light-blue
flowers

ᜪ **'Spring Beauty'** • A robust
cultivar that produces large flowers
on sturdy stems. Flowers are a
beautiful bright, brilliant porcelain-
blue, the deepest blue form of this
species. One of the best, most popular
cultivars, well worth planting.
Also listed as *S. atrocaerulea.*

Scilla siberica

Bluebells

You may know these lovely little plants as members of genus *Scilla*, but bluebells have recently been classified in their own genus, *Hyacinthoides* (which means hyacinth-like). Bluebells bloom around the same time as late-flowering tulips and prefer partial shade or dappled sun. They're perfect for the east side of a house, a woodland garden or a mass planting under deciduous trees and shrubs. They also look great in shadier areas of rock gardens or borders, used in mixed perennial beds or tucked in among groundcovers. Start with 25 bulbs; within a few seasons you'll have a broad carpet of sweet-scented flowers. For the most dramatic show, plant a drift in a single colour rather than a mix.

Plant bluebells 5 cm deep, 7 to 10 cm apart, in rich, well-drained soil. The plants produce numerous offsets, so if you don't want to divide a clump, space them generously—up to 15 cm apart. Bluebells cannot tolerate hot, dry conditions, so plant in partial shade. Once you transplant the bulbs, leave them undisturbed except to divide or revitalize the clumps. After flowering has finished, remove the flowerheads unless you want the plants to self-seed. Bluebell foliage must be allowed to die back on its own. It is heavy and coarse, and can look a little messy as it dies down; companion perennials like ferns and hostas hide it well. Provide consistent moisture until the foliage dies. Bluebells self-seed readily—some might say aggressively—and may quickly overgrow an area. When the clump becomes overgrown, bluebells produce fewer, smaller blooms and smaller, weaker leaves. Simply dig up the bulbs when the foliage has almost died down. Respace and replant the healthy bulbs.

Hyacinthoides hispanica 'Excelsior', 'Rosabella' and 'Alba'

Hyacinthoides hispanica *(H. campanulata, Endymion hispanicus, Scilla campanulata, S. hispanica)*

Common names ✍ Spanish bluebell, wood hyacinth
Height ✍ 25–40 cm
Blooming season ✍ Mid to late spring
Hardiness ✍ Zones 3–8

Sturdy, showy Spanish bluebells are good for borders, mixed perennial flowerbeds and rock gardens. Try them behind shorter, earlier spring-flowering bulbs. **Flowers** ✍ *H. hispanica* produces 6 to 15 bell-shaped flowers on long, sturdy stalks. They typically bloom in May and early June. They make lovely cutflowers that last up to a week in a vase. Spanish bluebells are scentless. **Requirements** ✍ These bulbs grow best in nutrient-rich soils with a good supply of moisture and good drainage, though they will tolerate almost every type of soil, provided it is well drained. They grow and multiply easily, thriving in shadier gardens. This species and its cultivars are often sold as a mix in garden centres.

✍ **'Excelsior'** • Bright violet-blue flowers striped with pale blue

✍ **'Bluebird'** • Dark-blue flowers

✍ **'Rosabella'** • Soft-pink flowers

✍ **'Alba'** • White flowers

Hyacinthoides non-scripta *(Endymion non-scriptus, Scilla non-scripta, S. nutans)*

Common names ✍ English bluebell, common bluebell, harebell, wild hyacinth
Height ✍ 20–30 cm
Blooming season ✍ Mid spring
Hardiness ✍ Zones 5–7

The traditional bluebell, these bulbs are excellent in woodland gardens. They also grow well under trees and deciduous shrubs and in mixed borders. They differ from Spanish bluebells in that the plants are slenderer, the raceme is one-sided and the flowering stems have a nodding tip. They are also slightly shorter and bloom earlier in the spring. They are also not as hardy or as adaptable. **Flowers** ✍ The lightly fragrant flowers grow on one side of the stem, 6 to 12 blossoms per stem. Individual blooms are very narrowly bell-shaped, and the petals curl back. **Requirements** ✍ *H. non-scripta* prefers a cooler, shady setting in well-drained woodland soil.

✍ **'Alba'** • White-flowered cultivar that produces up to twelve icy-white, fragrant, bell-shaped blooms on each stem

✍ **'Rosea'** • Pink-flowered cultivar

Tulips

If you were to ask someone to give an example of a bulb, chances are the answer would be the tulip. Tulips are readily identifiable and are very easy to grow, hardy and reliable. When you first plant a new tulip bulb in the garden, it already contains a flower, and the larger the bulb, the larger that flower will be.

The popularity of tulips today is undeniable. The Netherlands produces the majority of the world's flower bulbs, approximately nine billion per year; of these, almost a third are tulips. Worldwide, nearly 10,000 hectares are devoted to the commercial production of tulips, more than any other bulb.

Hybrid tulips are some of the most versatile bulbs available. They come in an incredible range of flower colours, bloom shapes, plant heights and growth habits, and need only sun to bring them to fruition. Hybrids are perfect in mass plantings, mixed beds and features. They also make exquisite spring cutflowers.

Species tulips are a bit more particular in their needs, and the more closely you can provide these conditions, the better they will do. They prefer well-drained, lean, gravelly soils that dry out rapidly after rains and bake in the summer sun. This makes them a great choice for rock and alpine gardens.

Whether you prefer the large, glorious flowers of the hybrids or the tough, subtle habits of the species, tulips deserve a place in your garden. The information in the following pages will help you choose the varieties that are best for you.

Type
True bulb

Planting season
Fall

Blooming season
Spring

Hardiness
Zones 3–8

How many
*At least 5 bulbs
of a single variety*

Golden Rules

- Never plant a single
  bulb by itself—plant
  tulips in groups
- Plant in well-drained
  soil
- Provide a full-sun
  location

Hybrid Tulips

Tulipa spp.

Tulips are the world's most popular bulbs, and this fascination has held for centuries. During the early 1600s, Holland was gripped by Tulipmania. People paid thousands of dollars for a single tulip bulb, hoping it would produce a mutant, a new colour or new form. The peak of this mania lasted from 1634 to 1637. Then the bubble burst. Prices fell suddenly, and many tulip speculators were ruined. The irony is that Tulipmania was caused in large part by a virus. The virus, spread by aphids, travels into the bulb, infecting the embryonic flower. It partly suppresses anthocyanin, the plant's colouring material, resulting in the unusual and bizarre transformation of single-coloured tulips to so-called broken-coloured flowers. No other flower is so beautiful when it's infected by disease, and no other flower has had such economic power.

Hybrid tulips remain popular today both in the garden and as cutflowers. And some of our present-day tulips are nearly identical to varieties first identified hundreds of years ago, a testament to the staying power of these gorgeous flowers.

Single late tulip 'Esther'

The word *tulip is derived from the Turkish word* tulbend, *meaning turban. The name is believed to reflect the shape and colour range of the original flowers.*

Order of Tulip Flowering, by Division, Earliest to Latest

a. greigii
b. kaufmanniana
c. fosteriana
d. single early
e. double early
f. triumph
g. Darwin hybrid
h. single late
i. double late
j. lily-flowered
k. fringed
l. parrot
m. viridiflora
n. Rembrandt

Microclimates play an important role in bloom time. Tulips planted in warm, sheltered spots will bloom earlier than the same tulips planted in cooler, exposed locations.

PLANTING

- Plant early in the fall. The bulbs need at least 3 weeks of daytime temperatures above 10°C to ensure proper root development.
- Full sun. In Zones 7 and 8, plant in light shade: tulips do not tolerate extremely hot sun well.
- Well-drained soil. Tulips prefer a slightly alkaline soil, but tolerate any soil type as long as it is well drained. If you are planting tulips as perennials, choose a spot where the soil is warm and dry through the summer.
- Apply bulb fertilizer when you plant the bulbs.
- Plant 15–20 cm deep if you want to treat tulips as perennials. If you intend to replant annually, plant 8–10 cm deep (to make the bulbs easier to dig up).
- Spacing varies by variety and aesthetic preference. Space tulips one to three times the height of the bulb apart.

Did you know it normally takes 15 to 25 years to bring a new tulip variety to market? It's because there are no shortcuts to breeding tulips—they grow and reproduce at nature's pace. Breeding takes years of trial and error as the hyridizer tests different crosses. Once the desired variety has been developed, many more years are required to build up enough stock to release the bulb commercially. Each new variety introduced is celebrated with great ceremony and, in keeping with tradition, champagne is poured over the flower as a way of baptizing the variety. This ritual goes back more than 400 years.

Triumph tulip 'Striped Bellona'

Single early tulip 'Duc Van Tol'

GROWING

- The bulb you plant in the fall dies after it has produced its flower. During the growing season, the bulb is replaced by several more bulbs, called daughter bulbs or offsets, that develop between the scales of the original. The two largest daughter bulbs are normally big enough to produce flowers the following spring; the others usually require another season's growth. With proper care and growing conditions, this pattern may continue for several years, until the clump becomes overcrowded and requires division. That said, tulips bloom best in their first year, so for the biggest burst of colour, replant annually.

- Deadhead tulips you want to rebloom the following year. Tulips use up to 30 percent of their energy producing seeds.

- After blooming, water foliage once a week if the soil is dry.
- Apply bulb booster or a feeding of liquid all-purpose fertilizer after flowering.
- Always allow the foliage to die back naturally. The leaves produce nutrients necessary for future growth and flower production. When the foliage turns brown, it indicates the nutrients have been stored in the bulb. Only then is it OK to remove the foliage. It should come away easily with a light tug.
- Tulips are planted deep in the soil relative to many other bulbs. You can plant smaller bulbs or bedding plants over tulips without disturbing the bulbs.

According to legend, when a young Persian man heard his beloved wife was dead, he mounted his horse and galloped off a cliff, killing himself. As the blood seeped out from his many wounds, bright-red tulips sprung up from the ground around him. For this reason, red tulips, not red roses, represent true love in the language of flowers.

With proper care, most hybrid tulips will rebloom fairly reliably for three to five years

*Multi-flowering
tulip 'Georgette'*

*Kaufmanniana tulip
'Heart's Delight'*

Single late tulip 'Blushing Beauty'

Tips

- If you live in a zone where spring temperatures rise quickly, plant earlier-flowering tulip varieties: their blooms will last longer when the weather is cool. The cooler the weather, the longer tulip flowers will last.

- In areas with cool, wet summers, lift tulips after the foliage has died and replant the stored bulbs in the fall. Lift the bulbs when you can wind the dry foliage and stem around your finger without snapping it. If you lift the bulbs too soon, they will not have enough energy stored to produce flowers the following season.

- Grow tulips for cutflowers in a very sunny location. A vegetable garden works well because it doesn't matter that the sometimes-unsightly tulip foliage is left to die there. It's easy to tuck a row or two into the vegetable garden since tulips require little attention. Remember that cutflower tulips are harvested with their foliage, so treat these as annual plantings.

*Over the years 4000 to
5000 varieties of tulips
have been developed.
Only about 500 remain
in commercial production
today.*

- Tulips with multiple flowers or very large blooms do not last as long because the blooms get too heavy for the stem. The shorter the stem and the lighter the blooms, the longer the flowers will last.

- If your tulips are getting smaller and sparser, something may be eating them underground or the daughter bulbs may not be growing to flowering size. Dig up the bulbs after the foliage has died, select the largest offsets and store them in a cool, dark location until fall. Some of the offsets may be too small to flower the following season and will need another year or two in the garden to grow large enough to produce flowers. In the meantime, replant the area with new, fresh bulbs.

- If rodents are a problem, plant the bulbs deeper (up to 18 cm deep) and place a screen or length of chicken wire over the planting area.

- In very warm climates (Zone 8 and warmer), tulips require chilling before planting. See the method on page 20. If you live in Zones 10 and 11, tulips won't do well in the garden: it's just too hot! (See page 300 for a list of tulips that grow in very warm climates.)

Lily-flowering tulip 'Aladdin'

It's easy to recognize when a bulb is too small: it has only enough energy to produce a single leaf and nothing else. Eventually, however, even these bulbs will produce blooms. Water and fertilize underachieving bulbs, and allow the foliage to die down and dry. In a couple of years, with proper care, small bulbs will grow large enough to produce flowers.

Parrot tulip 'Black Parrot'

Double early tulip 'Abba'

Each spring Herve Benoit's garden bursts into bloom with a variety of tulips

IN THE GARDEN

- Tulips are versatile flowers and can be well used in mass plantings, as accents in mixed beds, as feature plantings and in rock gardens.

- Always plant tulips in groups, never in rows. A mass of twenty tulips in the same area is much more impressive than a sprinkling of small groups of four or five throughout your yard. Plant them in formal patterns, or in irregular clusters in mixed flowerbeds.

- If you want to create formal garden designs, treat tulips like annuals. Dig up the bulbs and replace them every year. Imperfections are much easier to spot in formal plantings; if two or three tulips fail to return the next season, the effect is ruined.

- When using tulips as a focal point, mass plantings of a single vibrant colour make a great impact. However, if you want to mix varieties, choose varieties that flower together. If you mix early-flowering and late-flowering varieties, the impact is lost.

- Most hybrid tulips are not well suited to naturalizing—try species tulips (see pages 266–76) instead.

TRY THESE!

There are 15 classifications of tulip cultivars.

Division 1 •
Single early tulip

Traits ᔢ Large, single, egg-shaped flowers, most with pointed petals, produced on short stems
Height ᔢ 20–30 cm
Blooming season ᔢ Early spring
Hardiness ᔢ Zones 3–8

This relatively small group includes short, stocky varieties, many of which are fragrant. These tulips are suitable for mixed flowerbeds, borders and rock gardens; many cultivars are great for indoor forcing. They also make great cutflowers and can be grown in containers in areas with mild winters.

Single early tulip 'Christmas Dream'

Division 2 •
Double early tulip

Traits ᔢ Double flowers with pointed petals, produced on short, sturdy stems
Height ᔢ 20–30 cm
Blooming season ᔢ Early spring
Hardiness ᔢ Zones 3–8

Do not confuse double early tulips with double late tulips. Double late tulips flower in the late spring and their petals tend to have rounded tips. Double early tulips are generally a bit

Double early tulip 'Peach Blossom'

shorter and have tight double blooms; the flowers are wider than they are high and bloom in early spring. Most of today's double early varieties derive from the nineteenth-century variety 'Murillo' and its sports. As a result, the tulips in this group are among the most homogeneous in height and bloom time. Because they are short and sturdy, these varieties stand up to wind well. Try them in mixed flowerbeds, borders and rock garden. They also make great cutflowers and are suitable for indoor forcing.

Division 3 • Triumph tulip

Traits ᔢ Single flowers on medium stems
Height ᔢ 25–40 cm
Blooming season ᔢ Mid spring
Hardiness ᔢ Zones 3–8

This division, the most important group of tulips today, was created by hybrid crosses of cultivars from the single early and Darwin divisions. The result is tulips with strong, sturdy stems bearing large flowers with a gorgeous traditional shape in a wide range of colours. These varieties are also extremely tolerant of poor weather. They're terrific in mixed flowerbeds, borders and mass plantings. They make outstanding cutflowers; many cultivars are also suitable for indoor forcing.

Tulip Divisions

Division 1
Single Early

Division 2
Double Early

Division 3
Triumph

Division 4
Darwin Hybrid

Division 5
Single Late

Division 6
Lily-flowered

Division 7
Fringed

Division 8
Viridiflora

Division 9
Rembrandt

Division 10
Parrot

Division 11
Double Late

Division 12
Kaufmanniana

Division 13
Fosteriana

Division 14
Gregeii

Division 15
Miscellaneous

Division 4 •
Darwin hybrid tulip

Traits ✺ Large, single flowers produced on long, strong sturdy stems
Height ✺ 30–50 cm
Blooming season ✺ Mid spring
Hardiness ✺ Zones 3–8

Darwin hybrids were developed by crossing cultivars from the Darwin and fosteriana tulips. When the first few crosses were made, the only flower colours available were oranges and reds. Today there are yellow and pink varieties, some with speckles and stripes on their petals, but the flowers colour range is still fairly limited. This group has large flowers with long stems, and flowers in the mid spring. It is the most popular group cultivated commercially for cutflowers and accounts for fifteen percent of the tulips grown in the Netherlands. These tulips grow quite tall, so plant them in a sheltered location.

Division 5 •
Single late tulip

Common names ✺ May-flowering tulip, cottage tulip, Darwin tulip, breeder tulip
Traits ✺ Single flowers produced on long stems
Height ✺ 70–80 cm
Blooming season ✺ Late spring
Hardiness ✺ Zones 3–8

'Cottage tulip' is an older classification applied to single late-flowering tulips said to have been found in traditional English gardens. Cottage and Darwin tulips have been so intercrossed that it became impossible to tell the two groups apart; they were eventually combined to form this group. (It is not unusual to see both types listed in books or catalogues.) These tulips look wonderful in mass plantings, mixed perennial beds and borders. They also make excellent cut flowers.

Darwin hybrid tulip 'Daydream'

Lily-flowered tulip 'Burgundy'

Division 6 •
Lily-flowered tulip

Traits ✍ Single flowers with pointed, outward-curving petals on medium to long stems
Height ✍ 35–75 cm
Blooming season ✍ Mid to late spring
Hardiness ✍ Zones 3–8

This group was originally included with the cottage tulips. It contains a limited number of cultivars but also includes some of the most elegant tulips, bearing slender flowers on long stems. The stems tend to be quite thin, which makes them susceptible to wind damage, so choose a sheltered location. These tulips work well in mass plantings, mixed flowerbeds and borders. They also make lovely, graceful cutflowers.

Division 7 • Fringed tulip

Traits ✍ Single flowers with fringed edges on medium to long stems
Height ✍ 35–75 cm
Blooming season ✍ Mid to late spring
Hardiness ✍ Zones 3–8

This is a relatively new category of tulips and many people are not familiar with them. The fringed tulips are actually mutants culled from the other divisions. Their only common characteristic is their delicately fringed petals; the individual heights and flowering times vary widely.

Fringed tulip
'Burgundy Lace'

Division 8 •
Viridiflora tulip

Common names ♒ green tulip
Traits ♒ Single flowers, shaped like
lily-flowered tulips; all have some
green on the petals; medium to long
stems
Height ♒ 35–75 cm
Blooming season ♒ Late spring
Hardiness ♒ Zones 3–8

This is probably the least significant
division, but the tulips in it have been
around since the 1600s. These unusual
tulips are closely related to the single
late tulips and share many characteristics. The important difference is the
green stripes or bands on the petals of
all viridiflora tulips. One of the great
advantages of viridiflora tulips is that
their flowers hold so long and so well,
at least three weeks—even longer in
areas with cooler springs. Use these
tulips in mixed flowerbeds, in borders
and as cutflowers.

Rembrandt tulips

Division 9 •
Rembrandt tulip

Traits ♒ Long-stemmed single flowers with broken patterns on the petals;
background colour is generally red,
white or yellow; markings are brown,
bronze, black, red or pink
Height ♒ 55–60 cm
Blooming season ♒ Late spring
Hardiness ♒ Zones 3–8

These tulips have been bred to
resemble the beautiful but virally infected tulips that caused Tulipmania in
the 1600s. The historical tulips were
banned when researchers discovered a
virus was causing the broken patterns
on the flowers. Present-day Rembrandts are pretty but are no longer
available in the beautiful shades of
brown, gold and purple of the original
Rembrandts. The petal markings may
be stripes, streaks or other indistinct
patterns. The tulips in this group are
not always available, but when they
are they tend to come as a mixture,
often as a historical collection. These
tulips look superb in feature plantings
and mixed flowerbeds. They also make
outstanding cutflowers.

Viridiflora tulip 'Spring Green'

Parrot tulip 'Estella Rijnveld'

Division 10 • *Parrot tulip*

Traits ✺ Single bicolour and tricolour flowers, one colour of which is always green; curled, rippled and twisted petals on short to medium stems
Height ✺ 35–50 cm
Blooming season ✺ Late spring
Hardiness ✺ Zones 3–8

The tulips in this division arose from sports, or mutations, of regular tulips, and the division includes some of the most exotic tulips. They are called parrot tulips because the budding flowers resemble a parrot's beak. The flower buds remain green for quite a while, to the point that a first-time grower may believe something is wrong. As the flower develops and opens, however, vibrant colours manifest themselves. The petals open wide, almost flat, revealing a black, star-shaped centre and large, bright-yellow stamens. Although the flower stems are thick and strong, the extra-large flowers will be damaged in windy, exposed locations, so plant these tulips in a sheltered area. This group is also more sensitive than other groups to prolonged cold, wet conditions in the spring, although a few cultivars flower in mid spring. These unusual flowers are best used in feature plantings or among other flowers so that they can be viewed at close range. Parrot tulips are available as cutflowers, but are underrated because they look unspectacular at the bud stage. But if you ever have the chance to purchase a bouquet of parrot tulips, do so and watch their amazing transformation before your eyes.

Division 11 •
Double late tulip

Common names ❧ peony-flowered tulip
Traits ❧ Large (10-cm) double flowers produced on long stems
Height ❧ 30–40 cm
Blooming season ❧ Late spring
Hardiness ❧ Zones 3–8

Double late tulips are often called peony-flowered tulips because the flowers resemble peony blossoms; the flowers are always large and double. These traits make them susceptible to damage by heavy rains and wind. Plant these tulips in a protected area of the garden where their gorgeous, long-lasting flowers can be easily viewed up close. If you live in a zone with very cold winters and late springs, these tulips are an excellent choice; they perform well in mixed flowerbeds, in borders and as cutflowers.

Division 12 •
Kaufmanniana tulip

Common names ❧ waterlily tulip
Traits ❧ Single, short-stemmed flowers with a multi-coloured base that open fully to resemble a star; foliage may be mottled, speckled or striped
Height ❧ 10–20 cm
Blooming season ❧ Very early spring
Hardiness ❧ Zones 3–8

This group includes cultivars, subspecies, varieties and hybrids that have characteristics of the species *Tulipa kaufmanniana*. It is one of three groups referred to as botanical tulips. These are the earliest-flowering hybrid tulips. Each bulb produces more than one flower stem. The exterior of the petals often has a rosy blush and an obvious yellow area at the base of each flower. On sunny days, the flowers open wide like stars; on cloudy days, they remain closed, showcasing different shapes and colours. This group naturalizes easily and is very hardy and weather resistant. These tulips are great in rock gardens, borders and low mixed flowerbeds. They can also be grown in containers in milder climates.

Kaufmanniana tulip 'Chopin'

Division 13 • Fosteriana tulip

Common names ᜫ emperor tulip
Traits ᜫ Large, elongated, single flowers produced on medium to long stems; foliage is very broad, may be mottled or striped
Height ᜫ 25–30 cm
Blooming season ᜫ Early spring
Hardiness ᜫ Zones 3–8

Another of the botanical tulip groups, this division includes cultivars, subspecies, varieties and hybrids of species *Tulipa fosteriana*. These tulips have large, slender flowers; they are the largest and tallest of the early-flowering tulips. Many varieties are red-flowered. These tulips are excellent in mass plantings, mixed flowerbeds, borders and rock gardens. They also naturalize, but less readily than the kaufmanniana group.

Fosteriana tulip 'Orange Emperor'

Division 14 • Greigii tulip

Traits ᜫ Single, short-stemmed flowers, mainly red, yellow and white, with variable forms; foliage is usually mottled, spotted or striped
Height ᜫ 20–30 cm
Blooming season ᜫ Early spring
Hardiness ᜫ Zones 3–8

These tulips include cultivars, subspecies, varieties and hybrids derivative of *Tulipa greigii* and currently represent the largest group of botanical tulips. Their most outstanding trait is their beautiful mottled or striped, ground-hugging foliage. The leaves spread out, arching toward the ground. The flowers of this group are very large relative to the final height of the plant; in full sun the blooms open wide to create a stunning display. This is one of the best groups for use in borders and rock gardens; it is also great for mass plantings and naturalizing. These tulips may be grown in containers in areas with milder climates.

Greigii tulip 'Cape Cod'

Division 15 • Miscellaneous

This division is not, in fact, a cultivar group, but a collection of all species, varieties and cultivars in which the wild species is evident, not belonging to any of the above-mentioned cultivar groups. These are treated separately as species tulips, beginning on page 266.

Tulipa praestans *'Fusilier'*

Tulipa praestans

Height ∿ 20–25 cm
Blooming season ∿ Early spring
Hardiness ∿ 3

Native to Central Asia, this species is perfect for mass plantings, mixed flowerbeds, naturalizing and container growing (in areas with mild winters). **Flowers** ∿ The plant produces a single, larger central flower with several smaller ones on the sides, all forming on a single short stem. These tulips flower easily and readily for three years with minimal care.

∿ **'Fusilier'** • Luminous vermilion-red flowers

∿ **'Unicum'** • Orange-red flowers; leaves have a yellow edge

∿ **'Van Tubergen's Variety'** • Vermilion-red blooms

∿ **'Zwanenburg Variety'** • Bright-red flowers

Multi-flowering tulips

Multi-flowered tulips (also called bouquet tulips) are a collection of cultivars that have in common their multi-flowering habit. When the stem emerges, it splits into several smaller stems, each producing a flower. The number of flowers produced is determined by the cultivar and the size of the bulb—it varies from three to seven blooms. Several cultivars belong to the single-late tulip division; the others belong to the *T. greigii* division. Some authorities list the multi-flowered varieties within their true divisions, with which they share a majority of their characteristics. We have singled them out to reflect common cataloguing practices.

Species Tulips

Tulipa spp.

Type
True bulb

Planting season
Fall

Blooming season
Spring

Hardiness
Zones 3–8

How many
*Start with 9 to 13
bulbs of a single
species*

Golden Rules

- Plant in full sun
- Provide excellent drainage
- Keep dry and hot during the summer

Species tulips are very different from their hybrid cousins. They are tough, hardy plants, native to the dry, mountainous areas of Europe and central Asia, and they don't like to be pampered. Give them a hot, dry location where the sun bakes the soil all summer long and, provided the spot is well drained, species tulips will thrive. They also prefer to be somewhat isolated in the garden: they don't like to have other plants' foliage smothering them, crowding them or covering the ground around them.

Species tulip bulbs are much smaller than hybrid bulbs, and the flowers are smaller and subtler; they also cost less than the hybrids. As it is in other areas of gardening, interest in wild bulb species is on the rise. Species tulips are a great choice for anyone who wants a more natural-looking, low-maintenance garden.

Tulipa tarda *is considered the single most important true botanical species*

Planting

- Full sun. A location that is hot and dry during the summer is best.

- Well-drained, lean, gravelly soil. Species tulips require excellent drainage. Incorporate some kind of drainage material, such as coarse sand or gravel, into the soil when you plant. Prepare an area several centimetres wider and deeper than the bulb hole itself to prevent water from accumulating near the roots. If possible, plant on a gentle slope or in a raised bed to maximize drainage.

- Plant deep. Plant the bulbs to at least 12–20 cm to ensure the foliage does not develop before winter. In milder climates, plant species tulips late in the fall to prevent premature emergence.

- Space 5–15 cm apart (see chart, page 268). Tulips recommended for close planting have a thinner, more upright growth habit, while species recommended for wider spacing have a spreading growth habit and are multi-flowered.

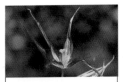

Species tulip spacing

5 cm apart
T. acuminata
T. batalinii
T. turkestanica
T. urumiensis
T. kolpakowskiana
T. linifolia
T. saxatilis
T. sylvestris

8 cm apart
T. bakeri
T. clusiana
T. clusiana
    var. chrysantha
T. eichleri

10 cm apart
T. pulchella

12–15 cm apart
T. tarda

*You may have seen
'Little Beauty' listed
among the species
tulips in a catalogue.
This species is, in fact,
Tulipa 'Little Beauty,'
a cultivar resulting from
crossing T. hageri and
T. aucheriana. It is
a beautiful plant with
fragrant reddish-pink
flowers and dark-blue
centres surrounded by a
pink ring. The flowers
grow 10–15 cm tall
and bloom in the early
spring.*

Tulipa *'Violet Queen'*

GROWING

• Do not water species tulips during the spring unless the weather is exceptionally dry. They will get the moisture they need from rainfall. Water regularly in the early fall to promote good root development.

• You must allow the foliage of species tulips to die back on its own if you want the bulbs to bloom the following season.

• Most tulip varieties won't produce seed capsules or even set seed in a home garden, but a few do. *Tulipa tarda* has particularly attractive seed pods. Remove the flower heads of species that produce seed so the plant's energy is directed to producing daughter bulbs.

• Species tulips prefer lean soils and do not require supplementary fertilizer.

TIPS

• Try to locate species tulips in areas of the garden where they will not receive water from artificial sources such as sprinklers or automatic watering systems. Avoid planting in low areas where water may pool.

IN THE GARDEN

Species tulips are rugged-looking plants best suited to rock gardens and alpine collections. They naturalize well, either by self-sowing or by producing stolons (runners), extending 30 cm or more, at the end of which new daughter bulbs form.

- *Tulipa clusiana* var. *chrysantha* competes well with dense vegetation. This feature, combined with its tall, thin, elegant growth habit, makes it an excellent choice for planting among ornamental grasses.
- *Tulipa acuminata* looks stunning planted in a mixed perennial flowerbed.
- Try *Tulipa bakeri* mixed with 'Tête-à-Tête' or 'Hawera' miniature daffodils.
- For something different and really pretty, try mixing *Tulipa tarda* with the taller *T. turkestanica*.
- Species tulips are not well suited to planting in lawns because they don't compete well with the grass. The soil beneath the turf tends to be cool and often wet. Species crocuses are a much better choice for planting in grassy areas.

The Big Issue

The taxonomy of species tulips is challenging. Although we have grouped the species under a single name, you may find other taxonomy and naming conventions. The following list provides the rationales for our category decisions and explains other potential naming.

- *T. bakeri* and *T. saxatilis* are often confused. *T. bakeri* has a slightly more compact growth habit and slightly smaller flowers. *T. bakeri* is most commonly listed as cultivar *T. bakeri* 'Lilac Wonder'.

- *T. batalini* is closely related to *T. linifolia*—the major difference is flower colour. Some authorities consider *T. batalini* to be a cultivar of *T. linifolia*.

- *T. clusiana* var. *chrysantha* is a highly variable species. Authorities disagree about its synonyms; many are listed as separate species. Similarly, some authorities consider *T. eichleri* to be a variety of *T. undulatifolia*; we have listed *T. undulatifolia* as a synonym.

- The International Register of Tulip Names lists *T. pulchella* as a cultivar of *T. humilis*, so we have followed this practice; the variety is more often sold as *T. pulchella*. *T. humilis* is a highly variable species, and there is wide disagreement about how certain synonyms should be listed. The distinctions between species are unclear, so we have listed this large, popular group under a single heading.

- *T. australis* is sometimes listed separate from *T. sylvestris*, but the main distinction between the two is their natural distribution; hence, we have listed them together. And although we have listed *T. dasystemon* as a synonym of *T. tarda*, *T. dasystemon* is a separate species that produces fewer leaves and a solitary, pure-yellow flower. It is rarely cultivated, however, and for many years *T. tarda* was sold as *T. dasystemon*. Today, the listing *T. dasystemon tarda* indicates that the variety is *T. tarda*.

- *T. biflora* is similar to its synonym *T. turkestanica*, but is larger, flowers later and produces more flowers. *T. biflora* also smells sweet, whereas *T. turkestanica* has an unpleasant odour. Many authorities consider *T. polychroma* to be a variant form of *T. turkestanica*.

TRY THESE!

Although there are well more than 100 known species of wild tulips, we have touched on the most significant ones.

Tulipa acuminata
(T. cornuta, T. stenopetala)

Common names ✧ horned tulip
Height ✧ 40–50 cm
Blooming season ✧ Mid spring
Hardiness ✧ 4

This is a tulip for people who like something really different. It's not really showy enough for large bedding displays, but it looks great against foliage plants, which highlight the curious, twisted flowers. It is too tall for use in rock gardens, but it's stunning planted in a mixed perennial flowerbed. This tulip naturalizes easily. **Flowers** ✧ The 8- to 13-cm flowers have unusual, narrow, twisted red-and-yellow petals with a greenish blush on the outer side. This species is native to Turkey and is one of the parents of the lily-flowered hybrid tulips.

Tulipa acuminata

Tulipa bakeri

Height ✧ 15–20 cm
Blooming season ✧ Mid spring
Hardiness ✧ Zone 3

T. bakeri is great for mixed flowerbeds, rock gardens and naturalizing. It is native to Crete. **Flowers** ✧ This species produces large, soft-purple flowers. **Requirements** ✧ *T. bakeri* is very stoloniferous—that is, it produces numerous underground stems, which is the reason it spreads so quickly and easily.

✧ *T. bakeri* **'Lilac Wonder'** • Delicately fragrant lilac flowers with yellow centres ringed with white

Tulipa bakeri *'Lilac Wonder'*

Tulipa batalinii *'Bright Gem'*

Tulipa batalinii

Height ᠉ 10–15 cm
Blooming season ᠉ Early spring
Hardiness ᠉ Zone 3

This is a popular, widely known species tulip. It is sometimes grouped
with *T. linifolia*. Native to Central Asia,
this species is great in mixed flowerbeds, rock gardens or natural plantings. **Flowers** ᠉ It features fragrant,
clear-yellow petals with brown or
golden-yellow centres and grey-green
leaves with wavy margins. There are
currently six varieties of *batalinii* tulips
in cultivation, but only 'Bright Gem'
is produced in sufficient quantities to
be available commercially. The others
are sometimes found in mail-order
catalogues.

᠉ **'Apricot Jewel'** • Golden-yellow
flowers with orange-red outer petals

᠉ **'Bright Gem'** • Fragrant, sulphur-
yellow flowers with orange tones on
petals

᠉ **'Bronze Charm'** • Fragrant,
creamy-yellow, bronze-feathered
flowers

᠉ **Regell 'Red Gem'** • Bright
scarlet-red flowers with a black base,
pale-yellow veins and vermilion-pink
outer petals

᠉ **Regell 'Yellow Jewel'** • Yellow
flowers tinged rose with a greenish-
yellow base

Tulip clusiana var. chrysantha
*(T. chrysantha, T. clusiana var.
stellata, T. stellata chrysantha, T.
aitchisonii, T. aitchisonii casmeriana,
T. chitralensis, T. clusiana)*

Common names ᠉ lady tulip,
candlestick tulip, peppermint stick
Height ᠉ 30–35 cm
Blooming season ᠉ Mid spring
Hardiness ᠉ 3

These bulbs are lovely in mixed flowerbeds, rock gardens and naturalized
plantings. The bulbs are native to Iran,
Afghanistan and the Kashmir region.
Flowers ᠉ The tapered flowers vary
in appearance, depending on whether
they are open or closed. When closed,
the pointed petals are crimson with
a narrow yellow edge; when open,
they resemble golden stars on long,
slim stems with slender blue-grey
leaves. This species produces numerous
underground stolons and naturalizes
easily.

᠉ **var. stellata** • Outer petals very
pale pink; the flowers lack dark blotch
at the base

Tulip clusiana *var.* chrysantha

Tulipa eichleri

᠅ **'aitchisonii'** • Brilliant-red flower opening to a flat star; small purplish-black basal blotch on each flower. Short species—average height 12–15 cm.

᠅ **'chrysantha (stellata)'** • Small yellow or red flowers with narrow, bluish-green foliage

᠅ **'cluisiana'** • Very old cultivar. Broad flowers shaded red with pinkish-white vertical stripes on the petals; flowers form an elegant star when fully open.

᠅ **'Cynthia'** • Larger flowers than 'chrysantha (stellata)'; ruby-red petals with a narrow greenish-yellow edge, opening to a light-yellow star. Shorter cultivar—average height 15–20 cm.

᠅ **'Lady Jane'** • Robust variety. Outer petals are soft red with narrow white edge; when closed, flowers resemble the stripes on a candy stick.

Tulipa eichleri *(T. undulatifolia, T. boeotica, T. scardica)*

Height ᠅ 25–30 cm
Blooming season ᠅ Early spring
Hardiness ᠅ Zone 4

This tulip increases rapidly by offsets and was considered a weed in the cultivated fields of Eastern Europe, Turkey, Iran and Central Asia, its native range. It suits mixed flowerbeds and rock gardens; it is excellent for naturalizing. **Flowers** ᠅ This species produces shiny scarlet flowers with a hint of yellow near the base of the petals; the flower centre is black, surrounded by a distinct yellow ring.

Tulipa humilis *(T. pulchella, T. aucheriana, T. violaceae)*

Common names ᔣ red crocus tulip
Height ᔣ 10–15 cm
Blooming season ᔣ Early spring
Hardiness ᔣ Zone 3

This group of tulips has one of the largest number of cultivars of any species. It is also one of the lowest-growing tulips, which makes it a superb choice for rock and alpine gardens. The common name derives from the fact that the flower resembles a crocus. This species grows wild in the Middle East. **Flowers** ᔣ It produces fragrant, long-lasting, pink to rosy-purple or magenta flowers with bluish-black, olive-green or yellow centres, often with white or yellow margins. **Requirements** ᔣ This is a reliable, easy-to-grow group, but unlike most species tulips the bulbs need moisture in the spring or the flower buds do not develop.

ᔣ *'albocaerulea-occulata'* • Very pale-mauve flowers with a deep steel-blue base; tends to flower earlier than the species

ᔣ *'aucheriana'* • Fragrant, bright-pink flowers with a yellow central blotch and pointed petals; one of the later-flowering cultivars; not widely available

ᔣ *'pulchella'* **(actually** *humilis* **'Pulchella')** • Pale-purple flowers with a navy basal blotch edged in white; height to 10 cm

ᔣ *'pulchella* **var.** *violaceae'* • One of the most widely available cultivars; bright purple-violet flowers with yellow centres; blooms very early

ᔣ *'violaceae'* **(actually** *humilis* **'Violacea')** • Similar to *pulchella* but flowers are purplish-rose with a yellow base margined with indigo or greenish-black; height 10 cm

ᔣ **'Eastern Star'** • Magenta-rose flowers with bronze-green flames and a yellow base

ᔣ **'Magenta Queen'** • Lilac flowers with yellow centres whose outside petals are flamed green

ᔣ **'Obalisque'** • Light-purple flowers with rosy-red outer petals and a yellow base

ᔣ **'Persian Pearl'** • Bright cyclamen-purple flowers with carmine-red outer petals, purple interior and soft-yellow base

ᔣ **'Violet Queen'** • Rich violet-red flowers

Tulipa pulchella var. violaceae

Tulipa linifolia

Tulipa kolpakowskiana

Height ✣ 15–20 cm
Blooming season ✣ Mid spring
Hardiness ✣ Zone 4

Another easy-to-grow species, perfect for mixed flowerbeds, rock gardens and naturalizing applications. When the buds of this species first emerge, they nod forward, straightening as the flowers open. This is also another variable species, so don't be surprised if the flowers differ slightly from each other. This tulip is native to Afghanistan and Central Asia. **Flowers** ✣ This fragrant, multi-flowered species produces several stems, each with a single small yellow flower. Each flower has a red spot at the base surrounded by a green blush; the leaves are wavy-edged and lie nearly flat against the ground.

Tulipa linifolia
(T. maximowiczii)

Height ✣ 10–15 cm
Blooming season ✣ Mid spring
Hardiness ✣ Zone 3

One of the best overall performers in colder climates, this tulip is native to Iran, Afghanistan and Uzbekistan. It is good in low mixed flowerbeds, rock gardens or naturalized settings. **Flowers** ✣ The plant forms fluorescent-red flowers with pointed petals, blackish purple centres, often with a yellow edge, and narrow grey-green leaves with wavy margins, occasionally edged in deep red or pink. Each flower only lasts a few days, but established clumps produce new blooms for almost a month, making this one of the longest-blooming species tulips.

✣ **'maximowiczii'** • Red flowers with black centres bordered with cream; tends to be a slightly shorter variety

Tulipa saxatilis

Common names ✣ candia tulip
Height ✣ 30–40 cm
Blooming season ✣ Early spring
Hardiness ✣ Zone 4 (may require protection)

One of the best performers in milder climates, this tulip is great in mixed flowerbeds, rock gardens and naturalized settings. It is native to Crete. **Flowers** ✣ It produces lightly scented, soft lilac–pink flowers with clearly defined yellow centres edged with white and covering almost one–third of the petal area; the blotch is visible from the outside of the flower. It has glossy bright-green leaves. **Requirements** ✣ This species is particularly sensitive to poor drainage, so be sure to provide a well-drained location. It must bake in the summer months to initiate embryonic flower buds, which produce next season's flowers. This is another stoloniferous tulip. It produces numerous stolons, extending 30 cm or more; new daughter bulbs form at the ends of the stolons.

Tulipa sylvestris
(T. celsiana, T. australis)

Common names ❧ Florentine tulip
Height ❧ 45 cm
Blooming season ❧ Late spring
Hardiness ❧ Zone 5

This multi-flowering tulip (3–7 blooms) is terrific for mixed flower-beds and naturalized gardens. **Flowers** ❧ It produces musk-scented, lemon-yellow flowers whose outer petals are feathered with green tones. **Requirements** ❧ *T. sylvestris* is unique among the species tulips because it actually prefers light shade. It is one of the taller species tulips. Its stems are

Tulipa saxatilis

brown, which is unusual but contrasts beautifully with the yellow flowers and narrow greyish-green leaves. This species tolerates more moisture and shadier conditions than most of the species tulips. It spreads by stolons.

Tulipa tarda *(T. dasystemon,*
T. dasystemon tarda)

Height ❧ 12–15 cm
Blooming season ❧ Mid spring
Hardiness ❧ Zone 3

If you are going to try only one species tulip, this should be it! Even the seed pods are extremely attractive. *T. tarda* is one of the most reliable species, persisting for years in the garden with little care. This species is very hardy and wind resistant, and it multiplies readily because it is stoloniferous. It will grow virtually anywhere, including banks and bare spots. It is also one of the few tulips that will tolerate partial shade. **Flowers** ❧ *T. tarda* produces fragrant,

Tulipa sylvestris

bright-yellow, six-petalled flowers with white tips, which open flat to resemble stars, with spreading, strap-like, bluish-green leaves. Each stem produces five or six flowers. This species is excellent in low mixed flowerbeds, rock gardens and naturalized gardens. It is native to Central Asia.

Tulipa turkestanica
(T. biflora, T. polychroma)

Height ✿ 20–25 cm
Blooming season ✿ Early spring
Hardiness ✿ Zone 4

Tulipa turkestanica is native to Central Asia through northwestern China. It's great in mixed flowerbeds and rock gardens, and naturalizes well. **Flowers** ✿ The long, arching stems produce two to five (usually three) white flowers with pointed petals and an orange basal blotch that covers about a third of each petal. The flowers have a horrible smell. The linear leaves are greyish green. **Requirements** ✿ This species is one of the best choices if you want to try to force species tulips indoors.

Tulipa turkestanica

Tulipa urumiensis

Height ✿ 7–10 cm
Blooming season ✿ Late spring
Hardiness ✿ Zone 3

Native to Iran, this species resembles a perfect miniature tulip. It is a very pretty variety but not widely available. If you do find the bulbs, they will make a worthwhile addition to the garden. **Flowers** ✿ *T. urumiensis* produces one or two fragrant, pure-yellow flowers on each stem. **Requirements** ✿ The plant is extremely low growing and not very vigorous, so plant it in a spot with little competition and lots of sun. This species is best for rock gardens. It naturalizes well but slowly.

Tulipa urumiensis

For the Adventurous

This section includes several dozen excellent bulbs you may want to try. Many of these bulbs are well known and readily available; some are harder to find, require special care or are strictly for indoor use. All will lend great colour, texture, fragrance or interest to the garden or home. Because common names vary widely, these bulbs are listed in alphabetical order of their Latin names. Where appropriate we have listed specific cultivars.

If you would like to try something a little different, we encourage you to experiment and learn more about the following bulbs.

Hardiness Guide

Cool	Zones 1–4
Temperate	Zones 4–7
Warm	Zones 7–9
Subtropical	Will not overwinter in areas cooler than Zone 10

Sample Entry

common name

(other common names)

Latin name (other Latin names)

Height Average plant height in centimeters or meters

Seasons *Planting* time; *Bloom* time

Planting *Depth* to the base of the bulb; *Spacing* between bulbs; *Soil* requirements

Hardiness General zone categories (see chart at left)

Light Includes locations

Description including bulb type, flowers, foliage and uses.

ゝ Significant cultivars or species • flower colour

orchid pansy

(mother's tears, widow's tears, hot water plant)

Achmines spp.

Height 30 cm

Seasons Plant in early spring; blooms late spring through early fall

Planting 2 cm deep; 6 bulbs per 15 cm pot; top-quality potting soil

Hardiness Subtropical

Light Partial to full, warm shade outdoors; bright indirect light indoors

Rhizome. Masses of short, trumpet-shaped, 5–8-cm flowers in white, lilac, purple, blue, peach, pink, orange or yellow. Leaves are dark green and velvet-like. Use in containers or as indoor plant.

African lily

(lily of the Nile)

Agapanthus spp.

Height Up to 100 cm

Seasons Plant in spring; blooms in summer

Planting Depth just to cover rhizome; space 20 cm; well-drained, moisture-retentive fertile soil

Hardiness Warm

Light Full sun

Rhizome. Blue or white, 5-cm trumpet-shaped flowers borne in loose clusters on long, leafless stems. Strap-like basal leaves. Use in borders and containers.

Agapanthus *sp.*

belladonna lily

Amaryllis belladonna

Height 60–90 cm

Seasons Plant in spring; blooms late summer

Planting Depth so neck of bulb is just above soil surface; space 20 cm; well-drained, sandy soil, rich in organic matter

Hardiness Warm

Light Full sun

True bulb. Clusters of 6 to 12 fragrant, rose-pink, lily-like flowers on tall, thick stalks that appear after foliage has died down. Strap-like leaves produced in spring, die down in early summer. Use in flowerbeds or mixed borders with southern exposures, and as cutflowers.

lords and ladies

(cuckoo plant)

Arum italicum

Height 25–30 cm

Seasons Plant in spring; blooms mid spring

Planting Depth 10–15 cm (roots develop from the tops of tubers); space 20–30 cm; well-drained, moist, deeply prepared, humus-rich soil.

Hardiness Warm

Light Sun in a sheltered location

Tuberous root. Leaves are large, arrow-shaped, wavy-edged, glossy dark green with silvery veins. Foliage appears in fall and lasts until spring. Use in borders, rockeries and woodland gardens.

baboon flower

Babiana stricta

Height 30 cm

Seasons Plant in spring; blooms in summer

Planting 5 cm deep; space 5 cm; well-drained soil, rich in organic matter

Hardiness Warm

Light Afternoon sun

Corm. Star-shaped purple, blue or mauve flowers arranged in clusters, spiralling up the stem. Leaves hairy and ribbon-like. Use in sheltered location for borders and as indoor plants.

Belladonna lily

hardy orchid

(Chinese ground orchid)

Bletilla striata

Height 30 cm

Seasons Plant in spring; blooms in late spring or early summer

Planting 3 cm deep; space 10 cm; well-drained, sandy soil with compost

Hardiness Warm

Light Partial shade

Rhizome. Produces 5 to 10 miniature orchid-like flowers per stem. Flowers can be purple, pink, blue, red or white with a ruffled lower lip of a darker colour. Use in mixed flowerbeds, borders or smaller containers.

↬ **'Alba'** • White-flowered cultivar

fancy-leaf caladium

Caladium x *hortulanmum*

Height 30–45 cm

Seasons Plant in late winter; usually no blooms—grows actively late winter to early fall

Planting Cover with 5 cm soil; grow singly in a pot; plant with top-quality potting soil

Hardiness Subtropical

Light Indoor in bright, indirect light; outdoors in partial to full shade

Tuber. Tropical plant grown for its beautifully coloured, shapely foliage. Leaves may be mottled, splashed or veined with combinations of green, red, pink or white. Best grown in containers.

Camassia *sp.*

Indian quamash

Camassia spp.

Height 60–90 cm

Seasons Plant in fall; blooms late spring to early summer

Planting 15 cm deep; space 20 cm; humus-rich, well-drained soil

Hardiness Temperate

Light Full sun to part shade

True bulb. Noted for producing spikes of star-shaped flowers, in white or shades of blue and purple. Use in beds, borders or rock gardens, or for cutflowers.

↬ *C. cusickii* • Pale-blue flowers; the earliest *Camassia*

↬ *C. leichtlinii* • Creamy-white flowers

↬ *C. leichtlinii* **'Alba'** • Pure-white flowers

↬ *C. leichtlinii* **'Caerula'**• Light-blue flowers

↬ *C. quamash* (*C. esculenta*) • Deep-blue flowers; the latest and shortest species

perfumed fairy lily

(delicate lily)

Chlidanthus fragrans

Height 20–30 cm

Seasons Plant in spring; blooms in summer

Planting 3 cm deep; space 10 cm; well-drained sandy soil rich in organic matter

Hardiness Subtropical

Light Full sun

True bulb. Produces one to four very fragrant, lily-like, pale-yellow flowers on leafless stalks. Grey-green leaves appear after the flowers. Use for borders, flowerbeds and containers, and as cutflowers.

kaffir lily

Clivia miniata

Height 30–45 cm

Seasons Plant in fall or spring; blooms late winter to early spring

Planting Cover with 1 cm of potting soil; grow singly in pot; use top-quality potting soil

Hardiness Subtropical

Light Bright light; avoid direct sunlight in summer

Rhizome. Umbels of 12 to 20 upright, fragrant, funnel-shaped flowers in orange, red and yellow; petals often tipped with yellow or green. Leaves are evergreen, strap-shaped, clump-forming. Best grown as a houseplant.

crinum lily

(swamp lily)

Crinum powellii

Height 60–100 cm

Seasons Plant in spring; blooms late summer to early fall

Planting Depth so neck of bulb is just above the soil; space 45 cm; well-drained, moist, fertile soil

Hardiness Subtropical

Light Full sun

True bulb. Up to 8 or 10 fragrant, pink lily-like blossoms cluster on the stem and open in succession from late summer to fall. Best grown individually in containers or as an indoor plant.

✧**'Alba'** • Cultivar with pure-white flowers

Montbretia

Crocosmia spp.

Height 60–90 cm

Seasons Plant in spring; blooms late summer to early fall

Planting 15 cm deep; space 10 cm; well-drained, moist, organic soil

Hardiness Warm

Light Sun

Corm. Thin, arching stalks bear spikes of brightly coloured starry flowers in yellow, orange or red. Leaves are sword-shaped.

Crocosmia *sp.*

Use in containers, borders, beds or perennial gardens.

∾ **C. x crocosmiiflora 'Emily Mckenzie'** • Large orange flowers with reddish-brown throats

∾ **C. masoniorum 'Lucifer'** • Large bright-red flowers

∾ **C. flora** • Golden-yellow flowers

cyclamen

Cyclamen spp.

Height 10 cm

Seasons Plant in fall; bloom times vary with species

Planting 5 cm deep; space 10–15 cm; humus-rich soils, rich in calcium and well-composted leaves

Hardiness Temperate

Light Partial shade

Tuber. Shuttlecock-shaped 2-cm flowers. Round leaves. Use in rock gardens, among trees and shrubs, and in woodland gardens. C. persicum (florist's cyclamen) is available only as a potted plant year-round.

∾ **C. coum** • Violet-purple, pink or white flowers with solid-green leaves. Flowers late winter through early spring.

∾ **C. hederifolium (C. neapolitanum)** • White to deep-pink flowers with marbled leaves. Flowers late summer through early fall.

eucharist lily

(Amazon lily)

Eucharis x *grandiflorum* (*E. amazonica*)

Height 45–60 cm

Seasons Plant in spring; blooms any season but typically between late fall and early spring

Planting Keep neck of bulb exposed just above soil surface; space 10 cm or 3–4 bulbs per 20-cm pot; top-quality potting soil indoors, organic soil outdoors

Hardiness Subtropical

Light Bright indirect indoors; bright, warm shade outdoors

True bulb. Umbels of 3 to 6 fragrant, white, narcissus-like, nodding blooms atop stemless stalks. Leaves are broad, deep green and lush. Use in containers outdoors or as a houseplant or cutflower.

pineapple lily

(pineapple plant)

Eucomis spp.

Height 30–60 cm

Seasons Plant in spring; blooms mid to late summer

Planting Just cover bulbs with a thin layer of topsoil, bulb neck barely exposed; space 15 cm; well-drained, sandy soil with lots of organic matter

Hardiness Subtropical

Light Full sun, sheltered location

True bulb. Plant resembles a pineapple. Masses of tiny, star-like, green, white or pink blooms are borne on a thick stalk tipped with a rosette of small green leaves. Excellent for containers; use in beds and borders or as cutflowers. Can be used as indoor plant in plentiful bright light.

∾ **E. comosa (E. punctata)** • White, pink or purplish flowers

∾ **E. bicolor** • Pale-green flowers with purple edges

∾ **E. bicolor 'Alba'** • White flowers

∾ **E. autumnalis** • Green flowers

Eucomis sp.

Fressia *x* hybrida

freesia

Freesia x *hybrida*

Height 30–45 cm

Seasons Plant in spring; blooms naturally in late summer to early fall; available commercially as cutflower year-round

Planting 3–6 cm deep; space 10 cm; fertile, sandy soil which drains quickly and well

Hardiness Subtropical

Light Part shade to full sun in warm, sheltered location

Corm. Fragrant, single or double, tubular 5-cm long flowers in white, yellow, bronze, pink, red, violet or blue. Flowers grow on one side of wiry stems. Use in containers, as a potted plant or as cutflowers.

summer hyacinth

Galtonia candicans (*Hyacinthus candicans*)

Height 90–120 cm

Seasons Plant in spring; blooms mid to late summer

Planting 15 cm deep; space 20 cm; well-drained, sandy soil with lots of organic matter

Hardiness Subtropical

Light Full sun to light shade

True bulb. Fragrant white flowers with green tinge at the base; lobed, bell-shaped, hanging from single stalks. Leaves are long, green, strap-like. Use for containers and mixed flowerbeds.

climbing lily

(glory lily, gloriosa lily)

Gloriosa spp.

Height 2 m

Seasons Plant in spring; blooms in summer

Planting 5 cm deep; space 35 cm or 1 bulb per 15-cm pot; top-quality potting soil with excellent drainage

Hardiness Subtropical

Light Full sun in warm, sheltered location

Tuber. Climbing vines with lily-like flowers in yellow, orange or red with yellow; reflexed petals. Best grown in containers with trellis or other plant support. Can also be grown as houseplant if light is abundant.

- **G. rothschldiana** (G. superba 'Rothschildiana') • Crimson-red flowers with yellow base; outlined in yellow

- **G. superba** • Flower colour changes from yellow-green to deep orange and red as plant ages

- **G. superba 'Lutea'** • Slightly smaller yellow cultivar

Gloriosa rothschldiana

blood lily

(cape tulip)

Haemanthus katharinae (Scadoxus multiflorus ssp. Katharinae, S. multiflorus, S. coccineus)

Height 30–40 cm

Seasons Plant in spring; blooms in late summer or early fall

Planting Neck of bulb should be just above soil surface; 1 per 13-cm pot; top-quality potting soil with excellent drainage

Hardiness Subtropical

Light Warm, light shade; partial shade in very hot climates

True bulb. Spherical 15-cm flowerheads composed of 10 to 20 spiky red flowers resembling a bottle brush on a leafless stalk. Leaves are large and oblong. Best grown in containers; can be grown as a houseplant if light is abundant.

amaryllis

Homeria ochroleuca

amaryllis

(hybrid amaryllis, florist amaryllis)

Hippeastrum hybrida

Height 30–90 cm

Seasons Plant in fall; blooms in winter to early spring

Planting Keep 1/3 to 1/2 of bulb above the soil surface; 1 bulb per 15-cm pot (prefers the smallest pot possible); top-quality potting soil

Hardiness Subtropical

Light Bright indirect

True bulb. Huge trumpet-shaped flowers, 20–25 cm, produced on strong stalks, ranging in colour from white to salmon, pink, orange, red or bicolour. Streaked cultivars also available. Leaves are broad and strap-like. Use indoors as a potted plant; commercially available as a cutflower.

cape tulip

Homeria spp.

Height 50 cm

Seasons Plant in spring; blooms in summer

Planting 7 cm deep; space 10 cm; well-drained, sandy soil

Hardiness Subtropical

Light Full sun

Corm. Star-shaped flowers standing upright on slender stems. Flowers open in

succession, extending the bloom period for several weeks. Leaves are long and narrow. Plant in borders, flowerbeds and containers.

- **H. flaccida (H. aurantiaca)** • Yellow or orange flowers
- **H. ochroleuca (H. collina var. ochroleuca)** • Pale-yellow flowers

sea daffodil

(spider lily, Peruvian daffodil)

Hymenocallis spp. (*Ismene festalis*)

Height 30–60 cm

Seasons Plant in spring; blooms late spring to early summer

Planting Neck just above the soil surface; space 20 cm or 1 bulb per 13-cm pot; well-drained soil rich in organic matter

Hardiness Subtropical

Light Full sun in sheltered location

True bulb. Fragrant pale-white to yellow flowers resemble daffodils; borne in umbels on leafless stalks. Leaves are broad and strap-like. Use in borders and containers.

- **H. festalis** • Fragrant white flowers flushed with green
- **H. festalis 'Zwanenburg'** • Improved *H. festalis*
- **H. 'Advance'** • Fragrant white flowers
- **H. 'Sulphur Queen'** • Fragrant, cream-yellow flowers

Ipheion uniflorum

spring starflower

Ipheion uniflorum (*Tritelia uniflora, Brodiaea uniflora*)

Height 10–20 cm

Seasons Plant in fall; blooms in mid spring

Planting 10–13 cm deep; space 3–10 cm; well-drained soil

Hardiness Warm

Light Full sun to light shade in sheltered location

True bulb. Blue or white-tinged blue, 3-cm, star-shaped flowers. Leaves are narrow and strap-like. Use in rock gardens and woodland gardens.

corn lily

(wandflower)

Ixia spp.

Height 30–45 cm

Seasons Plant in spring; blooms early to mid summer

Planting 7 cm deep; space 7 cm; well-drained, sandy soil

Hardiness Warm

Light Full sun

Corm. Star-like flowers in a wide range of colours are borne on spikes. Sword-shaped leaves. Use in rock gardens, perennial beds and pots, or as a cutflower.

Hymenocallis *sp.*

Siberian lily

(tartar lily, ixia lily)

*Ixiolirion tartaricum (I. pallasii,
I. montanum)*

Height 35–45 cm

Seasons Plant in spring; blooms in late
spring to early summer

Planting 8 cm deep; space 8 cm; well-
drained, compost-rich sandy soil

Hardiness Warm

Light Full sun in a sheltered location

*True bulb. Funnel-shaped, starry, blue-
violet flowers on slender stems. Grass-like
leaves. Use for borders or containers.*

snowflake

Leucojum spp.

Height 40–60 cm

Seasons Plant in fall; blooms in spring

Planting 10 cm deep; space 12 cm;
well-drained, moist, sandy soil with
lots of organic matter

Hardiness Temperate

Light Partial shade

*True bulb. Each stem produces 3 to 5
white, bell-shaped, 6-petalled, nodding
flowers with yellow-green spots at the tip
of each petal. Leaves are green and strap-
like. Use in borders, in rock gardens, and
under trees and shrubs.*

- *L. aestivum* **(summer snowflake)**
  • White flowers in mid spring. Most
  widely available species; best cultivar
  is *L.* 'Gravetye Giant'.

- *L. autumnale* **(autumn snowflake)**
  White flowers in late summer. Rare
  species; grows to 13 cm.

- *L. vernum* **(spring snowflake)**
  White flowers in early spring. Less
  common species.

Lilium *spp.* 'Stargazer'

lilies

Lilium spp.

Seasons Plant in spring; blooms in
summer

Hardiness Temperate

Light Full sun (will tolerate light shade)
in sheltered location

The *Lilium* species are among the
most complex bulbs to organize and
describe. Although all true lily species
grow from bulbs, the majority are sold
as actively growing perennials—many
are not even available as bulbs.

We have limited our discussion of this
important group for several reasons.
Some lily categories, such as Asiatics,
are sold in limited quantities as dry
bulbs, but the newest, widest selection
of cultivars is available only as green
plants in the spring.

The genus itself is also expanding.
With greater access to areas that were
unreachable only a few years ago—
such as Turkey and northern China—new species are being discovered,
providing exciting new parentages,
and leading to many novel hybrids and
divisions.

Lois Hole's book *Perennial Favorites* deals with a number of lilies in detail. For this reason, we have chosen to touch only briefly on a few divisions of this large group, primarily those that are sold to consumers as dry bulbs.

trumpet hybrids
Height 120–180 cm

Planting 15 cm deep; space 30 cm; well-drained, rich soil; these bulbs prefer cool soil in root zone

True bulb. Very fragrant, large, trumpet-shaped blooms that face outward or downward. Each stalk bears 12 to 15 blooms. Use in perennial beds; great cutflowers.

- ᔟ**'African Queen'** • Soft-orange flowers

- ᔟ**'Golden Splendour'** • Golden-yellow flowers

- ᔟ**'Pink Perfection'** • Pink flowers

- ᔟ**'Lilium Regale'** • White flowers; purple outer petals

Lilium pumilum

oriental hybrids
Height 70–100 cm

Planting 15 cm deep; space 30 cm; well-drained, rich soil; these bulbs prefer cool soil in root zone

True bulb. Fragrant, large, showy flowers are bowl-shaped or flat-faced. Use in perennial beds or containers; great cutflowers.

- ᔟ**'Stargazer'** • Bright reddish-pink blooms with lighter edges and dark spots

- ᔟ**'Casablanca'** • Pure-white blooms; classic wedding lily

species lilies
Height Varies with species

Planting 15 cm deep; space 25–45 cm, wider spacing for fuller plants; well-drained, rich soil; these bulbs prefer cool soil in root zone

True bulb. Taller varieties must be staked. The hardiest lilies—will naturalize once established. Use in background plantings, in perennial flowerbeds and as cutflowers.

- ᔟ***L. auratum* (golden-rayed lily)** • White flowers with yellow flowers and brown spots; 150–240 cm high

- ᔟ***L. bulbiferum* (*L. aurantiacum*)** • Trumpet-shaped, orange flowers with purple spots; 60–120 cm high

- ᔟ***L. candidum* (madonna lily)** • Up to 12 pure-white flowers per stem; 100–150 cm high

- ᔟ***L. speciosum*** • Fragrant, white, slightly pendulous flowers covered with numerous red spots and stripes; 90–150 cm high

- ᔟ***L. speciosum* var. *rubrum*** • Subspecies of *L. speciosum* with deep carmine-red flowers

- ᔟ***L. pumilum* (*L. tenuifolium*)** • Produces 7–20 fragrant, pendulous scarlet flowers; 60–90 cm high

spider lily

Lycoris spp.

Height 45–60 cm

Seasons Plant in spring; blooms in late summer to early fall

Planting 8–10 cm deep; space 15 cm; fast-draining, sandy soil rich in organic matter

Hardiness Warm

Light Full sun in sheltered location

True bulb. Showy clusters of recurved, six-petalled, star-shaped flowers with long, prominent stamens. Leaves are strap-shaped and linear. Use in borders, mixed flowerbeds and containers.

⚘ **L. africana (L. aurea, Amaryllis aurea)** (hurricane lily, golden spider lily) • Yellow flowers with wavy-edged petals

⚘ **L. radiata (Amaryllis radiata)** • Deep-red or deep-pink flowers with wavy-edged petals

⚘ **L. squamigera (magic lily, resurrection lily, hardy amaryllis)** • Large, rose-pink flowers with smooth-edged petals

Nerine bowdenii

Ornithogalum thyrsoides

Guernsey lily

Nerine spp.

Height 35–90 cm

Seasons Plant in spring; blooms late summer to early fall

Planting 5 cm deep—so neck of bulb is just above the soil; space 20 cm; fast-draining, sandy soil

Hardiness Subtropical

Light Full sun in a sheltered location

True bulb. An umbel of deep-pink, trumpet-shaped flowers with wavy, reflexed petals forms on a leafless stalk. Use in containers and for borders; good cutflowers.

⚘ **N. bowdenii** • Pink flowers; by far the most common cultivar

⚘ **N. undulata** • Fringed pink flowers

⚘ **N. flexuosa 'Alba'** • White flowers

star of Bethlehem

(chincherinchees)

Ornithogalum spp.

Height varies with species

Seasons Plant in spring; blooms in summer through early fall

Planting 5–10 cm deep; space 8–12 cm; well-drained, moist soil

Hardiness Subtropical

Light Full sun

True bulb. White or cream star-like flowers. Use in perennial gardens; good as cutflowers.

✧ **O. arabicum (true star of Bethlehem)** • Fragrant white flowers; 80 cm high

✧ **O. saundersiae (giant chincherinchee)** • White flowers with shiny green-black centres; 100 cm high

✧ **O. thyrsoides (wonder flower)** • White pyramid-shaped flower cluster; 35 cm high; most common species

oxalis

(wood sorrel, clover, shamrock, good luck plant)

Oxalis spp.

Height 8–30 cm

Seasons Plant in spring; blooms entire summer

Planting 5 cm deep; space 5 cm; well-drained, sandy soil

Hardiness Warm

Light Full sun; tolerates warm, light shade

Tuber, rhizome or true bulb; varies with species. Wide open, funnel-like flowers with shamrock leaves. Use in rock gardens, mixed flowerbeds and containers; can be invasive. Some species make good houseplants.

✧ **O. adenophylla** • Lilac-pink flowers; best garden variety

✧ **O. deppei (lucky clover)** • Pinkish-red flowers

✧ **O. deppei 'Iron Cross'** • Cultivar of *O. deppei*; leaves have dark blotch at base

✧ **O. regnelli** • White flowers; excellent houseplant

Oxalis deppei *'Iron Cross'*

tuberose

Polianthes tuberosa

Height 45–90 cm

Seasons Plant in spring; blooms mid to late summer

Planting Barely cover bulb with soil; space 20 cm; moist, well-drained soil rich in organic matter or top-quality potting soil

Hardiness Subtropical

Light Full sun in sheltered, very warm location

Tuber. Spikes of white, waxy-looking, very fragrant, tubular flowers are borne on the upper portion of the stems. Use in containers or indoors; good cutflowers.

Persian buttercup

Ranunculus asiaticus

Height 30–60 cm

Seasons Plant in spring; blooms in summer

Planting 2–5 cm deep; space 8 cm; well-drained, sandy soil

Hardiness Warm

Light Full sun

Tuberous root. Small, peony-like flowers in white, yellow, pink, gold, orange or red. Ferny foliage. Use in borders and flower-beds; taller varieties grown commercially as cutflowers.

rhodohypoxis

Rhodohypoxis spp.

Height 5–10 cm

Seasons Plant in spring; blooms in late spring through early fall

Planting 5 cm deep; space 10 cm; fast-draining, sandy soil

Hardiness Subtropical

Light Full sun in sheltered location

Corm. A dwarf plant with narrow leaves and pink, white or red flowers, produced in succession. Use in rock gardens and small containers.

roscoea

Roscoea spp.

Height 20–30 cm

Seasons Plant in spring; blooms in summer

Planting 10 cm deep; space 15 cm; well-drained, moisture-retentive, compost-rich soil

Hardiness Subtropical

Light Partial shade, heavy shade in very warm zones

Tuberous root. Orchid-like flowers tubular with an upper hooded petal and a large lower lip in yellow, red, pink, blue or purple. Use in borders and rock gardens.

✿ **R. auriculata 'Beesiana'** • Creamy-white flowers with purple stripes

✿ **R. scillifolia** • Pink flowers

Schizostylis coccinea

gloxinia

Chinese-lantern lily

(Christmas bells)

Sandersonia aurantiaca

Height 60 cm

Seasons Plant in spring; blooms in mid summer

Planting 7–10 cm deep; space 10–15 cm; extremely well-drained, fertile soil

Hardiness Subtropical

Light Full sun in warm and sheltered location

Tuber. Single, orange, lantern-shaped flowers form on a thin stem in the axil of each leaf. Use in containers or flowerbeds.

river lily

(crimson lily, kaffir lily)

Schizostylis coccinea

Height 45–70 cm

Seasons Plant in spring; blooms late summer through mid fall

Planting 10 cm deep; space 10 cm; moisture-retentive, well-drained soil rich in organic matter

Hardiness Subtropical

Light Full sun in warm, sheltered locations; this bulb prefers high humidity

Rhizome. Flower spikes resembling miniature gladioli produce 5–20 pink or red, crocus-like flowers on each. Sword-like green leaves. Use in flowerbeds or perennial gardens.

gloxinia

(temple bells, canterbury bells)

Sinningia speciosa

Height 25 cm

Seasons Plant in late fall/winter; blooms in spring and summer

Planting 5 cm deep; 1 bulb per 15-cm pot; top-quality potting soil

Hardiness Subtropical

Light Bright indirect light

Tuber. Large (8–15 cm), upright, velvety, bell-like flowers, white, blue, pink, red or bicolour. Best grown indoors as houseplant.

Tigridia pavonia

harlequin flower

(wand-flower)

Sparaxis tricolor

Height 25–40 cm

Seasons Plant in spring; blooms late spring to early summer

Planting 5 cm deep; space 7 cm; well-drained, sandy soil

Hardiness Warm

Light Full sun

> *Corm. Narrow, sword-shaped leaves and spikes of large, brightly coloured, star-shaped, white, yellow, orange, red, purple or pink flowers; solid or bicolour. Use in containers, rock gardens or borders.*

Aztec lily

(jacobean lily, St. James lily)

Sprekelia formosissima (*Amaryllis formosissima*)

Height 30–40 cm

Seasons Plant in spring; blooms late spring to early summer

Planting Just cover with soil; space 15 cm; fast-draining, organic, sandy soil

Hardiness Subtropical

Light Full sun in sheltered location

> *True bulb. Velvety red, orchid-like flowers; foliage is dark, narrow and strap-like. Use in flowerbeds, borders and containers.*

lily-of-the-field

(autumn daffodil)

Sternbergia spp.

Height 8–20 cm

Seasons Plant in spring; blooms late summer to early fall

Planting 12 cm deep; space 12 cm; very fast-draining, sandy, chalky soil

Hardiness Warm

Light Full sun

> *True bulb. Golden-yellow crocus-like flowers. Linear grass-like leaves. Use in rock and alpine gardens.*

✎ **S. lutea** • Golden-yellow flowers; most widely available and reliable species

✎ **S. clusiana (S. macrantha)** • Larger yellow flowers that bloom before the leaves appear

tiger flower

Tigridia pavonia

Height 45–60 cm

Seasons Plant in spring; blooms mid summer to early fall

Planting 8 cm deep; space 10–15 cm; fast-draining, organic, sandy soil

Hardiness Subtropical

Light Full sun in sheltered location

> *True bulb. White, cream, yellow, pink or red flowers have three larger outer petals, usually without markings, and three smaller*

inner petals, with red, brown or maroon blotches or spots. Foliage is basal, sword-like—like gladiolus. Use in containers, borders and flowerbeds.

brodiaea

(spring starflower)

Triteleia laxa (Brodiaea laxa)

Height 45–60 cm

Seasons Plant in late spring; blooms early summer

Planting 10 cm deep; space 10 cm; very well-drained, sandy soil

Hardiness Warm

Light Full sun in a sheltered location

Corm. Star-like, funnel-shaped, deep-blue to white flowers borne on long, leafless stalks. Leaves are grass-like and grow in clumps at the base of the plant. Use in flowerbeds and borders; commercially available as cutflowers.

↳ **'Queen Fabiola'** • Large lilac-blue flowers

↳ **'Candida'** • Pure-white flowers

tritonia

(blazing star)

Tritonia spp.

Height 30–60 cm

Seasons Plant in spring; blooms late spring to early summer

Planting 15 cm deep; 1 bulb per 15-cm pot; top-quality potting soil

Hardiness Subtropical

Light Full sun in a warm, sheltered location

Corm. Cup-shaped, starry blooms in red, pink and white on wiry stems. Leaves are strap-like. Use indoors as a houseplant or outdoors in containers.

↳ ***T. crocata*** • Orange, pink or cream flowers; best grown as a houseplant

↳ ***T. rosea*** • Taller, pink, funnel-shaped flowers; best choice for outdoors

rain lily

(fairy lily, zephyr lily, coca flower, flower of the west wind)

Zephyranthes spp.

Height 15 cm

Seasons Plant in spring; blooms in fall

Planting 10 cm deep; space 7 cm; well-drained, sandy soil

Hardiness Subtropical

Light Full sun

True bulb. Narrow, grass-like foliage and star-shaped, crocus-like white, pink or yellow flowers; each stalk produces a single flower. Use in rock gardens.

↳ ***Z. candida*** • White flowers

↳ ***Z. rosea*** • Pink flowers

Triteleia laxa

How to Force Garden Bulbs

One of the marvels of bulbs is that they contain everything a new plant needs to grow. That fact makes many bulbs ideal for forcing—that is, stimulating them to bloom indoors. The practice of forcing bulbs is old and popular, probably because it yields such terrific results. Forced bulbs add colour and fragrance to our homes during the bleak days of winter, and are a great way to introduce children to the wonders of plants and gardening.

When you force a bulb to flower, you're 'fooling' it into blooming earlier than it normally would. Temperature, light and moisture are manipulated to simulate a favourable blooming environment. If you provide the right artificial environment, the plant will respond just as it would in its natural environment. Bulbs are typically forced in either water or soil.

Bulbs forced in water

September is bulb-forcing season in Canada and the northern United States. Paperwhites, amaryllis and hyacinths are among the most commonly forced bulbs; these three—and others—can be grown in a vase of water. Choose the largest, healthiest bulbs you can find. Large paperwhite bulbs should produce three or four bloom stalks per bulb; large amaryllis bulbs can produce six to twelve flowers, potentially four blooms per stalk. Here's the method.

Purchase pre-chilled bulbs and a forcing vase (any vase with a neck narrow enough to support the bulb over water will do). Fill the vase with water and place the bulb in the vase. Be sure the base of the bulb is close to the water level but not touching the water. Place the vase in a cool but sunny spot and wait for flowers to appear. Be patient: blooming times vary, and flowers take at least a couple of weeks to appear. You should see roots start to develop in just a few days, a signal that the bulb is actively growing. Keep the water level in the vase consistent: the water should never be higher than just up to the base of the bulb.

Note that some bulbs, such as hyacinths, require a long cold treatment before they bloom. Many garden centres carry pre-chilled bulbs (also called prepared or pre-cooled bulbs), which cuts down significantly on the amount of

---

Quick Steps to Forcing

1. Purchase bulbs. Select firm, unblemished bulbs.

2. Chill bulbs if necessary.

3. Provide the proper initial growing environment: growing medium, light and temperature.

4. Adjust the environment as growth progresses. Transplant the growing bulb to a larger pot if necessary.

5. Enjoy your bulb!

time you have to keep them in your refrigerator. But if the bulbs have been sitting on the garden centre shelf too long, they will lose much of their accumulated chill. Place the bulb and vase in the refrigerator for at least eight weeks, until you see pale, thin roots emerging from the base of the bulb. (Be careful to place the vase well away from ethylene-producing fruits and vegetables [see chart on page 297]. Ethylene gas may retard flower development in the bulb.) Remove the vase from the fridge and put it in a warm, brightly lit location. Flower spikes will begin to appear two to three weeks later. The warmer the room, the faster they will appear. To prevent the plant from leaning toward the light, turn it every couple of days. Once all of the flowers have appeared, you can place the vase anywhere you like.

You can also force hyacinths in a bowl filled with stones. Nestle the bulb atop the stones, and fill the bowl with water just up to the base of the bulb. The rocks will hide the emerging roots. Coloured marbles or decorative stones create an even more attractive display.'

Triumph tulip 'Kees Nelis'

Bulbs Forced in Soil

Some bulbs must be forced in soil, including tulips, crocuses, daffodils, bulbous irises, muscari and many lilies. Amaryllis, which can be forced in water, is often more robust when forced in soil. Plant the bulbs in a 15-cm pot. (If you want to force several bulbs in a single pot, use a larger pot.) Check that the pot has drainage holes and use a high-quality soilless mix as your planting medium.

Fill the pot with 3 cm of soilless mix. Place several bulbs on this layer but ensure they don't touch. Cover the bulbs with soil to fill the pot to 3 cm from the top. (Growing bulbs heave up the soil, so leave a bit of space to prevent spilling.) Water the bulbs in well and store the pot in the fridge or cold storage at 4–10°C. After 16 weeks, place the pot near a bright, sunny but cool window. After about a month, shoots will emerge, followed shortly by flowers. Water sparingly; let the edges of the soil dry out before each watering.

Fall bulbs can be forced only once, but some can be planted outdoors in the garden after they have finished blooming, and may bloom the following season. Oriental and Asiatic lilies, muscari, daffodils and hyacinths usually bloom in the garden in the season after they've been forced. When you plant these bulbs in the garden, be careful not to disturb the foliage. The bulbs will need help to grow large enough to rebloom the following spring, so if you replant these bulbs in the garden, fertilize them every two weeks with 20-20-20 while they're growing indoors. Forcing uses up 80 percent of the bulb's energy, so forced bulbs will never be peak performers in the garden. You're better off to buy new ones rather than trying to coax forced bulbs into blooming again.

Best Bulbs for Forcing

Anemone blanda
Chionodoxa spp.
Eranthis cilicica
Fritillaria meleagris
Galanthus spp.
Iris danfordiae
Iris histrioides 'George'
Iris reticulata 'Harmony'
Muscari armeniacum
Scilla tubergeniana

Hyacinths
'Amsterdam'
'Anna Liza'
'Anna Marie'
'Atlantic'
'Blue Star'
'Carnegie'
'Delft Blue'
'Jan Bos'
'L'Innocence'
'Pink Pearl'
'Splendid Cornelia'

Crocus
'Jeanne d'Arc'
'Pickwick'
'Remembrance'

Double early tulip 'Monte Carlo'

Best Hybrid Tulips for Forcing.

Single Early
'Apricot Beauty'
'Brilliant Star'
'Charles'
'Christmas Dream'
'Christmas Marvel'
'Flair'
'Joffre'
'Merry Christmas'
Double Early
'Abba'
'Kareol'

'Monsella'
'Monte Carlo'
'Montreux'
'Queen of Marvel'
'Stockholm'
'Verona'
'Viking'
Triumph
'Abra'
'Blenda'
'Golden Melody'
'Hibernia'

'Inzel'
'Kees Nelis'
'Merry Widow'
'Prominence'
'Snowstar'
'Thule'
Double Late
'Angelique'
'Wirosa'

Best Daffodils for Forcing

trumpet cultivars
'Arctic Gold'
'Ballade'
'Brighton'
'Dutch Master'
'Exception'
'Foresight'
'Goblet'
'Golden Harvest'
'Gold Medal'
'Las Vegas'
'Magnet'
'Mount Hood'
'Princewinner'
'Royal Gold'
'Spellbinder'
'Standard Value'
'Unsurpassable'

**large-cupped
cultivars**
'Accent'
'Carlton'
'Flower Record'
'Fortissimo'
'Fortune'
'Gigantic Star'
'Ice Follies'
'Johan Strauss'
'Juanita'
'Salome'
'Scarlet O'Hara'
'Slim Whitman'
'Yellow Sun'

**cyclamineus
cultivars**
'February Gold'
'Jack Snipe'
'Peeping Tom'

tazetta cultivars
'Cragford'
'Grand Soleil d'Or'
paperwhites ('Bethle-
hem', 'Chinese Sacred
Lily', 'Galilee', 'Israel',
'Jerusalem', 'Nazareth',
'Ziva')

Ethylene-producing fruits and vegetables

Relative Ethylene Fruit/Vegetable	Production
Cherry, grape, strawberry, root vegetables	Very low
Cucumber, pepper, pineapple	Low
Banana, tomato, honeydew	Moderate
Apple, apricot, avocado, cantaloupe, kiwi, peach	High
Passion fruit	Very high

HOW TO
NATURALIZE BULBS

The term *naturalizing* refers to the process of planting bulbs with the intention of letting them become self-tending perennials. In other words, nature does the work. A naturalized area involves an investment of time initially, to prepare the planting area; but once the bulbs are in the right environment, they will do what they do best, allowing you to sit back and watch the show.

The naturalized garden

Naturalized plantings can be introduced successfully in large garden areas—as features or understorey—in meadow gardens and in rock gardens. Think of woodlands: drifts of colour dotting the landscape. The planting flows into the surrounding plants, changing size and shape each year.

Masses of crocuses naturalized in a lawn make a spectacular show each spring

If you are very ambitious, you can plant bulbs of different varieties that bloom at different times of the year. Provided you plant species with similar cultural requirements, your naturalized area may quickly become a rotating display of low-maintenance blooms.

The key to a naturalized planting of any size is allowing the plants to follow their natural growth cycle. Don't deadhead the flowers—you must let the plants self-seed—and allow the foliage to die down on its own.

Naturalizing the Lawn

A particular application of naturalizing involves grassy areas. Naturalizing your lawn is a fun way to turn the everyday carpet of grass into a colourful, showy extension of your garden.

The key to naturalizing bulbs in the lawn is that you cannot mow the grass until the growth cycle is complete—that is, when the foliage dies back naturally and the seed pods have ripened and shed their seeds. When you see flower buds on the emerging plants, feed them once with liquid fertilizer. As the plants flower, apply a weekly liquid feed. When all the flowers have died, let the foliage wither naturally. Continue feeding until the dying leaves turn pale. After the foliage has died completely, you can mow the lawn.

Stick with shorter bulbs for naturalized lawns, such as crocuses (especially *Crocus tommasinianus, C. chrysanthus* and *C. vernus*), *Iris reticulata* 'Harmony', *Muscari armeniacum, Scilla campanulata, Scilla siberica* and very early-flowering *Narcissus* varieties. Winter

How to plant bulbs for naturalized areas

1. Choose bulb varieties suitable for naturalizing (see the lists that follow). You will require several dozen bulbs; plan to use at least 50 to 100 bulbs per square metre (an area of 1 m by 1 m)—more (125 to 150) with very small bulbs.

2. There are two planting systems: dig and scatter, or scatter and then dig.

   a) If you are putting in a new garden, dig out the area to be naturalized to the appropriate depth; cover with a thin layer of soil. Now, throw handfuls of bulbs onto the planting area in odd numbers: five bulbs in one area, seven in another, three in another and so on. Allow the bulbs to rest where they fall unless there is less than 15 cm between one bulb and another—leave at least this distance between bulbs. Cover the bulbs with good-quality garden soil enriched with compost.

   b) If you are planting in an established area, gently scatter the bulbs, either randomly by tossing them or intentionally by setting them in a loose, informal bluff. Wherever you have set a bulb, dig a hole of appropriate depth and line with a shallow layer of coarse soil. Set the bulb in the hole, pointed end up, and fill the hole with good-quality soil enriched with compost (you may want to sprinkle in some granular bulb fertilizer as well).

3. Water the area thoroughly and leave the bulbs to work their magic. Apply protective mulch to insulate the bulbs and help the soil retain moisture.

aconites, chionodoxa and snowdrops complete their growth cycle within a month and are also good choices. Colchicum is an excellent fall-flowering choice for naturalizing, but you must allow the foliage to die down in the spring and must stop cutting the lawn before the flowerbuds emerge—usually around the end of August.

To naturalize a lawn, plant the bulbs as directed above. Note that bulbs with blue or purple flowers are less effective because the blooms tend to blend into the green grass. Yellow and orange varieties contrast beautifully.

Best Daffodils for Naturalizing

Several *Narcissus* cultivars naturalize well. They come primarily from three divisions: the large-cupped daffodils, the small-cupped daffodils and the botanical daffodils.

Small-cupped daffodils	Large-cupped daffodils	Botanical daffodils
'Actaea'	'Carlton'	'February Gold'
'Barrett Browning'	'Flower Record'	'Hawera'
'Birma'	'Fortune'	'Jack Snipe'
	'Ice Follies'	'Minnow'
	'Salome'	'Peeping Tom'
		'Suzy'
		'Tête à Tête'

Best Cultivar Tulips for Naturalizing

The following varieties will spread vigorously for more than three years.

T. kaufmanniana varieties	Single early	'Holland's Glorie'
'Guiseppe Verdi'	'Charles'	'Oxford'
'Heart's Delight'	'Christmas Marvel'	'Striped Apeldoorn'
'Shakespeare'	'Coûleur Cardinal'	'Apeldoorn's Elite'
'Showwinner'	'Princess Irene'	**Lily-flowered**
'Stresa'	**Double early**	'Aladdin'
T. fosteriana varieties	'Peach Blossom'	'Ballade'
'Candela'	**Triumph**	'Maytime'
'Red Emperor' (aka	'Abu Hassan'	'Red Shine'
'Madame Lefeber')	'Cassini'	'White Triumphator'
'Orange Emperor'	'Don Quichotte'	'West Point'
'Princeps'	'Golden Melody'	**Fringed**
'Purissima'	'Kees Nelis'	'Arma'
T. greigii varieties	'Merry Widow'	'Burgundy Lace'
'Plaisir'	'Peerless Pink'	**Parrot**
'Red Riding Hood'	**Darwin hybrid**	'Estella Rijnveld'
'Toronto'	'Apeldoorn'	**Double late**
'Yellow Dawn'	'Beauty of Apeldoorn'	'Angelique'
	'Golden Apeldoorn'	

Allium caeruleum

Pest-Resistant Bulbs

The following bulbs have two sterling qualities: they are beautiful and mammals find them unpalatable.

Allium spp. (ornamental onion)
Camassia spp.
Chionodoxa spp. (glory of the snow)
Colchicum spp.
Crocus tommasinianus
Eranthis spp. (winter aconite)
Fritillaria spp
Galanthus nivalis (snowdrop)
Hyancinthoides hispanica (Spanish bluebell)
Hyacinthus spp. (hyacinth)
Leucojum spp. (snowflake)
Muscari spp. (grape hyacinth)
Narcissus spp. (daffodil)
Ornithogalum spp. (star of Bethlehem)
Oxalis spp.
Scilla spp.

Best Tulips for Warmer Climates

If you live in a warmer climate and would like to try growing tulips, refer to page 20 for the proper chilling method and give any of these varieties a try.

Single Late
'Halcro'
'Queen of Night'
'Renown'
'Menton'
'Maureen'
'Makeup'
'Temple of Beauty'
'Blushing Beauty'
'Blue Aimable'
'Hocus Pocus'

Single Early
'Apricot Beauty'
'New Design'

Parrot
'Estella Rijnveld'
'Orange Favourite'
'Texas Gold'
'Flaming Parrot'

Double Late
'Angelique'
'Mount Tacoma'

Darwin Hybrid
Most varieties

Lily-Flowered
'White Triumphator'
'Red Shine'
'Mona Lisa'
'Marilyn'

Species
'Linifolia'
'Tarda'
'Saxtilis'

Lily-flowered tulip
'White Triumphator'

GLOSSARY

anther: The pollen-bearing part of the STAMEN.

axil: The angle between a twig or leaf and the stem.

axillary (of buds or branches): Growing in an AXIL.

basal plate: The hardened, compressed stem portion within a bulb.

bloom (not a flower): A powdery, usually whitish coating.

bract: A modified leaf structure associated with a flower.

bud: An undeveloped flower or leaf.

bulb: A short underground stem covered by enlarged, fleshy leaf bases and containing stored food.

bulbil: A secondary bulb produced by the mother bulb. May also be called a bulblet. Bulbils sprout easily and must grow for an additional season or more before they are large enough to produce flowers. Tiger lily is an example of a plant that produces bulbils.

calcareous (soil): Containing or consisting of calcium carbonate.

calyx: Refers collectively to the green, leaf-like parts (SEPALS) that protect the flower in bud; typically found beneath the open flower.

campanulate: Bell shaped.

channelled: Having deep, gutter-like, longitudinal grooves.

companion planting: Planting particular species to repel or trap harmful pests, or to attract beneficial insects. Planting species close together to gain a particular cultural benefit.

compressed: Tightly formed.

corm: A dense, thick, underground stem covered with dry scales; shaped much like a flattened sphere.

cormel: A miniature corm formed at the end of the fleshy stem and produced from the base of the corm. A cormel is harder and more pointed than a new corm, which forms on the upper surface of the old one. Cormels must be grown for at least one additional season before they are large enough to produce a flower. Gladiolus is an example of a plant that produces cormels.

corolla: The flower structure formed by a union of petals; a collective word for petals.

corona: An interior flower structure, found between the COROLLA and the STAMENS, that resembles a crown.

corymb: A flat-topped flower cluster in which the central flowers typically bloom last.

cultivar: A variety of plant found only under cultivation. The term is a contraction of *cultivated variety*.

damping off: A generic term for young seedlings that die shortly after germination or emergence. Three diseases are largely responsible for damping off: species of pythium, phytophthora and rhizoctonia. These diseases exist naturally in most garden soils.

disc floret: On an Asteraceae plant, a small, tube-shaped flower.

eye: An undeveloped stem or leaf on an underground plant part such as a TUBER or TUBEROUS ROOT.

filament: The stalk of the STAMEN.

geophyte: A plant propagated by means of underground buds, taking the form of a true bulb, corm, tuber, tuberous root or rhizome.

glabrous: Smooth, hairless.

glaucous: Covered with a waxy or powdery BLOOM.

gravitropism: The phenomenon that causes plants to grow toward or away from gravity.

hardiness: A plant's ability to withstand specific environmental conditions. See also WINTER HARDINESS.

inflorescence: The flowering structure; an arrangement of flowers on the plant.

interplanting: Locating one species of plant alongside another, often to take advantage of mutual benefits.

involucre: The bract or collection of bracts beneath a flower cluster.

involute: Turned inward.

laciniate: Leaves that take the form of narrow, pointed segments, with fringed or serrated edges.

non-tunicate: Not bearing a TUNIC, a dry outer sheath.

offset (or offshoot): A lateral shoot that develops from the base of the main stem.

peltate: A leaf arrangement with the stalk in the centre.

pendent: Hanging.

pedicel: The stem of a flower within a floral cluster; the flower stalk or neck.

perianth: Refers to the petals and SEPALS taken together.

petiole: The leaf stalk.

pistil: The part of the flower that accepts pollen; the female reproductive part of a flower.

raceme: A flower cluster that blooms from the bottom up.

ray floret: On an Asteraceae plant, a straplike flower, often growing on the outer edge of the flower structure.

ray: The stalk of an UMBELLET in a compound UMBEL.

reflexed: Bent backward.

revolute: Turned outward. Fully revolute means the margins of the rays overlap or approximate each other.

rhizome: A thick, horizontal, elongated underground stem that produces upright shoots.

runner: A specialized stem that grows horizontally along the ground to form a new plant. May be called a STOLON.

scape: A leafless flowering stalk.

sepal: An individual part of the CALYX; usually green and leaf-like.

spadix: An INFLORESCENCE of many tiny flowers clustered on a central stalk.

spathe: A showy, modified leaf that encloses a flower cluster.

species: Plants that can interbreed to produce similar-looking offspring. Unlike CULTIVAR, species refers to plants as they are found in nature, unmodified by selective breeding.

sport: A plant that is distinctly different from its parents, resulting from a natural mutation.

stamen: The part of the flower that produces pollen; the male flower part.

stolon: A horizontally growing stem that produces adventitious roots. May be called a RUNNER.

tessellation: Checkered patterning.

top dress: To spread a thin layer of organic matter, fertilizer or mulch atop the soil surrounding plants.

top size: The largest size of true bulbs; a retail description.

tuber: The thick, fleshy, underground portion of a stem. It is covered with eyes and has no TUNIC or BASAL PLATE.

tuberous root: A structure similar to a TUBER but composed of root tissue rather than stem tissue.

tubular floret: See DISC FLORET.

tunic: The dry outer scales on some bulbs.

tunicate: Bearing a TUNIC.

twijfelmaten: The Dutch term for a bulb that is of borderline size for flowering. The bulb may not be large enough to produce blooms.

umbel: A flower arrangement in which the stalks originate at a single point.

umbellet: Refers to a small UMBEL or a single flower within an umbel.

underplanting: Deliberately creating or introducing a canopy or garden layers by planting taller-growing species alongside shorter-growing species, particularly with trees and shrubs.

vernalization: Extended exposure to cold temperatures.

whorl: A circular collection of three or more leaves, branches or flower stalks arising from the same point.

winter hardiness: Refers to traits in a plant's genetic makeup that make it more or less able to survive cold.

References

Bidwell, R.G.S. *Plant Physiology*. New York: Macmillan, 1974.

Bowles, E.A. *A Handbook of Crocus and Colchicum for Gardeners*. London: Martin Hopkinson & Company, 1924.

Cassleman, Bill. *Canadian Garden Words*. Toronto: Little, Brown and Company (Canada) Limited, 1997.

The Complete Book Of Garden Flowers, How to Grow Over 300 of the Best Performing Varieties. Vancouver: Whitecap Books, 2000.

Cooke, Ian. *The Gardener's Guide to Growing Cannas*. Portland, Oregon: Timber Press, 2001.

Davies, Dilys. *Alliums: The Ornamental Onions*. Portland, Orgeon: Timber Press, 1992.

Day, Sonia. *Tulips Facts and Folklore about the World's Most Planted Flower*. Canada: Key Porter Books, 2002.

De Hertogh, August. *Holland Bulb Forcer's Guide*. Fifth edition. Hillegom, The Netherlands: The International Flower Bulb Centre, 1996.

Dobbs, Liz. *Tulip*. London: Quadrille Publishing, 2002.

Ellis, Barbara W. *Taylor's Guide to Bulbs*. New York: Houghton Mifflin Company, 2001.

Hartmann, Hudson, Dale Kester and Fred Davies, Jr. *Plant Propagation: Principles and Practices*. Fifth edition. Englewood Cliffs, New Jersey: Prentice Hall, 1990.

Heath, Becky and Brent. *Daffodils For American Gardeners*. Washington: Elliot and Clarke Publishing, 1995.

Heitz, Halina. *Success with Begonias*. London: Merehurst, 1994.

Hessayon, D.G. *The Bulb Expert*. London: Transworld Publishers, 1999.

Leatherbarrow, Liesbeth and Lesley Reynolds. *Best Bulbs for the Prairies*. Calgary: Fifth House, 2001.

Mathew, Brian and Philip Swindells. *The Complete Book of Bulbs, Corms, Tubers and Rhizomes*. New York: Reed International Books, 1994.

Mead, Chris and Emily Tolley. New York: Clarkson Potter/Publishers, 1998.

The Netherlands Flower Bulb Information Centre/USA. International Flower Bulb Centre. Last accessed 14 February 2003. <http://www.bulb.com>.

Pratt, Kevin and Michael Jefferson-Brown. *The Gardener's Guide to Growing Fritillaries*. Portland, Oregon: Timber Press, 1997.

Raven, Peter H., Ray F. Evert and Susan E. Eichhorn. *Biology of Plants*. Fifth edition. New York: Worth Publishers, 1992.

Rees, Alun. "Four Centuries of Tulips." *The Garden*, April 1994.

Ross, Marty. *All About Bulbs*. Des Moines: Ortho Books, 1999.

The New Royal Horticultural Society Dictionary. *Manual of Bulbs*. Portland, Oregon: Timber Press, 1995.

Whiteside, Katherine. *Forcing, etc*. New York: Workman Publishing Company, 1999.

Williams, Greg and Pat. "'Pest-Resistant' Flower Bulbs." *HortIdeas*, Volume 18 Number 9 (September 2001).

The success of this book is due entirely
to the hard work of the staff of Hole's Greenhouses & Gardens
over the course of three years including, but not limited to, the following people.

CONTRIBUTING WRITERS	Jim Hole
	Valerie Hole
	Marlene Willis
	Earl J. Woods
EDITOR	Leslie Vermeer
EDITORIAL DEVELOPMENT	Linda Affolder
	Christina McDonald
BOOK DESIGN	Gregory Brown
PRINCIPAL PHOTOGRAPHY	Akemi Matsubuchi
OTHER PHOTOGRAPHY	Valerie Hole
	Jill Fallis
	Internationaal Bloembollen
	Centrum Hillegom, Holland
	Geoff Bryant
ILLUSTRATIONS	Donna McKinnon
BULB TRIALS	Hilary Allen
	Cheryl Dembecki-Lep
	John Gabriel
	Jenyse Green
	Maggie Nielsen
PERENNIAL BULBS	Bob Stadnyk
	Jan Goodall
FLORAL DESIGN	Lesleah Horvat
	Colleen Kwiatkowski
INDOOR BULBS	Judith Fraser
	Gwen Hanes
PROJECT CONSULTANTS	Nancy Brink
	Christine Cassavant
	Pat Lewis
	Scott Messenger
	Tanja Pickrell
	Stephen Raven
	Betty Sampson
PUBLICATION MANAGEMENT	Bruce Timothy Keith